INTRODUCING DATA ANALYSIS FOR SOCIAL SCIENTISTS

SECOND EDITION

INTRODUCING DATA ANALYSIS FOR SOCIAL SCIENTISTS

SECOND EDITION

David Rose and Oriel Sullivan

OPEN UNIVERSITY PRESS
Buckingham • Philadelphia

Open University Press
Celtic Court
22 Ballmoor
Buckingham
MK18 1XW

and
1900 Frost Road, Suite 101
Bristol, PA 19007, USA

First published 1993

First published in this second edition 1996

A catalogue record of this book is available from the British Library

ISBN 0 335 19617 9

Library of Congress Cataloging-in-Publication Data
Rose, David, 1947 Feb. 17–
 Introducing data analysis for social scientists/David Rose and
Oriel Sullivan.
  p.   cm.
 Includes bibliographical references and index.
 ISBN 0–335–19617–9 (pb)
 1. Social sciences – Statistical methods.   2. Social sciences – Research.
I. Sullivan, Oriel, 1957–   II. Title.
HA29.R79   1996
300'.1'5195 – dc20
96–4035
CIP

Typeset by Type Study, Scarborough
Printed in Great Britain by Redwood Books, Trowbridge

To Nickie, John and the
Sullivan extended family

Contents

Part IV Inferential data analysis in social research

Part V Introduction to multivariate analysis

Preface

This is a book designed for those with no previous knowledge of statistics, and only a very elementary recall of school mathematics. The emphasis throughout is on understanding the underlying *principles* of data analysis, and on bringing these out with reference to simple but realistic worked examples. The hope is that those who go on subsequently to do their own research and analysis will feel confident that they have a thorough grounding in the basics of data analysis before getting thrown head first into the increasingly sophisticated statistical techniques which are available to them at the touch of a computer key.

The bulk of the text may be worked through as a basic course-book, and includes some exercises which could be used for course or self-assessment purposes. A floppy disk containing a sub-set of data for analysis is included in the price. The book also offers simple computing instructions in SPSS, as well as the formulae for a few statistics, but understanding is the key throughout. The final part of the text contains an introduction to some of the most useful multivariate techniques, in particular log-linear analysis and event-history analysis (including a short discussion of the uses and availability of longitudinal data). This introduction is not intended to serve as a complete guide to performing such analyses (which would involve a much more substantial exposition) but it is included for two major reasons. First, it is intended that those beginners who follow this text right through will be in a better position to understand and interpret the analyses of others. This being so it seems necessary to address the fact that, with recent developments in statistical theory and computing, published books and articles in social research are becoming increasingly sophisticated. It is hoped that the introduction provided in Part V will be comprehensible on an intuitive level to those who are familiar with the content of the preceding parts of the text, and will enable them to grasp the underlying principles of such analytic techniques, without introducing the possibly confusing details that need to be grasped before embarking on such analyses themselves.

Second, while the main body of the text deals exclusively with cross-sectional data (the majority of data used in social research being of this form) we also felt it important to provide a simple introduction to the nature and analysis of longitudinal data. With an increasing number of longitudinal data-sets available, it is becoming more and more likely that readers will come across and need to be able to interpret the kinds of analyses appropriate to them.

By emphasizing the understanding of basic principles, we are not, of course, implying that we believe that the detailed assumptions and problems surrounding any particular analysis are unimportant – far from it – and anyone who goes on to do research will need to go into these in some depth. Our hope is that those who absorb the information contained here will be in a position to move on both to more advanced statistical texts, and to more sophisticated statistical procedures on a computer, with a solid grounding in the fundamental principles of data analysis which will ensure they need not feel out of their depth.

Preface to the second edition

The second edition of *Introducing Data Analysis for Social Scientists*, incorporating SPSS FOR WINDOWS, has been expanded and restructured to a new textbook format, including additional features such as a glossary of methodological and statistical terms, and key concepts and multiple choice questions at the end of each substantive chapter. It is hoped that these changes will make the text both more visually accessible and more 'user-friendly' to students. A new section on how to use the text is included below in order to aid study.

One of the most significant changes is that computer instructions and new data-sets have been added in order to enable students to learn and use an increasingly popular alternative version of the Statistical Package for the Social Sciences (SPSS): SPSS FOR WINDOWS. This is the version of SPSS which is used from the Microsoft WINDOWS environment on IBM PCs and their look-alikes. Consequently the two chapters which contain detailed instructions on how to use SPSS (Chapters 4 and 6) have been substantially rewritten, and the data-disk updated to include SPSS FOR WINDOWS data files in addition to those for SPSS/PC+.

Another substantial change is that, since the first edition was written, the British Household Panel Study (BHPS), which provided the data for one of the data-sets available on the accompanying data-disk, has produced two more waves of data. We have therefore made available on the data-disk a longitudinal data file using data from all three of these waves. The chapter on longitudinal analysis (Chapter 12) has been expanded to take on board discussion of the analysis of cross-wave panel data, and a fifth exercise, in using panel data, has been added in order to help students get to grips with the explanation in the text. To aid in this an annotated example of an SPSS analysis using the new data-set has been included on the data-disk.

Finally, the authors would like to thank all those students and teachers who contributed the useful suggestions which we have done our best to incorporate in this new edition. In particular, we would like to thank Vernon Gayle and Mel Read for their interest and comments. Oxford University Press kindly gave us permission to extract entries for the

Glossary of methodological and statistical terms from *The Concise Oxford Dictionary of Sociology*. Jane Worton again supplied infinite patience and care in the secretarial work for the drafting of this edition, and Mark Taylor produced the data files and annotated example analysis on the data-disk. We are very grateful to them both.

The organization of the text and how to get the most from it

Key concepts

At the end of each chapter of the second edition we have included a list of key concepts for that chapter. The first time in each chapter that a key concept appears it is highlighted in **bold**. At the end of each chapter students should therefore make sure that they have understood the meaning of the key concepts for that chapter.

Multiple choice questions

At the end of each substantive chapter dealing with statistical procedures there are between three and six multiple choice questions, which you can use as a small test of whether you have absorbed some of the main ideas and/or statistical techniques contained in that chapter. Answers to these questions are provided on pp. 255–6 at the end of the book.

The exercises

There are five more substantial exercises involving doing data analysis tasks on the computer, which are found at the ends of Chapters 6, 7, 8, 10 and 12. These exercises combine the computing skills which you need to undertake specific pieces of analysis, with an understanding of the statistical procedures presented in the relevant chapters. In addition, they involve writing a brief report on each analysis, which will give you practice at writing up results.

The glossaries

At the end of the book a new glossary of methodological and statistical terms based on the key concepts and entries from *The Concise Oxford Dictionary of Sociology* (Marshall, 1994) has been included for you to use as a reference guide. In addition there is a short glossary of computing terms at the end of Chapter 4.

Computing instructions

Chapter 4: 'Getting to know the computer: DOS, WINDOWS and SPSS' and Chapter 6: 'Univariate descriptive statistics using SPSS' are primarily concerned with getting across the main points that you will need to know about doing data analysis using SPSS on a PC. The basic information about computing and SPSS are elucidated first, and thereafter instructions for those using SPSS/PC+ (indicated by ∗) and those using SPSS FOR WINDOWS (indicated by #) are separated. You only need to follow those instructions relevant to the version of SPSS that you are using.

Acknowledgements

All writers borrow ideas from the work of others and it is usual to acknowledge this in the text. While we have made attributions where we can, we cannot be sure that we have always been able to acknowledge all sources properly. Books that develop from teaching notes, from ideas culled from other books and from one's own teachers, risk something close to plagiarism, especially in an area such as data analysis. What we wish to do first, therefore, is to pay a personal tribute to those whose teaching inspired us. In David Rose's case (as is obvious in parts of the book) Jim Davis was an important influence. In the case of Oriel Sullivan, John Osborn at the London School of Hygiene and Tropical Medicine and Mike Murphy at the London School of Economics introduced a world that had to that point seemed completely impenetrable. However, while we have tried extremely hard to acknowledge other sources, it is possible that we have used the ideas and examples of others without proper acknowledgement. If this should be the case, we apologize and hope the original authors will be flattered rather than offended.

Finally, we wish to extend our thanks to our colleagues Tony Coxon, Jacqueline Scott, Alan Taylor and Graham Upton for their careful reading of our first draft and the many useful comments they made. We are also grateful to Ray Pawson and Janet Siltanen for their most generous comments and encouragement when we first decided to write this book. The successive drafts of this book were processed by Carole Allington, Sue Aylott and Jane Worton. We are indebted to them all for the care and diligence (as well as good humour) they gave to the task. Of course, the lectures on which the book is based were written for our students and they have been our most important critics. We thank them for the help and stimulation which they gave us. The usual caveats apply: any errors are ours alone. We hope more statistically sophisticated readers will recognize that it is sometimes necessary to simplify in order to introduce students to the challenges of data analysis.

Part I

The logic and language of social research

1 Introducing data analysis

Aims

- To understand the underlying principles of data analysis and the relationship with the experimental method.
- To describe the various 'levels of measurement' of variables.

The ability to understand and interpret quantitative data is a skill required by all social researchers, regardless of theoretical or epistemological persuasion. Marx could not have produced his penetrating analysis of capitalism without being able to read and interpret the British government 'Blue Books'.[1] Durkheim could not have written *Suicide* without the ability to interpret official data on suicide.[2] Weber's earliest work involved quantitative analysis of Prussian agriculture. Thus, sociology's classical triumvirate taught us an important lesson: it is not sufficient for social researchers to be merely literate; they must also be numerate. Moreover, this requirement is an even more demanding one in the computer age. Not only is an appreciation of **data analysis** important to understand and evaluate the work of many social researchers, but also much of what we read, hear and see in the media, and in official publications. In addition, many of the problems which we wish to analyse as social researchers can be examined via secondary analysis of data collected by others and then deposited in data archives.

Nevertheless, it remains the case that many social researchers, both students and professionals, are afraid of numbers and largely ignorant of quantitative data analysis. After all, many of us found mathematics at school a complete mystery and persuaded ourselves that anything numeric or (worse) algebraic was incomprehensible. Part of the purpose of this book, therefore, must be to persuade people that anything quantitative, let alone formally expressed, is not beyond their grasp. It is not necessary to be a mathematician or statistician in order to develop an understanding of quantitative data and how they can be analysed. That is why this book is described as dealing with *data analysis*; data analysis is *not* an alternative to the term 'statistics' but has its own distinct meaning.

Statistics refer to formal mathematical procedures as they are applied to data. *Data analysis* refers to the practical application of such procedures to, in this case, the analysis of social science data. That is, data analysis is concerned with sensitizing social researchers to the use, interpretation and evaluation of relevant data rather than with the more formal understanding of statistics. It involves the understanding of certain statistical techniques in terms of knowing which techniques apply to which sort of data or which can best deal with certain kinds of problems in analysis; but this understanding takes the form of appreciation and awareness rather than any particular mathematical facility. The more familiar we become with techniques of data analysis, the better we can think about data in general. This is because a proper understanding of data analysis improves the way in which we think about, interpret, evaluate and plan empirical research. It is therefore an indispensable skill for any professional social researcher or aspiring student.

This last point reminds us that data analysis is not somehow disembodied or otherwise separated from the other concerns of social researchers. Too often research methods of all kinds have been taught or written about as if they were ends in themselves rather than means to ends. Yet the object of data analysis should be to aid us in arriving at a better understanding of the operation of social processes. We have questions which we wish to answer *but* those questions must always derive from theory; and it follows that what we measure in order to produce data, and how we analyse those data, is also a theory-guided process which leads in the end to new ways of thinking about the world, and to more theoretical puzzles. For this reason, Part I deals with certain epistemological issues which have a bearing on data analysis.

Finally, it should be understood that what follows is only intended as a basic introduction to the problems and possibilities of both social science data analysis and computing. As such it will provide a foundation on which to build a more sophisticated understanding of the process. There are many more advanced forms of analysis and specialized techniques which have been developed to inform particular problems which are not discussed here.

The book is divided into five parts. Part I deals briefly with general issues relevant to data analysis – the logic of social research, questions of measurement and the particular logic for analysing social science variables on a computer. In this part, certain fundamental terms and ideas are introduced. Part II deals with a discussion of how data, once collected, are prepared for computer analysis, and introduces readers to the basic computing skills. Part III discusses particular well-known techniques of data analysis, interspersed with discussion of how to employ such techniques on the computer using the computer program *SPSS* – the *Statistical Package for the Social Sciences* in both the SPSS FOR WINDOWS and SPSS/PC+ versions. Part IV is concerned with the extension to making generalizations about a population from statistics calculated for a sample taken from that population. Finally, Part V discusses some more complex types of analysis in simple terms, and introduces the idea of analysing data collected longitudinally rather than cross-sectionally, i.e. across time rather than at only one point in time.

The data

Some of the examples used in the text, and the exercises in analysis suggested in Part III, use data from the British Class Survey of 1984 and from the British Household Panel Survey (1991–). The survey of social class in modern Britain was undertaken as part of an international project whose aim was to investigate the effect of recent economic change on class structure and class related behaviour in advanced capitalist societies (see Marshall *et al.*, 1988). The British project set out to examine the strengths and weaknesses of three different class models. These are the models of John H. Goldthorpe (1980), Erik Olin Wright (1979 and 1985) and the Registrar General (the 'official' class model used in government data).[3] The British Household Panel Survey is a longitudinal study, and is discussed in Chapter 12. We have selected a limited number of variables from these data-sets, and these sub-sets are available as both SPSS FOR WINDOWS and SPSS/PC+ data files on the floppy disk provided with this book. The Appendix at the end of the book tells you how to use this disk.

Data analysis: some preliminary considerations

In the remainder of this chapter, we are going to introduce some of the most basic ideas required for an understanding of data analysis. First, we convey in simple terms the purpose of data analysis and its place in social scientific explanation and procedures. Here we introduce the idea that data analysis concerns the description and explanation of **variance**. Second, we place this idea in the broader context of the logic of social research or what we call '**socio-logic**'. We also introduce the idea of the experiment as the scientific method for establishing causal relationships and briefly examine how this relates to social scientific analysis. In the experimental situation the scientist directly manipulates the factors with which s/he is concerned; in social research we cannot generally do this but we can still follow the logic of the experiment in our analyses. In the next section of the chapter we examine measurement in the social sciences and the way in which we move from the language of theory to the

language of research. This leads into a discussion of the nature of variables and the different levels at which they can be measured. However,
we begin with the most basic question of all: what *is* data analysis? To
answer this question we need to make a brief excursion into some theoretical and epistemological issues.

Empirical social science research is concerned to explain the patterns
and regularities we believe society exhibits. We want to explain these patterns. When we consider how social researchers *explain*, or where their
explanations begin from, the answer is from *theory*, but what is a theory?
Theory is a form of selective focusing: that is, it is a way of separating out
from the confusing world which assails our senses those elements of
reality which concern us as social researchers, rather in the same way that
we put blinkers on a horse to prevent it from being distracted. In other
words, data do not suddenly appear from nowhere: they are constructed
by being placed in some kind of context which gives them meaning from
the viewpoint of a particular discipline. For us the meaning context is
called 'Sociology' or 'Political Science' or 'Geography'. For example, to
be a sociologist or to do sociology is to place the world around us within
a particular meaning system. Put baldly, sociologists are concerned with
the study of social relationships. That is, we look at the world around us
and we separate it, first, into what is 'social' and what is 'non-social'. We
then develop a language with which to discuss the social world: that is,
we construct concepts and theories. Concepts are the building blocks out
of which we construct meanings. Theories link these meanings into claims
about how the social world or some part of it actually works. Concepts
create order out of chaos and theories link these concepts in an attempt
to explain the way the social world is.

Of course, there are many different ways of conceptualizing and theorizing the social world, and there are many disputes about how we can
legitimately study society. It is not part of our task here to pursue these
disputes. On the contrary, we assume that it is possible to study society
in a particular way, construct data in a particular way and analyse it with
particular methods.[4] For now, all we need to note is that before we can
observe anything useful about the social world we have to have a theory.
Moreover, that theory must be capable of being **operationalized** (made
amenable to some kind of measurement). Then, in order to generalize
from the observations which our theory allows us to make, we must
process those observations into data and analyse them. Here we present
a way of elucidating that process where the observations we make are
converted into numeric data and analysed via statistical methods. We
shall say more on these issues when we discuss the logic of social research,
the measurement problem and the logic of data analysis.

However, our discussion so far on meanings, data, theories and observations is sufficient to make a simple point: data analysis is the means by
which we test our theories about the social world and attempt to specify

the nature of the relationships between the observations our theories allow us to make. Above all, to put the matter slightly more technically, data analysis is concerned with *explaining variance*, with explaining why there is variability in some particular characteristic in a population or sample which is of theoretical importance to social researchers. Because we are interested in variance, we construct our data in the form of what we call *variables*. We shall say more about variables later but, as the name implies, a variable is a theoretically devised characteristic in terms of which people vary. For example, 'social class' is a variable. It is not something which is given: it is a theoretical construct. And it can be measured: some people are working class and can be classified as such; others are middle class and can be so classified. All we need is a rule by which to classify people into different classes, a procedure we shall discuss later. Once we have constructed our variables (by defining them and assigning numeric values according to the observations we have made – see below), we use data analysis to try and explain the variability we have observed. We call this *partitioning variance*, i.e. finding a way of categorizing a variable into two or more constants and thus explaining the observed variability. An example is necessary to explain this.

One common way of summarizing variance is to create some kind of average score for a variable. Say we ask a sample of people what their annual income is. For ease of explanation we will choose a small sample of six people. Our variable is 'annual income' and its values are given by the answer to a question intended to elicit how much each person earned in the same twelve-month period. The answers we get give us the following values:

Person	Annual income
1	£25k
2	£15k
3	£20k
4	£5k
5	£7k
6	£12k

Notice that each person gave a different answer and we want to know why there is variance – why their answers differ; why they don't all earn the same income. One way in which we could begin to answer the question we are posing is to *summarize the variance* by working out the average income for our sample. We do this by adding their incomes together and dividing by the number of individuals, thus:

$$\frac{£25k + £15k + £20k + £5k + £7k + £12k}{6} = \frac{£84k}{6} = £14k$$

So the average income is £14k; £14k *summarizes the variance* in annual income. That is, we have taken a variable and reduced it to a *constant* – one score, in this case £14k. One way of beginning to explain the variance in our sample's incomes would be to ask 'Why don't they all earn £14k?' Why do three people earn more than this and three people earn less? As we shall see, average scores are very important in data analysis because they provide us with a constant value as a first step in explaining variance. In the example we have just given, we could now begin to ask why cases 1–3 have more than the 'constant' value of £14k and why cases 4–6 have less. To do this, we would need to look for other ways in which people vary which might explain the differences from the average we have observed. Let us say that we also know the sex of our sample and that cases 1–3 are male and 4–6 are female. We could use the information about the 'average' or *mean* income of our sample to divide them into two groups – those who earn more than £14k (cases 1–3) and those who earn less than £14k (cases 4–6). Sex is already a two-category or *dichotomous variable* – male and female. Let us assign the letter X to the variable 'sex' and the letter Y to 'income'. If we now put together what we know about income and what we know about sex for our sample, that is, if we examine the *relationship* between X and Y, we would have

	Sex (X)	Case		Income (Y)*
X_1 {	M M M	1 2 3	Y_1 {	> £14k > £14k > £14k
X_2 {	F F F	4 5 6	Y_2 {	< £14k < £14k < £14k

* Note: > means 'more than'; < means 'less than'.

Now provided we had a theory which linked gender and income, we would have a paradigm case for the explanation of income by sex. We have *partitioned* the variance of income into two constants – above and below the average or *mean* score of £14k; and we have shown that all the males earn above £14k and all the females earn below £14k, i.e. we have explained the variance in income (Y) by reference to sex (X). When the value of X changes from female (X_2) to male (X_1), the value of Y changes from below £14k (Y_2) to above £14k (Y_1) or when $X = 2$ = female, $Y = 2$ = <£14k; but when $X = 1$ = male, $Y = 1$ = > £14k. If we put our results in a table, we would have

| | Sex | | |
Income	M	F	Total
> £14k	3	0	3
< £14k	0	3	3
Total	3	3	6

We have produced two constant values for Y (income) depending on the value of X (sex). Of course, in practice it is never so easy as this, but we hope the point is made. *Data analysis is about explaining variance – about finding a way of categorizing a variable which reduces it to two or more constants and thereby explains the variability concerned.* In the example above, we could go even further and make some claims about the value in income terms of being male or female. This again involves using the mean as a summary score. We calculated the mean for all our cases in the income variable, but we could also calculate the *within-category means*, i.e. the mean income for males and the mean income for females. The mean income for males is:

$$\frac{£25k + £15k + £20k}{3} = £20k$$

For females, mean income is:

$$\frac{£12k + £5k + £7k}{3} = £8k$$

We have already seen that the overall mean of £14k can be thought of as a constant value for income. Indeed, we can think of all variables as potential constants with 'errors' around them, so that each actual observation is an error term from the constant value which a measure such as the mean gives us. Explaining variance can be thought of as a way of explaining those 'errors'. In our paradigm example, we can explain the 'errors' by relating the sex category means to the overall mean. Thus we can say, in relation to the overall average of £14k, being female imposes a decremental value of (£14k–£8k) or £6k. In saying this, we no longer have an error of £6k from the constant value but rather an *explanation* of why some cases differ by that amount. The same goes for males. They have an income *increment* of (£20k–£14k) or £6k which implies that being male is worth an extra £6k a year. Hence, in such an example, we can explain the variance of income (Y) in respect of the variance of sex (X) – always provided we have a theory which leads us to believe that sex and income are related. It could, of course, have been true that cases 1–3 all have blue eyes and 4–6 all have brown eyes but it would never occur to a social researcher in our society that this could provide an explanation for the income differences observed because eye colour is not a variable which has social aspects to it. Of course, skin colour might be a different matter since we know there is discrimination in Britain on grounds of colour. Had cases 1–3 been white and 4–6 been black, we would have been more interested in this as a possible explanatory factor.

We can now further illustrate some of the points we have made so far about data analysis by considering the logic of social research and the concept of measurement.

The logic of social research

To reiterate, as social researchers we believe that patterns and regu-larities occur in society and that these are not simply random. The task we are faced with is to ask why these patterns exist; in other words to produce *explanations* of them. We couch these explanations in terms of *theories*. Theories allow us to select out from a mass of confusing material those elements of reality which are of concern to us. On the basis of theory we can develop hypotheses about relationships which ought to exist, if the theory is valid. Essentially the whole of this book is concerned with such theory and hypothesis testing procedures where the data to be analysed to test a theory or hypothesis are numeric.

Of course, in the social sciences there are many competing theories but nevertheless it can be argued that there is a similar underlying logic to the process of social research regardless of the particular theory being used. In other words, there are general points we can make about theories, concepts and forms of explanation in social research. As Mann (1981) has argued, while there is not one methodology, there is one 'socio-logic'. Socio-logic is the knitting together of theory, concept formation, the derivation of hypotheses, operationalization, observation, data analy-sis, causal inference and back to theory again. All these terms will become familiar as we progress. In the interim we can better appreciate what is meant by socio-logic from Figure 1.1. There are a number of points which are usefully elucidated by this. First, it confirms what has already been stated about the inextricable relationship between theory and method. For example, we can see that before one can observe anything, elements within the theory must be operationalized (i.e. made amenable to measurement of some kind); and before we can generalize from the observations made we must process and analyse data, and so on. Second, while the diagram should not be interpreted to imply any necessary sequential pattern in which we must work, it does illustrate some of the processes which must be followed in order to render a theory testable.

In analysing data we are ultimately concerned with one particular

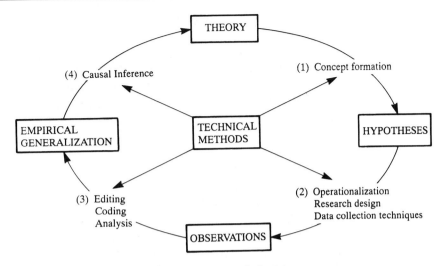

Figure 1.1 The logic of social research or 'socio-logic'
Source: After Wallace (1971).

method of theory testing called **multivariate analysis** (see Part V) and so we shall be following the elements in socio-logic from that viewpoint. Multivariate analysis is a method of theory testing which follows the logic of the **experiment.** The experiment is, of course, the principal natural scientific method for theory testing. Because the experiment is so useful in connecting cause and effect, techniques such as multivariate analysis have been developed which attempt to reproduce the main elements of experimental design in non-experimental situations. It is therefore worth examining briefly the basics of the experimental method.

The essence of the experimental method lies in the attempt to *control* all factors which might affect what is being studied in order to specify the causal relationships involved. However, to achieve this, what is being observed must be capable of being *measured.* When we can control and measure in this way we have a true experimental situation. The experimenter can then vary one or more factors in the situation in order to investigate the effects of this manipulation. These factors are known technically as *variables*. Since the essence of the experiment is that all variables are under the control of the experimenter and all can be measured, then it is possible to meet three necessary conditions of determining cause and effect:

(i) that two variables *co-vary* such that when the experimenter varies (manipulates) one variable, the second variable varies without being similarly manipulated;

(ii) *temporal order* – for something to cause something else to happen, it must happen first;

(iii) *control for rival or alternative causal factors* – we must be sure that other possible causes of the observed behaviour are controlled for.

Since the experimenter can manipulate *all* the variables in an experiment, it is relatively easy to establish (ii) and (iii); since measurement is possible, co-variation can be observed when it takes place. Obviously there is much more to experimental design than this indicates but the important point to note is that in the experiment the experimenter can directly manipulate the variables, and can in principle establish co-variation and temporal order, while controlling for rival or alternative potential causal factors.

However, true experiments, for a variety of fairly obvious reasons, are rarely possible in social research. Nevertheless, because of the obvious advantages of the experimental method in making causal inferences, social researchers have devised ways in which they can follow the logic of the experiment in *non*-experimental situations, with non-experimental data. How this is done raises two important issues. First, how do we measure? Second, how do we control? The first question addresses the *measurement problem* and the second addresses the *logic of data analysis*. These form the next two elements to be discussed. In the process we shall learn more of the language of social research, including the meanings of some of the terms which have been used in this brief discussion of the logic of social research. In the remainder of this chapter we discuss measurement; the logic of data analysis is the main topic of Chapter 2.

The measurement problem

The measurement problem is not peculiar to the social sciences but is a problem shared by researchers in all disciplines where the attempt is made to quantify observations. In social science, because of the nature of our objects of study, the measurement problem does, however, take a peculiar form. Indeed, whether one can measure at all in the social sciences has been the subject of much debate.

The problem can be stated in the form of a question: how do we move from the language of theory to the language of research? Or to put the question more simply, how do we know when we are observing something in the research process which represents a manifestation of our initial concepts and theories? Figure 1.2 illustrates the major problems to be discussed both here and in the next chapter on the logic of data analysis.

By definition, *concepts* are abstractions by which we select and order our impressions of the world. They are mental constructs and are, therefore, not observable. Since they cannot be observed they cannot be measured. Hence the tension between concepts and *indicators* is that

Figure 1.2 The tensions between theory and data
Source: Evans (1979), p. 15.

between the unobservable and the observable. If we wish to understand something about class (a concept, and, therefore, part of our theoretical language and not observable) what can we observe in the real world which manifests class? That is, what indicators can we use for class so that we can obtain data about class? This is the essence of the measurement problem; and when we link an unobservable concept with an observable indicator we are producing **operationalizations**. Operationalization refers to the rules we use to link the language of theory (concepts) to the language of research (indicators).

The second tension, that between causal relations and correlations, presents a similar problem. Since concepts are not observable, neither are the causal relations between them. Equally, by definition, indicators are observable and correlations between them can be measured, but does a correlation between two variables mean a causal relationship has been established? Obviously, stated in that form, the answer to the question must be 'No'. However, there are rules for linking correlations to causes which we will discuss later.

The final tension, that between the *general* and the *particular*, is the problem of inference. This is dealt with in more detail in Part IV. However, we can briefly illustrate the problem. Theories are expressed in terms of whole populations or sub-groups, i.e. they are general. However, it is usually the case in empirical research that data relate only to a small part or *sample* of the population. If we wish to generalize, it is therefore important that we should try and ensure that the samples we study are as representative of the population we wish to generalize about as possible. In other words, the third tension concerns *representation* and *generalization*.

For the present, however, we are concerned primarily with the first tension, the relation between concepts and indicators – the measurement problem. We saw that in an experimental situation the experimenter manipulates one variable to see what, if any, effects it has on another or others. The manipulated variable is known as the **independent variable** and is conventionally represented by the letter X; the variables hypothesized to be influenced by X are known as **dependent variables** and are conventionally represented by the letter Y. Hence we are interested in relationships of the type:

$$X \rightarrow Y$$

which can be expressed verbally in a variety of ways. We could say 'X leads to Y'; or 'X causes Y'; or 'Y is dependent on X'. However, it would be more exact to talk of X being associated with Y such that a knowledge of the value of X would give us a better indication of the value of Y. Indeed the more X and Y are correlated, the better would be our prediction of Y on the basis of knowing the value of X. In Part III, this way of expressing the $X \rightarrow Y$ relationship will be developed in our discussion of the measurement of association between variables, although we have already explained the basic idea with our first example of the relation between income and sex.

For the time being we can say that $X \rightarrow Y$ implies that if the value of X changes then it will lead to a change in the value of Y. This discussion helps us to understand the essence of variables: they are factors which have more than one value. If we think about concepts such as 'class', 'social status', 'anomie', or whatever, they are useful precisely because people vary in terms of them. There is more than one class and status group, just as there are different types of anomie. However, concepts are not observable or measurable whereas variables are. This is because variables are invented constructs which serve to bridge the gap between the language of theory and the language of research. Hence they must be defined in such a way that they (a) relate to some concept in a theory or hypothesis, and (b) can be observed and measured (turn back to the socio-logic diagram and you will see this process described). We can easily think of a number of variables – sex, occupation, income, religion, party political preference and so on, all of which take on different values among any random group of people.

So a variable is in effect a symbol to which numbers or values are assigned in order to represent its variation. It may have only two values (a *dichotomous variable*) or several or many values (*polytomous variable*). It may be a *categoric* or *discrete* variable, i.e. one in which values represent certain categories such as in sex or class; or it may be a *continuous* variable, such as age or income, which can assume any value, between two extremes, in quite small steps. Examples of variables which are both categoric and dichotomous, might be:

Sex   = 1 Female
                                  2 Male

or

Voting behaviour = 1 Labour
                                  2 Other

We can see that in the first example we have a true dichotomy – sex – which can only take on two values. In that sense we are concerned only with the presence or absence of some property, but most variables used in social research are polytomies. For example, in Britain, voting behaviour might more normally be expected to take on the following appearance:

Voting behaviour = 1 Conservative
                   2 Labour
                   3 Liberal Democrats
                   4 Nationalist
                   5 Other
                   0 Would not vote

Continuous variables such as age, income and IQ are often grouped into categoric variables for analytic purposes. This is generally achieved by *grouping* data in some way. Thus, for example, the ages of a sample of respondents may take on a range from 16–65 in a particular study of the working population. The variable age could then be expressed as follows:

Age	Number of cases
16	75
17	91
18	102
19	117
20	108
21	130
–	–
–	–
–	–
63	105
64	60
65	37

In this format age has already been reduced from a continuous variable to a discrete one by standardizing to whole years. However, we could also group the data, as follows:

Age	Number of cases
16–19	385
20–24	407
25–29	461
–	–
–	–
–	–
60–65	362

Any continuous variable can be transformed into a polytomy or dichotomy in this way. Of course, one of the problems of transforming any variable like this is a certain loss of information (in this case about the exact ages of the respondents). In analysis, as we shall see, we trade such a loss against the gain we can make for a simplified understanding of the real world. What does all this discussion tell us about the original question, 'what is a variable?'

What we are basically saying is that a variable is a sorting or allocation of cases into two or more mutually exclusive and exhaustive categories. In other words each case can be assigned to one category only, and all cases must be assigned – and what we assign when we put cases into categories is, of course, a numeral. As Davis (1971: 10) notes, every variable has four essential parts: (1) a name; (2) some sort of verbal definition; (3) a set of categories; and (4) a procedure for carrying out the sorting. So we could have a variable called 'party political preference' which we define as 'usual vote at general election' and divide into categories, Conservative, Labour, Liberal-Democrat, Nationalist, Other and None (because it must be totally inclusive) and a sorting procedure given by answers to the survey question 'In General Elections which party do you normally vote for?' Note that in the process we have moved from the language of theory to the language of research.

Imagine that, theoretically, we were concerned with the concept of political ideology. We have decided that one way in which political ideology is indicated is in terms of people's party preferences. So we have taken steps to measure this by developing a variable called 'party political preference' and the rule we have chosen to measure this is given by the question 'In General Elections which party do you normally vote for?' Hence this question is being used as an indicator of the original concept of political ideology as operationally defined in terms of party political preference. Note that we are therefore making an assumption, and this is where the tension between concept and indicator lies. The assumption is that the way in which people vote at General Elections reflects their political ideologies. You can perhaps begin to see why we would normally look for more than one such indicator of a concept such as political ideology. Nevertheless, the basic idea should be clear. In order to measure we must create a construct which relates to our unmeasurable concept. We do this in the form of one or more operational definitions which give meaning and content to a variable, i.e. which tells us what we must do in order to measure objects or people in terms of that variable. In this way we move from the language of theory to the language of research and eventually back again to theory, as indicated previously by the diagram of socio-logic (Figure 1.1).

It still remains to provide a more formal definition of measurement. Earlier it was stated that variables are useful because objects vary in respect of them. That is, we are interested in *variance* and consequently we must create variables as indicators of the concepts within our theory. Measurement is a way of describing variance. It is *the distribution of objects into two or more classes through the assignment of numerals according to rules.* Thus, at the most basic level, numeric measurement is simply a form of classification which tells us that one thing is different from another and we make that distinction clear by assigning numerals to each of the different categories of whatever variable we are dealing with. Measurement, then, helps us to describe something for a particular purpose. There is a strong heuristic component to measurement. However, it must be done according to *rules.* In the process we improve our theory by 'sharpening up' our concepts. This is because in trying to formulate rules for the empirical classification of objects and then trying to apply those rules, we often find that our original conception is inadequate because it is imprecise or deficient in some way.

Actually all that has just been said about measurement is simply another way of expressing the previous discussion about variables. After all, since a variable is used to measure something, it must meet the definition of measurement. A variable has a set of categories, each of which is distinguished by a different numeral; and it has a procedure for sorting cases into the different categories, i.e. rules which tell us which numeral to attach to each case on that variable. Variables are, therefore, measures and measurement is a form of description which allows us to analyse variance. The ways in which we can analyse variance therefore depend on the ways in which we measure. For instance, variables may be measured at different '**levels of measurement**' (depending on the type of variable), and the level of measurement will determine what *kinds* of analyses may be performed. Later, the implications for analysis of different levels of measurement will be made clear. At this point, however, it is important to know that there are four commonly distinguished levels of measurement, of which only three are normally used in the analysis of social data. They are distinguished as follows.

Nominal, ordinal, and interval and ratio measures

Nominal measures

Earlier we noted that measurement is simply a way of saying that, in respect of some variable, one case is *different* from another – not bigger or smaller, better or worse, but only different. When all that we are talking about is difference, we talk of a nominal measure. Many social variables are nominal. Our earlier example of party political preference is a nominal measure. If A votes Conservative and B votes Labour, we can only draw one conclusion: A and B vote differently. The fact that we assign, say, the code '1' to A and '2' to B for the purposes of numerical analysis does not mean B is bigger than A, let alone twice as big, but only that they are different in respect of their voting behaviour. Here we are only using numerals as labels to indicate difference.

Ordinal measures

Ordinal measures are measures which involve some kind of ranking but no basis for measuring the amount of difference between the ranks. In other words an ordinal scale involves a rank order that allows us to say 'bigger'/'smaller' or 'higher'/'lower' but does not allow us to say by how much. Measured in certain ways, social class is a good example of an ordinal measure.[5] Clearly, if we constructed a social class variable such that we had

    1 Working class
    2 Middle class
    3 Upper class

we would not simply be saying that each class is different. Since class has to do with command over economic resources, it is clear that the upper class has more command than the middle class, but the middle class has more command than the working class. Therefore, we can also say that the upper class has more command than the working class. In that sense the numeral 3 does indicate 'more than 1 and 2'. However, we cannot specify how much more, and so cannot say, for example, that the upper class has three times as much command as the working class, or is two units higher on the class scale. By definition all categorical variables are measured at the nominal or ordinal level.

Interval and ratio measures

In interval and ratio measures the numerals used are real numbers, not category codes. This means that we can perform a wider range of arithmetic operations on the data – add, subtract, multiply, divide, etc. We can therefore use the most powerful available statistical techniques on such data. Now in fact in social research there are very few examples of true interval level measurements, which is why we present interval and ratio measures together. This is because, strictly, *interval* measures have arbitrary zero points, rather than true zero points. For example, Fahrenheit temperature is an interval level scale. If A has a body temperature of 100° F and B a temperature of 98°F, we may draw three conclusions:

    1 A and B have different temperatures.
    2 A is hotter than B.
    3 A is hotter than B by an interval of 2°F.

However, the only conclusion we can draw about the *relative* temperature of A and B is to count the interval between our observation for A and that for B, hence the term 'interval scale'. We cannot say that A is hotter than B by a ratio of 100:98 because 0°F is not absolute zero.

In non-medical social research, however, there are few variables which have such characteristics. What we do have are ratio measures such as age and income. For example, if A has an annual income of £20k and B of £10k we can say the following:

1 A and B have different incomes [*property of a nominal measure*].
2 A has more income than B [*property of an ordinal measure*].
3 A has £10k p.a. more than B [*property of an interval measure*].
4 A has twice as much income as B [*property of a ratio measure*].

Because income has a true zero point, we can say the ratio of A's income to B's is 2 : 1. This represents our highest level of measurement.

The classification of levels of measurement thus has a hierarchical structure: we can see in the table below that each level of measurement has all the characteristics of a lower level, plus something extra:

Level	Classification	Order	Distance	Non-arbitrary zero
Nominal	✓	✗	✗	✗
Ordinal	✓	✓	✗	✗
Interval	✓	✓	✓	✗
Ratio	✓	✓	✓	✓

We can easily recall the four levels of measurement by the mnemonic NOIR – nominal, ordinal, interval, ratio.

The importance of all of this for data analysis will become clearer when we discuss descriptive statistics later. It should also be noted that, to add to confusion, variables measured at a ratio level are frequently referred to as 'interval-level variables'. This should not cause too many problems since true interval-level variables, as mentioned above, occur only rarely in social research. To conclude this discussion of measurement, we turn to two other terms which were mentioned earlier – **validity** and **reliability**.

Validity and reliability

Validity is concerned with whether what one is measuring is what one really intends to measure. Reliability refers to the consistency and dependability of measures. Validity is the more difficult to discuss because there are a number of different aspects to it. However, if we return to the tension between concept and indicator shown in Figure 1.2, perhaps the most important point to grasp is that validity is concerned with the issue of whether the indicator which is used is a valid one in relation to the concept to which it refers. So, when we ask if party political preference is an adequate indicator of political ideology, we are asking about the validity of the measure. In terms of our discussion of variables, we are questioning definitions and sorting procedures. In an earlier example, we said that party political preference could be measured by asking how people normally vote in a General Election, but would this be a valid indicator? The answer is probably 'No'. Some people, for example, may vote tactically. If you are a Labour supporter, committed to a socialist view, but choose to vote Liberal-Democrat because in your constituency Labour has no hope of beating the Conservatives, to know how you vote will not be a valid indicator of your true party preference and nor, therefore, of your political ideology.

Each of the tensions referred to in Figure 1.2 raises questions of validity. Indeed, we can pose questions not only about the validity of particular indicators but of whole pieces of research. When someone criticizes a piece of survey-based research designed to test a theory about class consciousness on the grounds that one cannot 'get at' class consciousness via a survey, then this is a critique of that survey's *internal validity*. On the other hand, if a critic were to say that the sample used was not representative of the population, this would be to criticize the survey's *external validity* or lack of generalizability. In other words, validity has epistemological and technical aspects but can be thought of simply as the degree to which we accept that a particular measure relates to a particular concept, or a particular method to the testing of a particular theory, or a particular set of cases or sample to a particular population, and so on.

Reliability asks about how far we can depend on the consistency of a measure. If the same person were to answer the same survey question one way today and a different way tomorrow; or if the person were to answer it one way when asked the question by interviewer A and in a different way if asked by interviewer B, the measure would not be reliable. After all, the variance which we measure in research must be assumed to reflect real variation and not some quirk in the data collection method.

Validity and reliability are, therefore, concerned with the *quality of measurement*. They are not perfectly independent of one another, since it is possible to have reliable measures which are not valid. For example, as Davis (1971) notes, we could measure IQ by standing subjects on a very accurate pair of bathroom scales and reading off their weights. This would give reliable measures but it would not, of course, be valid. Similarly, our example of the measurement of party preference via a question about voting behaviour was reliable for the Labour supporter who voted Liberal-Democrat but was not valid.

Conclusion

In this chapter we have been concerned to give some basic grounding for what will follow. We have explained that data analysis is different from statistics, and constitutes a vital aspect of the way social researchers think about the social world. Data analysis is geared to the explanation of variance and is guided by theory. Moreover, it is used to test theories by specifying the relationships between phenomena which our theory tells us should be related. Thus, data analysis has a place within an overall logic of social research, which we have termed (following Mann, 1981) 'socio-logic'. We have noted that underlying the various methods of data analysis which we shall be exploring is the logic of the experiment and we will develop this point in Chapter 2. We have also discussed the measurement problem in order to elucidate the relationship between theory and empirical research. We have seen the importance of variable construction to this process and we have examined what we mean by a variable. Finally we have defined measurement and the properties of different levels of measurement and we have introduced the ideas of validity and reliability. It is now time to put some of these ideas to work by elaborating on them. In the next chapter we turn to some aspects of the relationship between correlations and causes in non-experimental situations such as survey analysis.

Notes

1 However, we would not recommend any student to take Marx as an exemplar of a designer of questionnaires. His *enquête ouvrière* might qualify as one of the worst questionnaires ever produced. Nevertheless, it is interesting that Marx recognized the need for data collection on working conditions via a social survey (see Bottomore and Rubel, 1963).
2 Again, we would not argue that Durkheim's analyses of statistics on suicide are unproblematic. Apart from the well-known strictures about the meaning of suicide statistics, some of Durkheim's data analysis was weak, to say the least. However, it was a pioneering attempt to interpret social data in a scientifically useful way.
3 Each of these models is extensively discussed in Marshall *et al.* (1988) and in Marsh (1986).
4 There are many texts which explore these more philosophical aspects of social research but a good introduction can be found in Hughes (1980).
5 However, some class schemes are not ordinal but nominal. For example, Goldthorpe's scheme is not an ordinal one. The fact that the self-employed are

Class IV in Goldthorpe's scheme does not mean they have *less* command over economic resources than routine non-manual workers in Class III but that they have *different* work and market situations.

Key concepts

Make sure you have understood the following key concepts:

- data analysis
- socio-logic
- experiment
- variance
- dependent and independent variables
- operationalization
- levels of measurement
- validity and reliability

---

2 The logic of data analysis

Aims

- To understand the distinction between 'correlation' and 'causation'.
- To introduce the logic of the non-experimental manipulation of variable via 'control' variables.

In the earlier discussion of the logic of social research we noted that the experiment was the principal method for testing scientific hypotheses. This method involves an experimenter directly manipulating the variables in which s/he is interested. We also noted that such a procedure is rarely possible in social research. Both practical and ethical reasons limit its applicability at the individual level, and at the macro level the very idea of an experiment would be ludicrous. (Consider for example, how you would construct an experiment to test Weber's Protestant ethic thesis!) However, it is possible to follow the *logic* of the experimental method when doing social research. We have already discussed the measurement aspect of this process, and now we turn to the way in which the same logic may be applied in data analysis. The techniques of analysis discussed here involve the statistical manipulation of variables which cannot be directly manipulated by the researcher (so-called non-manipulated variables). In this chapter we outline the logic of the process (for further discussion see Rosenberg, 1968; and Hirschi and Selvin, 1967).

We saw earlier that, on the basis of some theory or hypothesis, we wish to examine relationships of the type $X \rightarrow Y$. While we know that nothing is ever so simple as this, nevertheless it is the beginning point in causal analysis. Initially X and Y are theoretical concepts which we hypothesize to be causally related. In order to test our hypothesis we then operationalize X and Y, i.e. we derive measurable indicators of these concepts. We then proceed to measure them so that we have data on X and Y as variables. The question now becomes one of, first, establishing whether these variables are *correlated*. While correlations are not causes never-theless we can argue that two variables which are not correlated cannot be causally related, either. A **correlation**, as we saw earlier, is a relation-ship such that we can more accurately estimate an individual's value on Y, if we first have some knowledge of that individual's value on X. So, for example, if you were asked to guess a person's politics (Y) at the time of the 1992 General Election, all you could reasonably do would be to guess that his/her politics were Conservative because more people voted Con-servative than for any other party. However, if in addition you were told that the person was working class (X = social class) you would do well to change your guess to Labour because more working-class people vote Labour than for any other party. That is, there is a correlation between class and voting behaviour. However, that is not the same thing as saying that class 'causes' voting behaviour. In order to make that statement we must (a) have some sound theoretical reason for there being a *necessary* link between class and voting; (b) remember that causal relationships are asymmetric (i.e. class causes voting is not the same thing as voting causes class) but correlations are symmetric (i.e. class and voting correlate both ways) and so, consequently, our theory must explain why it is that the cor-relation should be interpreted as $X \rightarrow Y$ and not $Y \rightarrow X$; and (c) we must be certain that X does 'cause' Y by making sure that we rule out *rival or alternative causal factors*. In other words, we must make sure that Y cannot be explained by another independent variable, say A, which also happens to be correlated with X. We need to be sure that the correlation between X and Y is 'genuine' and not 'spurious' in terms of causation.

Once we have done all of these things, we will want to undertake further analysis to **elaborate the relationship** between X and Y in order to understand its nature. The ways in which we establish correlations sta-tistically are examined later. Here we are concerned with the principles by which we test theories or hypotheses where the variables we have measured have not been directly manipulated by the researcher. Let us recall on the basis of Figure 1.2 that we are concerned here with the tension between causal relations in theory and correlations in data. Our theory tells us that a causal relation we have hypothesized can be tested by reference to a particular correlation. Once we have our data we examine that correlation and then seek to explain it via the process of statistical elaboration. An example should make the process clearer.

Say we want to investigate the relationship between the 'consumption locations' of individuals and their political ideologies. Let us further imagine that we have operationalized the concept of consumption location in terms of whether individuals rely on public or private pro-vision of a range of goods and services for which public and private alternatives exist, e.g. health care, transport, housing, education, etc.; and further that we have operationalized political ideology in terms of current voting intention, previous voting behaviour, class identification, attitudes to the welfare state, attitudes to 'privatization', etc. For purposes of simplicity, let us examine one possible relationship – that between the consumption of housing and voting behaviour. The British Class Survey interviewed a random sample of the British population and among the questions asked were:

1 Do you own or rent your home?
2 (If renting) who does own your home?
3 (If owner) what made you decide to become a home owner?
4 If there were a general election tomorrow, who would you vote for?
5 Have you ever voted for another party at a general election?
6 (If 'Yes' to 5) which other party or parties have you voted for at past general elections?

Suppose we were to look at the association between two variables derived from some of the above questions. From Question 1 we have derived the variable 'housing tenure' as our independent variable (X), with the categories (1) Owns and (2) Rents. From Question 4 we have derived the variable 'current voting intention' as the dependent variable (Y), with categories (1) Labour and (2) Other. The hypothesis we want to examine concerns the impact that owning one's own home has on the propensity to vote Labour. Let us now examine the resulting data presented in Table 2.1.[1]

Table 2.1 Voting intention by housing tenure

Voting intention	Owns	%	Rents	%	Total	%
Labour	304	30.1	275	52.8	579	37.8
Other	706	69.9	246	47.2	952	62.2
Total	1010	100	521	100	1531	100

We can see from this table that 1010 respondents own their homes and 521 rent them (column totals); 579 (37.8 per cent) would vote Labour and 952 (62.2 per cent) would vote for another party, or would not vote (row totals). When we put this information together and read across the first row we see some striking differences. Whereas, for example, 37.8 per cent of the sample overall would vote Labour, no less than 52.8 per cent of those who rent their homes would vote Labour, compared to only 30.1 per cent of those who own their own homes. In other words, distinguishing how people intend to vote by housing tenure gives us more information about how they are likely to vote. Suppose we had assembled our respondents in the Albert Hall, had then picked one out at random and

asked how does this person vote? If you had been given only the information provided by the variable 'voting intention' your best guess would
be 'Other' because this is the largest overall category, with 62.2 per cent
of respondents. However, if you were also told that the person rented
their home, you would change your guess to Labour because this is the
largest category for renters, consisting of 52.8 per cent of respondents. In
other words, what is obvious from Table 2.1 is that there *is* a correlation
between housing tenure and voting intention for this sample.

However, at this stage we can only really call this an *apparent* relationship. We certainly cannot conclude that housing tenure is causally related
to voting intention. Of course, we could have a narrative which leads us
to believe that they are causally related. It would not be difficult to construct a theoretical argument which would lead us to believe that those
who rent are more likely to vote Labour. Such a causal narrative would
also have to be sufficiently sophisticated to explain why this relationship
would not be *invariant*, i.e. would have to take the form that 'other things
being equal' $X \rightarrow Y$. Hence we never would have expected a result such
as that in Table 2.2 which shows a perfect correlation between X and Y.

Table 2.2 Voting intention by housing tenure

Voting intention	Owns	%	Rents	%	Total	%
Labour	–	–	521	100	521	34.0
Other	1010	100	–	–	1010	66.0
Total	1010	100	521	100	1531	100

Nevertheless, Table 2.1 certainly shows a strong correlation between the
two variables since over half of those who rent vote Labour, while over
two-thirds of those who own do not. So far, so good; but the next stage
of the analysis must be to rule out other explanations for voting intention. Now, of course, no one would argue that voting behaviour could ever
be wholly explained by one factor. When people vote they express many
things at the same time. Therefore, the question we must ask is whether,
as Table 2.1 seems to indicate, housing tenure is a major causal variable
in the propensity to vote Labour, or whether (1) it is merely disguising
something else which is antecedent to, and can account for, *both X* and
Y; or (2) there is something which intervenes *between X* and *Y* which can
better account for *Y*. In asking these questions we are beginning to elaborate our relationship by saying not

1 $X \rightarrow Y$

but either

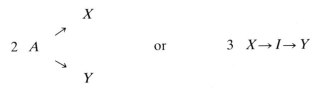

Here, *A* stands for *antecedent variable*, and *I* stands for *intervening variable*. We have observed an empirical relationship between *X* and *Y* which we now wish to understand more completely via the effects of introducing other variables into the analysis. For instance, in (2) above, we would effectively divide our sample into sub-sets in respect of *A*, the antecedent or **control variable**. This allows us to recompute the relationship between the two variables *X* and *Y* separately for each sub-sample, controlling for *A*. In other words we *partition* the original relationship and examine the resulting **partial relationships**. In the process we are beginning *multivariate analysis* by examining more than two variables together. This process will be examined in greater detail below, but for the moment let us be clear about why we need to undertake it. In part the answer is that we need to rule out other possible (rival or alternative) causal factors and further understand the original relationship. We have also said that this must be a theory-guided process.

However, we should also be clear about the nature of the non-experimental situation. In a scientific experiment the experimenter would have tried to control for possible rival causal factors *prior* to the study. In the non-experimental situation we have to collect data on possible rival causal factors and then control for them in the *analysis*. That is, we cannot have any prior control over the social processes which are under examination. For example, in the hypothesized study of the relationships between consumption locations and political ideology it would not be feasible (or ethical) to take a random sample of the population and then assign them to a particular housing tenure, insulate them from all other aspects of society which might affect their politics, and wait and see what effects this has on their voting behaviour. We must take the social world as it is. This is one reason why we need theories because theories should sensitize us to all those aspects of the real world which are relevant to the problems we are investigating. Therefore, any theory which tells us that consumption location is in part a determinant of political ideology ought also to alert us to other possible determinants of political ideology. In the research process we must find measures for these, too. After all, people do not differ solely in relation to, say, housing tenure and voting behaviour but in terms of a host of other variables relevant to the concerns of our hypothesized study, too. Moreover, housing tenure might be *an* important determinant of voting behaviour but the nature of society is such that it will presumably only be so *conjointly* with other variables, so that in particular cases, because of the effect of other variables, it will have its effect reduced or eliminated, and in others enhanced. This is what the technique of multivariate analysis allows us to investigate.

So, to return to the case we considered in Table 2.1, we might decide that social class would be a useful control variable. We could hypothesize that social class is an *antecedent* variable (A) in respect of X and Y, i.e. logically class occurs 'before' housing tenure and voting and so could be the cause of both. If it is the cause of both, then when we use class as a control variable in analysis, the relationship originally observed between X and Y may change. It may even be that because of the nature of the $A \rightarrow X$ and $A \rightarrow Y$ relationships we find an apparent $X \rightarrow Y$ relationship in which X and Y are not causally linked to each other at all but only to A. We can further illustrate this point by reference to the example in Table 2.3. This shows data for the variables housing tenure (X) and voting behaviour (Y) in respect of the control variable social class (A) such that:

In other words, as the diagram indicates, A is hypothesized to be antecedent to X and Y, and X and Y are not otherwise related. A correlation is apparent between them only because of their respective relationships with A. To match the logic of the way we measured X and Y for Table 2.1, social class is derived from the Registrar General's Social Class Classification with two categories: (1) Manual class; (2) Non-manual class.

Table 2.3 Voting intention by housing tenure controlling for social class

| Voting | Manual (548) | | | | Non-Manual (568) | | | | | |
	Owns	%	Rents	%	Owns	%	Rents	%	Total	%
Labour	142	42.9	124	57.1	86	18.8	40	36.4	392	35.1
Other	189	57.1	93	42.9	372	81.2	70	63.6	724	64.9
Total	331	100	217	100	458	100	110	100	1116	100

First of all note the structure of Table 2.3. The total in the rows has changed. This is because we do not have the information on class for all of the people who appeared in Table 2.1. This is due to the fact that those not in paid employment (e.g. students and housepersons) cannot be assigned a class position using the Registrar General's class schema. Nevertheless the proportions who would vote Labour and Other are similar for Tables 2.1 and 2.3 and it is vote we are ultimately trying to explain. The columns of the table have also changed. The sample has been sub-divided into social class categories so that voting behaviour for each of the categories can be compared. Whereas in Table 2.1 we had only two housing tenure groups – owners and renters – we now have four. We have (1) those who own in the manual class; (2) those who own who are non-manual class; (3) those who rent who are manual class; and (4) those who rent who are non-manual class. Having sub-divided the sample into manual and non-manual class, we have recomputed the relationship between the two original variables separately for each sub-sample.

So what can Table 2.3 reveal about the $X \to Y$ relationship in respect of A? First we can note that the sample divided roughly equally between the manual (548) and non-manual (568) categories. Of the manual classes we can see from the first two columns of row 1 that $142 + 124 = 266$ voted Labour; and from the first two columns of row 2 that $189 + 93 = 282$ did not vote Labour. We could make similar observations for other categories of the social class $(A) \to$ voting (Y) relationship, as we would have expected from the arrow diagram

What, then, of the $A \to X$ relationship between social class and housing tenure? Obviously, if the $A \to Y$ information is in the rows of Table 2.3, $A \to X$ must be in the columns. So, for example, column 1 tells us that $142 + 189 = 331$ owners are manual class; and in column 2, $124 + 93 = 217$ renters are manual class; and so on. Therefore when we take the observations about $A \to X$ and $A \to Y$ together we produce Table 2.3. Indeed (as we shall see later) this is what we have to do when we ask for a three-way cross-tabulation using SPSS. SPSS does not produce a table like Table 2.3 but two tables: one for $X \to Y$ for each value of A, as in Tables 2.4 and 2.5. So our first major observation is that Table 2.3 really contains three tables which give us, combined, the overall relationship $X \to Y$, and then $X \to Y$ for each value of A. Therefore, multivariate analysis is really only a way of combining the results of three or more bivariate (two-variable) analyses. For example, Table 2.3 is composed of Table 2.1 + Table 2.4 + Table 2.5.

However, it is easier to see the nature of the relationship between A, X and Y by examining Table 2.3 than by comparing across Tables 2.1, 2.4 and 2.5. What we need to do in order to see the effect of A (social class) is to make comparisons between the owns and rents columns of Table 2.3 with those of Table 2.1. For example, Table 2.1 showed that 30.1 per cent of all owners voted Labour; while Table 2.3 shows that 42.9 per cent of

Table 2.4 Voting intention (X) by housing tenure (Y) controlling for social class (A = Manual)

Voting	Owns	%	Rents	%	Total	%
Labour	142	42.9	124	57.1	266	48.5
Other	189	57.1	93	42.9	282	51.5
Total	331	100	217	100	548	100

Table 2.5 Voting intention (X) by housing tenure (Y) controlling for social class (A = non-manual)

Voting	Owns	%	Rents	%	Total	%
Labour	86	18.8	40	36.4	126	22.2
Other	372	81.2	70	63.6	442	77.8
Total	458	100	110	100	568	100

manual class owners voted Labour but that only 18.8 per cent of non-manual class owners voted Labour. In other words, the relationship between housing tenure and voting becomes more pronounced for non-manual class owners. This alters the nature of our Albert Hall guessing game. If you were told that one of the sample in the Hall was an owner, you would guess a non-Labour vote on the basis of Table 2.1, and you would be correct on average roughly two times in three (since 69.9 per cent of owners vote Other). If you were further told that the owner was manual class, you would be in a dilemma. You would still have to guess 'Other', since only 42.9 per cent of manual class owners vote Labour, but your chances of being right have diminished. In this case elaboration has *reduced* the relationship: manual class home owners are only slightly more likely to vote 'Other'. What about home renters? Table 2.1 shows a 52.8 : 47.2 split in favour of Labour among renters. However, Table 2.3 shows a 57.1 : 42.9 split for manual class renters – a slightly *increased* relationship; but a 36.4 : 63.6 split among non-manual class renters – the relationship has *reversed*: non-manual renters are more likely *not* to vote Labour.

We now have to interpret what all this means. It would appear that among owners, being manual class makes it much more likely that one will vote Labour than other home owners but less likely than either the manual classes as a whole (Table 2.4) or than if one were a manual class tenant. We might argue that whereas home ownership would normally be associated with non-Labour voting as in Table 2.1, being manual class *is* associated with Labour voting. There is, therefore, cross-pressure on manual class home owners. And we could go on to produce similar arguments in respect of the rest of the data in Table 2.3, and tie these arguments to a causal narrative.

However, we need to reflect on the process so far discussed in terms of data analysis procedures. We began with Table 2.1 which examines the relationship between one aspect of consumption location, housing tenure, and one aspect of political ideology, voting intention. The relationship which emerged in Table 2.1 was promising but needs to be examined further in order to make sure it is genuine rather than due to other factors (spurious). To do this we produced Table 2.3 which introduced social class as a control variable. Effectively we made our sample 'equal' with respect to social class to see what effect this had on the original relationship – i.e. we *controlled* for social class. What we discovered from Table 2.3 were the various effects such *partitioning* had.

We could extend the example provided by Table 2.3 much further. In analysis we would probably want to consider other control variables; we would want to examine other indicators of consumption location and political ideology; we would almost certainly want to further specify the relationship between A, X and Y in respect of particular sub-groups. Provided we had enough cases, we could, for example, divide the manual class into skilled, semi-skilled and unskilled categories and examine the new partial relationships this revealed. We must certainly exhaust all the possibilities which the data seem to open up for investigation. It is through this continual weaving together of theory and data that we can begin to infer causal relationships.

However, what has been discussed by no means exhausts all the procedures involved in the logic of data analysis. Inferring cause can be aided by a variety of other means which are discussed in the literature. So far we have examined only the case of an antecedent variable. We chose a measure of class as our antecedent variable because we knew it would be related to housing tenure and voting intention. Indeed, precisely because we know that class is related to tenure, its use as an antecedent variable could (a) demonstrate the importance and direction of the relationship; and (b) check that a spurious relationship between housing tenure and vote has not been produced by class. What we discovered in the process were *conditional relationships*. The $X \rightarrow Y$ relationship was not spurious but nor was it simple. There were *interaction effects* which require us to specify a separate causal model for each condition discovered.

There are, however, other forms of analysis which can help us further in understanding our data. For example, we can examine **component variables** (those *aspects* of independent variables which produce differences on dependent variables). Voting intention is a very crude way of measuring political ideology. How a person votes will not generally reflect the whole range of their political views. That is why political ideology was measured in a variety of ways in the British Class Survey. Because we have also measured political ideology in relation to people's attitudes on specific issues which might affect their voting behaviour, we could see how far people's attitudes to these issues are *components* of their voting intention and how far these issue components relate to housing tenure.

Equally, we can examine possible *intervening variables*. Earlier, a relationship of the type $X \rightarrow I \rightarrow Y$ was mentioned. Here I is an intervening variable between X and Y. Is the link between housing tenure and voting intention mediated via some other variable? We could hypothesize here that perceived class identification was an intervening variable. The British Class Survey also asked people to say which class they thought they belonged to – their self-rated class. It would certainly make sense to interpret self-rated class as an intervening variable since it has often been argued that, among working-class people, buying a house leads to a change in class *identity* from working class to middle class.

However, whether dealing with antecedent variables, component variables or intervening variables the logic of the analytic process is identical. All involve introducing a third variable into a bivariate relationship in the manner indicated in Table 2.3. It is the conclusions we draw which will differ according to how we are theorizing the relationship of our control variable to the other variables in our analysis. In the end we hope to put all our separate findings together in some way in order to show how all the variables examined interrelate, e.g.

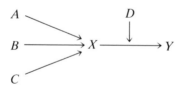

To summarize, we can use statistical procedures to 'control for' the effects of different variables. We can use the same procedures to specify the relationship between independent and dependent variables and to identify antecedent or intervening variables. Partitioning procedures of this kind are used to understand the ways in which variables are related, and thus to provide support for causal inferences in the realm of theory.

Conclusion

In this chapter we have introduced the logic which lies behind the forms of data analysis which are discussed later. This logic is sometimes referred to as the '*logic of analysing non-manipulated variables*' in order to distinguish it from the experimental situation in which the scientist directly manipulates the variables of interest. We have seen that statistical correlation satisfies the co-variation requirement of the experiment and that controlling for alternative or rival causal factors requires the researcher to measure a wide range of variables in order to use them as control variables in analysis. We have also noted, however, that correlation is not the same as causation. Both causation and the question of temporal order are largely a matter for theory (and common sense!). For example, we might have a theory which tells us that class of origin (say father's class) is related to educational attainment. Here the temporal order is clear since we are family members before we are educated. Logically our educational attainment cannot determine our class of origin. However, our own class position may well be affected by our educational attainment since we are educated before we enter employment. These are obvious examples of temporal order but it is not always so simple. Take the relationship between health and unemployment. It has often been noted that the unemployed are less healthy than the employed, but is this because being unemployed affects one's health or is it those who are less healthy who are more likely to become unemployed?

This is but one example of the problems we face when we are analysing non-manipulated variables. In the end we can never be sure we have the right answer. This is why it is so important to undertake exhaustive analyses using control and component variables. We must both challenge the relationships we find: that is, try to falsify them using different data; and elaborate relationships in order to gain a better understanding of the conditions under which X and Y are related. Our example of the housing tenure/vote relationship is an example of this process but, as we shall see in Part V, there are special forms of analysis which allow for a much more sophisticated approach to this type of problem.

So far we have discussed data analysis, measurement, variables and the logic of analysing non-manipulated variables. We have said very little, however, about how we derive data. Where do these data come from? How are they created? Data are not tablets of stone but are themselves the product of the procedures we use. It is to this aspect of research procedures that we now turn.

Note

1 We examine the construction of tables in Chapter 7.

Key concepts

Make sure you have understood the following key concepts:

- correlation
- partitioning variance/partial relationships
- elaboration of relationships
- control variables
- component variables
- multivariate analysis

Part II

From data collection to computer

3 Preparing the data

Aims

- To understand the principles of data preparation and coding for analysis.
- To discuss the implications of using 'open' and 'closed' questions.
- To understand the principles of entering numeric data into a computer.

All the forms of data analysis discussed in the two previous chapters could, in principle, be carried out with pencil and paper. However, in most instances social researchers use computers to do such analyses for them. This is because computers can calculate at immense speed using huge amounts of data. However, in order to take advantage of these capabilities we must first prepare the data in a form acceptable to a computer. The starting point in any operationalization is therefore to consider what form the data need to take in order to analyse them on a computer. We must always consider this question right at the start, since it will affect the way we collect the data and all the subsequent analyses.

In this chapter we consider the procedures involved in collecting and preparing data in a way which will enable us to analyse them using a computer. We are therefore continuing our discussion of the 'operationalization' stage of the socio-logic diagram (see Figure 1.1). We discuss the objects and principles of 'coding' data into a numerical format taking into account the design and structure of our questionnaire in helping us to achieve this. In other words, we are dealing with the procedures involved in moving from questionnaire design to the collation of data in a form suitable for entry into, and analysis by, a computer. The primary procedure for doing this is referred to as **data coding**.

Coding

When first discussing variables, we described the way in which we allocate a numeric code to each category of a variable. This *coding* process is the first step in preparing data for computer analysis. It constitutes the first step in mapping our observations into data. How we do this depends upon how we wish to use the data, and that, in turn, depends upon our *theoretical* concerns. Hopefully we know why we chose to make certain observations; those reasons will now determine how we map our observations into data. We use the word 'observations' because, of course, not all analysis depends on having survey-type data. There *are* computer programs which analyse textual or qualitative information, although even in these cases the analysis is often of a numeric type, as when, for example, the computer counts the occurrences or the juxtapositionings of a particular word or phrase.

Let us say, however, that our observations have been made via a survey. (It is still true, after all, that most data analysis in social research using a computer involves the analysis of survey data.) Of the questions we have asked in this survey, some are **structured** or 'closed' and some are **unstructured** or 'open'. Closed questions are those where we have decided *prior* to asking the questions what answers are possible and we have already assigned numeric codes to the range of answers. This process is known as 'pre-coding'. When asking such questions of a respondent we simply circle the number indicating the respondent's answer on the pre-coded questionnaire. This type of question is referred to as 'closed' precisely because the range of responses is predetermined.

Open questions, however, are those where we have not decided in advance on the range of possible answers in which we are interested. This might be because we cannot easily predict how people might answer, or because several variables will be derived from the answers, or because we want to make 'richer' observations. If we are to analyse such responses via a computer, we subsequently have to assign numeric codes. Inevitably this will involve a certain loss of information, which we choose to trade against the advantages of computer analysis. We can readily understand why the transformation of such observations into numeric codes is referred to as the *degradation of data*. Nevertheless, it is important to remember that we ask an open question with some definite purpose in mind and, therefore, we should be able to classify the answers according to our original purpose(s) in asking the question. We may thereby lose the uniqueness of each respondent's answer but we gain something as well – the ability to compare different responses on the same scale. Obviously a compromise is involved here.

Consider the following example. Suppose we have asked all respondents in a survey concerned with geographical mobility the question 'Where were you born?' Suppose also that to be included in the survey a person had to have been born in Britain. The question is open and most people will immediately respond with the name of the town or village where they were born. In coding the answers we now have to make a compromise. At one extreme we know that all our respondents were born in Britain and so we could assign the code '1 = Britain' to all respondents. However, this would make little sense because we could not analyse any variability between respondents. We no longer have a variable but a constant. At the other extreme we might find that each respondent was born in a different place from all the others and we could, therefore, give each one a unique code, e.g.:

1	=	Auchtermuchty	=	Respondent 1
2	=	Mousehole	=	Respondent 2
3	=	Steeple Bumpstead	=	Respondent 3
–	=	–	=	–
–	=	–	=	–
–	=	–	=	–
n	=	Somewhere in Britain	=	Respondent n

However, this, too, would be self-defeating as we now have too much variability for useful comparative analysis between respondents. We must find a compromise between the full richness of our observations and the complete reduction of them to a single constant. Of course, in either case the computer would be indifferent since it has numeric codes to work on. The point is that we could not produce any meaningful analysis.

So how *do* we decide upon a coding procedure? Obviously we had a purpose in asking the original question – indeed we may have had several. We now apply this to our coding problem. We said earlier that the survey was concerned with geographical mobility. One obvious purpose might be, therefore, to see how many people still live in the place where they were born. We will also, then, have asked each respondent 'Where do you live at present?' A simple comparison of answers could produce the following codes:

1 = Immobile
2 = Mobile $\Big\}$ in relation to birthplace

Or we might want to be more sophisticated, e.g.

1 = Same place as born
2 = Within 10 miles
3 = 10–49 miles $\Big\}$ from birthplace
4 = More than 50 miles

We might want to produce other categorizations of the observations we have made. For example, we could not only code as above but also, say:

1 = Rural birthplace
2 = Urban birthplace

or

1 = England
2 = Scotland
3 = Wales

Or we could code into Standard Regions. And so on. It all depends what we want to do in data analysis, which in turn depends upon why we made the observations which we did, i.e. *theory*. Potentially, there are many different ways to categorize the observations. Indeed we may have originally decided to ask an open question precisely because, in relation to the problem of geographical mobility, we wished to derive a number of different variables of the type exemplified above. After all, if we had only wanted to know whether respondents did or did not still live where they were born we could have asked that question and left it at that. This would then have been a closed question along the following lines:

'Have you always lived in the same city/town/village where you were born?'

Yes   1
No   2

Of course, if we do this, we have to be certain that we will not need any of the other information concerning birthplace when we do our analysis, because we will not have it!

As you may have noticed, all the points made here about coding procedures are just a re-statement of what was discussed earlier in relation to variables. The categories derived from the original question about place of birth all assume an underlying variable, e.g.

Categories	Variable
England Scotland Wales	Country of birth in Britain
Immobile Mobile	Geographical mobility since birth

If we have a hypothesis that people born in Scotland or Wales are more likely to be geographically mobile from their place of birth than those born in England, the variables just specified would give us a basis for testing the hypothesis. We follow the process below. As you read through this, notice how it reproduces the 'socio-logic' diagram in Chapter 1 (Figure 1.1).

Step 1	Theory	Population characteristics affect propensity to geographical mobility (Population characteristics = independent variable; Geographical mobility = dependent variable).
Step 2	Hypothesis	The characteristic 'Country of birth within Britain' affects propensity to geographical mobility when the latter is understood in terms of whether or not adults reside in the place where they were born.
Step 3	First operationalization	Country of birth in Britain is given by the three constituent countries, England, Scotland and Wales. Geographical mobility is given by place of current residence in relation to place of birth such that 'Same place now as birth = Immobile; Different place from birth = Mobile'.
Step 4	Collect observations	Survey questions asking for place of birth and place of current residence.
Step 5	Code as defined at Step 3 (final operationalization)	Take answers to questions about place of birth and current residence and code to categories defined at Step 3.
Step 6	Data analysis	Apply data analytic techniques to investigate the relationship between the relevant variables. (We will be going into this step in much greater detail in the remaining part of the book.)
Step 7	Inference	Draw conclusions about the hypothesis from the data analysis, which are then reviewed in respect of the theoretical statement at Step 1.

All of this might seem to have taken us a long way from where we began but it is necessary if we are to realize the crucial part which coding of observations into categories plays. In fact, as can be seen, Step 5 represents the final stage of the operationalization process. Earlier stages produced a variable and question(s) but this step is the actual coding itself. It should be becoming even more clear at this point why variables have to have (1) a name, (2) a clear definition of categories and (3) a sorting procedure which guarantees the mutual exclusiveness and exhaustiveness of categories. Unless all this is done there will be a high risk of measurement errors through the misclassification of observations. The computer can't help here: it will analyse according to how observations have been coded. It cannot put right any miscoded observations.

The codebook

In order to code accurately it is helpful first to produce a **codebook**. The codebook gives a complete listing of all categories and codes for each variable. Generally the variables derive from single questions in a survey. Hence the codebook tells the coder all the information s/he needs to assign a unique code for each variable category. In the case of closed questions this is generally unproblematic. The interviewer will have circled or in some way indicated the code in the interview schedule.

For open questions, however, a **code frame** is provided as a list of possible answers to a question. Code frames for open questions are generally constructed both deductively and inductively, i.e. partly on the basis of theory and partly on the basis of how people actually answered the questions. The reason for this is easy to see. Open questions are included in surveys for a number of reasons. For example, they allow the respondent to provide a fuller range of opinions and beliefs which researchers can examine for a variety of purposes, from constructing a number of different variables from the same data to the use of quotations for illustrative purposes in research reports. Equally, there are some issues which researchers require information on but where the likely variability of answers is not known prior to research and hence no structured question can be used. In this sense some open questions are *exploratory* in nature.

Whatever the case, however, all answers must be reduced to numeric form for computer analysis and so some way has to be found to code the answers to open questions. Theory will suggest some likely categories but the exploratory nature of the questions will require researchers to examine a sample of answers from the interview schedule, too. Answers are then classified into different types, and each type allocated a numeric code. Eventually a coding frame will be produced which looks similar to that for structured questions. This coding frame will then be checked by taking a new sample of questionnaires and seeing if the frame 'works' for that sample. In most surveys the number of open questions will be relatively small. In earlier stages of research, at pre-test and pilot phases,[1] researchers might use more open questions. They would then follow the procedure outlined above to construct closed questions for use in the main survey. After all, at some same stage all open questions have to be 'closed down' to permit numeric analysis.

Generally, then, the codebook will look very similar to the questionnaire, since many of the questions will be pre-coded or closed, but it will also contain codes for open questions. Additionally it will contain the name or number of each variable. Each question, or each part of a question, will be given a variable name or number and the answers to the question form the categories of the variable. Each category has a numeric code assigned to it. In the case of structured questions the rule for assigning responses to categories is given by the question the interviewer asks and any interviewer instructions attached. In the case of open questions the code frame and any necessary coding instructions provide the rules for assigning responses to categories. In fact, all we are doing here is to re-iterate what we said earlier about measurement, but in a slightly different way. That is, each variable has to have (1) a name, (2) a definition and (3) a sorting procedure. As an example, a typical extract from a codebook is shown overleaf.

We can see that the first question would have been coded by the interviewer during the interview itself. However, in the actual questionnaire the only responses would have been 'Yes', 'No' or 'Don't know'. The other two codes are office codes. 'Skip' is for cases where the question wasn't asked because it wasn't relevant to that particular respondent. 'Missing' is for where there is no answer given, presumably because the interviewer forgot to ask the question or the respondent didn't give an answer. These codes are included in the codebook and added in the office during coding. The second question is an open question for which a code frame has subsequently been devised. Since people might well have given more than one answer, coders are instructed to code up to five answers. There are 11 major codes and '12' is used for 'Other answers'. In that way all cases can be assigned to one of the codes.

Note also the use of variable names for each question. The first question is given a variable name 'SAMEINTS' which is short for 'same interests'. The question effectively defines the name. The second question requires five variable names: 'SAMEINT1–SAMEINT5'. This is because there are five possible answers to the question and the computer will treat each answer as a variable. The format of the variable name – 'SAMEINTn' – indicates the connection to the previous variable 'SAMEINTS'. The overall format of the variable names in this example has been determined by the requirements of the computer program SPSS which allows up to eight characters in a variable name. The only remaining item to explain is the term 'Column' and the numbers beneath it '355–356' and '357–366'. This takes us to the next stage of the analysis after coding. However, before we discuss this there are one or two more points to note about the coding process.

Variable name:	SAMEINTS	*Column*

Question 10(a): Do you think there are any issues over which those who run industry and those who work for them *share* the same interests?

Categories	Code	355–356
Yes	01	
No	05	
Don't know	−2	
Skip	−1	
Missing	−3	

Variable name:	SAMEINT1–SAMEINT5	

Question 10(b): What are these issues?
Instruction: Code up to 5 answers
Categories   357–366

Simple economic interests
Greater prosperity, pay, money, living standards.   01

Company interests
The survival of the company or industry.   02
The *profitability* of the firm or enterprise is in everyone's
interest.   03
To *expand or improve the company* (e.g. all have interests in
pulling together to 'make the firm more competitive', 'to win
new orders', 'to expand the firm').   04
Greater productivity (e.g. all have interests in increasing
productivity).   05
Safeguarding jobs (e.g. everyone has an interest in safeguarding or preserving jobs).   06
Company policy (e.g. all have interests in how the company is
run and in working conditions).   07
Effect of government policy on the industry or company (e.g.
all have an interest in how government policy affects their
industry or company).   08
Pride in the firm or the quality of its products (e.g. all feel
pride in the firm and the quality of its products).   09

National interests
The good of the country (e.g. all are working for the well-
being of the country).   10
Benefits of citizenship or being British (e.g. all share in the
benefits of living in Britain such as the welfare state).   11

Other answers
Don't know   −2
Skip   −1
Missing   −3

We noted earlier that to code observations in such a way that all answers were given the same code would be self-defeating. We would thereby produce not a variable but a constant. Since the object of data analysis is to explain variance, producing constants in this way prevents us from doing any analysis. However, it is equally useless to produce a unique code for every answer to a question because that way we have too much variability and again we can explain nothing. If we have been thoughtful, however, we should have designed questions and produced variables and categories which provide a reasonable amount of variability. We should, therefore, design code frames with this in mind and should not aim to produce any categories for which we have either no cases or only a few. As a rule of thumb we would generally want a minimum of around 30 cases in any category of a sample which we wish to analyse beyond univariate level.

Remembering, too, that in the process of data analysis we may want to reduce the coded categories of a variable still further, it helps if we can create generic headings for different kinds of codes. For example, in the extract from the codebook for the variables SAMEINT1–SAMEINT5, there are three headings: Simple economic interests; Company interests; and National interests. The responses under each heading are of that type. *For theoretical reasons* the researchers have identified these three types of answer as important and they have coded in such a way that, in analy-, sis, they can use the headings as codes. That is, they can give an instruction to the computer to put all codes under each major heading into the same category and thereby produce a three-category variable. In analysis, therefore, SAMEINT1 might appear as:

Category	Code
Simple economic interest	01
Company interests	02
National interests	03
Other responses	04

This is, then, yet another example of the importance of thinking backwards and forwards in the research process. Here the researchers have thought backwards to theory for the generic codes as well as forwards to analysis where the generic codes might be required.

Next, we should say something about the actual numbers which are assigned to the categories of each variable in coding. The two questions used in the codebook example above each give rise to nominal measures and hence the category codes only imply difference. If the codes used imply *order*, i.e. an ordinal measure, it would make sense for the numbers used as codes to show the order, e.g.

working class	1
middle class	2
upper class	3

For any level of measurement above the ordinal, the numbers will be 'real', as with age and income. Apart from this case, the numbers we use as codes are arbitrary. In the variable SAMEINTS the category 'Yes' was coded 01 and 'No' was coded 05. However, any two different numbers would have served the same purpose of indicating different categories. In this example 01 and 05 were chosen because they reduced the chance of coding errors which arise when Yes = 1 and No = 2 and coders sometimes forget which is which. But why the use of 01 and 05 rather than 1 and 5? This was simply the convention used in this particular piece of research. Because missing data (e.g. Skip, Don't know and Missing) were indicated by two characters (the minus sign and a number) all other codes have two characters, too. Once again this raises an issue not yet explained and which relates to the use of the 'Column' in the codebook, but first one more point should be made about coding conventions which will help to avoid mistakes.

Remember that in most circumstances the computer will accept any number we give it; anything we code incorrectly will still be accepted by the computer as long as that wrong code *could* be right. Hence if we coded 'Yes' as 05, the computer will accept it, even though this is a coding error. However, if every 'Yes' in our codebook is given the code 01 and every 'No' = 05, coders are less likely to make such a mistake. The rule, therefore, is that whenever we can, we should standardize codes throughout the codebook. It speeds the process and reduces error. So we use standard coding schemes for all variables with the same categories. We can now address the points so far left to one side – the meaning of 'Column'; and why, if we use –1 etc. for missing data we must also have double-digit category codes for every other category of that variable.

From codebook to computer

We go back to the questionnaires to explain this, noting that the observations they contain are principally of two kinds. Either they are circles around numeric codes (or ticks in boxes marked by numbers); or they are the words of a respondent transcribed by an interviewer. We have seen that the codebook is used to transform all question items into variable format. Response items for closed questions are just categories of a variable, and answers to open questions are examined for patterns and coded according to the different types of answers produced, thereby creating variable categories. We now have a way of providing numeric codes for every item in the questionnaire. We must next transfer these codes from the questionnaire via the codebook into the computer. That is, we must take each questionnaire and write down (or directly key into the computer) a numeric code for each question. For closed questions we can take the codes direct from the questionnaire; for open questions we must consult the codebook and match the answer to the appropriate code. We can therefore see the codebook as an intermediate stage between the completed interview schedules and having analysable data. The codebook shows us the operations we must perform to transform our observations into data, and we have seen that this involves giving numeric codes to each answer in the questionnaire. These numeric codes are then entered into the computer as a long series of numbers, each of which relates to a coded response from the questionnaires.

Since computer programs impose constraints on the way data are organized, we need to note certain features. The observations on the questionnaire are given a numeric value in coding and these numeric values are entered into the computer, row by row. Until relatively recently, it was normal practice to enter data into a **raw data file**, consisting only of these rows of numeric codes. These files, with row lengths consisting conventionally of 80 columns, could then be read into a statistical analysis program like SPSS to create a data file ready for analysis. It is nowadays more usual to enter data directly into an analysis program, creating a data file which can then be transferred, if necessary, to other analysis programs. This has the advantage of skipping the raw data file stage, and often allows greater flexibility in terms of row length. However, it is important to understand how to interpret raw data files, since this is the format in which they are often transported between computers for use by different analysts using different machines and programs.

We are now finally in a position to explain the meaning of 'Column' in the example codebook. It is a reference to the position of a particular piece of data in a row of numeric data. 'Col 355–56' means that data for variable SAMEINTS lies in Columns 55 and 56 of row 3 of the raw data file for each case. 'Col 357–366' means that data for the variables SAMEINT1–SAMEINT5 lie in Columns 57–66 of row 3, i.e. following on from the SAMEINTS data. Hence, imagine that in answer to Question 10(b) in our codebook example a respondent had said:

'We are all in it for the money. It's as simple as that.'

The coder would have entered in row 3 of that respondent's raw data in columns 57 and 58 the figures 01, i.e. the code corresponding to the answer given by the respondent. Now you can see why we require two columns for the answer; since in this codebook −1, −2, −3 are used for missing data, every category of every variable must have two columns, because every piece of information in the raw data file must appear in the same columns for every respondent. Therefore, if someone doesn't answer a question, we must put a code in the relevant column in the row which tells us s/he didn't answer it. So, for the example above, our respondent gave only one answer but we have the space to code for up to five, if necessary. Since this respondent only gave one answer, on row 3, in columns 57–66, we would enter:

Column	57	58	59	60	61	62	63	64	65	66
Row 3	0	1	–	3	–	3	–	3	–	3

This means for Row 3:

Variable	Columns	Code
SAMEINT1	57–58	01 ('We're all in it etc . . .')
SAMEINT2	59–60	−3 (Missing)
SAMEINT3	61–62	−3 (Missing)
SAMEINT4	63–64	−3 (Missing)
SAMEINT5	65–66	−3 (Missing)

In this way we enter all the information for all respondents on all variables into the computer as a raw data file.[2] Such a file, then, consists of rows and rows of numbers (an example of a small raw data file can be found in Chapter 4, pp. 70–1). The computer, of course, needs to know how to interpret those numbers. *We* know that row 3, columns 57–58 for each case always contains data on the variable SAMEINT1 but the computer does not. Therefore, in order to do any analysis, we also have to tell the computer how to interpret the data, i.e. which bits of data refer to which variables; and it also needs to know the names of the variables and what the categories mean. How this part of the job is done depends upon the computer program being used. In Chapter 5 we discuss how this is achieved using SPSS. Once the computer has all this information, we can begin to analyse our data. Simple ways of doing this are described in Part III.

The important points to remember from this chapter are the way in which information should be collected and coded into numerical format for computer analysis, and how this process involves the simultaneous consideration of both *theoretical* concerns (what concepts underlie the variable categories) and *methodological* ones (maintaining variability, category sizes). Before going on to think about analysis, however, we need to know exactly how we go about communicating with the computer, and how we can give it the information we have just said is necessary before we can begin analysis. Chapter 4 goes on to discuss these questions.

Notes

1 It is the normal practice in social scientific surveys to undertake pre-test surveys to check whether questions work in the field, and thus to improve the design of the final survey. Such pre-tests are normally followed by a pilot survey – a small dress rehearsal of the final intended survey. This is to make sure that all survey procedures work smoothly. For more detail, see Moser and Kalton (1971).

2 However, we should note that many modern techniques of data collection obviate the need for so many operations (and thereby reduce error). In recent years *computer assisted interviews* have become increasingly common. In these interviews, the interviewer enters the data into the computer as the respondent answers the questions. That is, the interviewer keys the data directly on to the disk of a computer from where it can later be transferred to a data file on the computer which will be used to analyse the data. The interview schedule itself no longer exists as a printed questionnaire but appears instead on a computer screen (see Saris 1991).

Key concepts

Make sure you have understood the following key concepts:

- data coding
- structured/unstructured questions
- pre-coding
- codebook/code frame
- raw data file

4 Getting to know the computer DOS, WINDOWS and SPSS

Aims

- To understand basic file handling procedures.
- To describe the different types of files in SPSS.
- To create data files in SPSS.

Having described the process of preparing data for analysis on a computer, the first part of this chapter provides an introduction to communicating with a computer, using either its built-in 'operating language', **MS-DOS**, or a user-friendly pictoral interface called WINDOWS (see below), to give it simple commands. In the second part of the chapter we introduce the basic command structure of the Statistical Package for Social Sciences (**SPSS**) in both its PC and WINDOWS versions, before moving on to the procedures involved in getting data into the computer in a form which will enable us to analyse them. Here we are launching into a practical, hands-on approach. There is a short glossary of simple computing terms at the end of this chapter.

We will leave aside for the moment the question of actually analysing data, the first principles of which are discussed in Chapter 5. In Chapter 6 we then put together some of the information contained in the preceding two chapters with some of those principles so that you can see exactly how you might undertake your own analysis of data on a computer. First, though, it is necessary to get to know how to use the computer. This chapter assumes that the reader has access to a computer operating under MS-DOS. All IBM-type personal computers (PCs) work using an underlying operating system language called MS-DOS. This is one of the major operating system languages for personal computers and the commands you will learn in this text to communicate with the computer are in the MS-DOS operating language (often just called DOS). WINDOWS is a more recently developed user interface with DOS, using pictoral symbols to represent packages and files, which you will be shown how to use by pointing and clicking a 'mouse'. This has the effect of accessing DOS commands without you actually having to learn and type them out!

(If you are working in a WINDOWS environment you have a choice about how to use the first part of this chapter: if you only want to use the file handling facilities (e.g. copying, deleting) of WINDOWS then simply ignore the structure of the DOS commands which are outlined here. If you would like to learn the DOS commands as well then you should be able to access the DOS command prompt (C:\>) from the WINDOWS program manager by double-clicking the MS-DOS icon with your mouse. To return to the program manager just type: exit at the command prompt.)

Whether you are using DOS commands or WINDOWS, unless you have access to a PC yourself – in other words if you are working in a computing lab for which you need authorization – then as a first step you will have to identify yourself to the computer. The computer will only respond if you have already obtained authorization to use it, and have a name and/or password that it recognizes. You should first, then, obtain such authorization from the relevant people. Having obtained this authorization the way that you introduce yourself is by logging in. When you have finished you log out. Logging in is the method by which you identify yourself to the computer; logging out is the way you tell the computer you have finished. It is possible that the system which you are using will be slightly different in respect of certain key terms (for instance LOGIN may be replaced where you are working by LOGON). Obviously you will need to check this, but the basic principles we elucidate here are not specific to any particular site. Below we present a sample session.

Logging in and out

Logging in

To log in you press [ENTER] or [RETURN] (the [↵] key) to arouse the computer. When you get the login prompt you type your login name:

Login: <name> [↵]

You will then be asked to type your password – do so, but remember that your password is secret and therefore does not appear on the screen. You are logged in successfully when

C:\> (the DOS command prompt)

appears on the screen, or, in WINDOWS, when the WINDOWS 'program manager' window appears.

Listing files

Once the name and password have been entered and you are success-fully logged in, you may want to see a directory of all **files** on the disk in drive C: (Drive C: indicates the hard disk actually inside the machine. Drives a: and b: are floppy disk drives.)

∗ Listing files in DOS

To do this in DOS, the command is: dir_c: (it doesn't matter in DOS whether you use upper or lower case letters). So you typè (from the C:\> prompt):

   C:\> dir_c: [↲]   (the _ means leave a space here)

A number (possibly a large number!) of file and sub-directory names will then appear on the screen (we will explain what these are shortly), and then you will find yourself back at the C:\> prompt.

Listing files in WINDOWS

In WINDOWS you need to access the 'File Manager' window to do this. You will find the icon for this (called Winfile, which looks like a filing cabinet!) in the 'Main' window of the program manager. You simply position your mouse pointer (an arrow) on the icon and double-click the left-hand button of your mouse, and you should then see the 'File Manager' window appear. The file icons (shown on the right-hand side of the window) look like sheets of paper. By default all the files and sub-directories (we will explain what these are shortly) shown on the right- and left-hand side of the window, respectively, are those stored on the hard disk C:. To return to the program manager simply click the top left-hand corner of the 'File Manager' window and select (i.e. click) 'Close' from the drop-down menu.

Listing files on the data disk

If you try to look in the same way at the files on a new floppy disk in drive a:, the computer will tell you that you have no files on the disk in a: (since you have not yet created any for it to store for you). In order to see what would happen if you did have files on a floppy disk in drive a: first insert the disk (the 'data disk') that comes with the book into drive a:. Then:

∗ DOS

In DOS type:

   C:\> dir_a: [↲]

the computer should respond with:

CLASS	SAV	40360	02/08/95	10:41
BHPS1	SYS	317600	02/08/95	11:34
CLASS	SYS	72272	02/08/95	11:26
BHPS123	SYS	264888	02/08/95	11:44
EXAMPLE	SPS	2001	03/08/95	9:46
READ	ME	13891	02/08/95	11:57
BHPS123	SAV	219168	02/08/95	11:09
DEMO	DAT	224	02/08/95	12:07
BHPS1	SAV	214744	02/08/95	10:35

9 files 1145148 bytes
309248 bytes free

There are nine files, which are called READ.ME, DEMO.DAT, CLASS.SYS, CLASS.SAV, BHPS1.SYS, BHPS1.SAV, BHPS123.SYS, BHPS123.SAV and EXAMPLE.SPS (we explain about file names below). It also tells you about their size (in 'bytes') and the date and time they were created. You are then informed about the total number of bytes taken up by all the files put together, and how much space is still left on the disk.

WINDOWS

In WINDOWS select (click) the 'Winfile' icon again, and this time when the 'File Manager' window appears select drive a: by clicking the box (labelled 'a') that looks like a disk drive slot in the row of such boxes which run along the top of the window. You will then see in the right-hand side of the window the files listed above appear (we explain about file names below). You can see how much space each file takes up (in bytes) and the date and time they were created (if these are not shown automatically) by clicking the 'View' drop-down menu and then clicking the item 'All File Details'.

Logging out

Every time you want to stop using the computer you should log out. You do this by typing (after the DOS C:\> prompt)

    logout [↵]

The computer then understands that you have finished and it returns to the 'login' prompt ready for the next user.

Basically all this is done using a keyboard (and, in WINDOWS, a mouse) connected to a computer and a VDU (visual display unit) screen. You put information into the computer via the keyboard (and/or the mouse) and receive information back via the screen. Remember that the computer doesn't process anything until you either press the ENTER([↵]) key or, in WINDOWS, click the left-hand button of the mouse. So if you make an error in something you have typed, you can correct it before pressing ENTER or clicking the mouse. For example, you can delete the last character you typed by positioning your cursor (the flashing positional indicator) just to the right of the character concerned and pressing the backspace ([<-]) key. If you keep pressing this key, you will delete steadily backwards along the line.

Within the WINDOWS environment, you still need to be able to use a keyboard for editing and word-processing, but in addition the special feature of WINDOWS is that you can select (click) words or pictures (icons) with your mouse, which has the effect of accessing DOS commands without you actually having to learn them and type them out.

Useful keys on the PC

In general, the keyboard is very similar to that for a typewriter. However, in addition there are a number of keys that are given a special interpretation by the computer.

[←] BACKSPACE	Deletes the previous character.
[⇑] SHIFT	Used with other keys, gives the symbols shown on top of those keys.
[Ctrl] CONTROL	This key provides another set of characters, called 'control characters', in a similar way to the shift key. They are not printing characters, but mostly appear on the screen ('echo') as the corresponding alphabetic character, preceded by a circumflex (^). For example, [Ctrl] [C] echoes as ^C.
[↵] ENTER or RETURN	Normally used to end a line. Remember that the computer will generally not respond until the ENTER/RETURN (or the ESCAPE) key is pressed.
[Esc] ESCAPE	This key is usually represented by [Esc]. For our purposes, its primary use is for moving between menus in SPSS/PC+ (see the following section).

Floppy disk

This is your own portable disk, on which to store the information that you put into the computer. A **floppy disk** with files already on it is provided with this book (the data disk). However, we do not recommend that you use this disk to store your own work on. To get a new floppy disk you will need, therefore, to obtain one for your computer from the relevant source. Once the disk has been 'formatted' you will be able to create and store files of your own on it. Most floppy disks now come preformatted, but if you have an unformatted disk then to 'format' it place it in the floppy disk drive a: and do the following:

* Formatting disks in DOS

In DOS (with the C:\> prompt showing on the screen) type:

    format_a:

Formatting disks in WINDOWS

In WINDOWS get into the 'File Manager' window by double-clicking the 'Winfile' icon. Then, from the disk drop-down menu, select 'Format Disk' and click the 'OK' button.

The machine will whirr and click for a while; the best way to conceptualize what is going on is to think of it making 'tracks' in your disk equivalent to vinyl disk tracks, which are then ready to store information. Eventually it will respond to inform you that it has successfully formatted your disk. If it informs you instead that there is an error, or 'bad sectors' on your disk, seek assistance; sometimes the disks are defective and will need to be replaced. Assuming that you have a formatted disk you are now ready to proceed. The disks you have will hold a certain amount of information (normally 1.44 megabytes of data) – this should be more than enough for your needs.

Remaining bytes

* In DOS you can always check how many bytes are left on a disk by typing:

    C:\> chkdsk_a:

In WINDOWS you can see how many bytes are still free on the floppy disk from the information given along the foot of the 'File Manager' window.

This will tell you how many bytes on your disk in drive a: are taken up by files already and how many are free.

Hard disk (C:)

This is the disk belonging to the computer on which the programs such as SPSS that you will be using are stored. Disk C: is known as the 'default drive' – in other words the computer automatically assumes that disk C: is the drive from which you want to work. So when you don't specify a disk drive then it will just assume drive C:.
    You have already learned how you can see what is stored on disk C:.

∗ In DOS by typing:

C:\> dir/w   (where the 'w' means wide format, i.e. list files
                              across rather than down the screen, since
                              there may be many files in drive C:).

In WINDOWS through accessing the 'File Manager' by double-clicking the 'Winfile' icon from the program manager window.

When you are working from disk C: in a teaching lab you must remember to copy any files that you want to store from disk C: either on to another hard disk or on to your floppy disk in drive a:, since usually all extraneous files on disk C: will be deleted at regular intervals! The instructions on copying files given in the next section below will show you how to do this.

Files

All the information which is stored 'in the computer' is recorded in files. Files contain stored information and are identified, like books, by their names. All file names should be of the form:

<name.extension> (e.g. FILE1.SYS, VOTER.DAT, SPSS.LST)

where:

name =   the name which whoever created the file gave it. The name
            can involve a string of up to eight alphanumeric characters
            (i.e. eight letters or numbers)

extension = a three-character adjunct to the name designed to inform the user what sort of information is contained within the file. By convention, each extension has a particular meaning. For example:

1 The extension .DAT generally denotes a raw data file.
2 The extension .SYS denotes an SPSS/PC+ system file containing data ready to be analysed in SPSS/PC+.
3 The extension .SAV denotes an SPSS FOR WINDOWS save file containing data ready to be analysed in SPSS FOR WINDOWS.
4 The extension .LIS denotes that the file is an output file from an SPSS/PC+ analysis.
5 The extension .LST denotes that the file is an output file from an SPSS FOR WINDOWS analysis.

There are of course numerous other extensions. You are strongly advised when creating your own files to follow the conventions outlined above. It is also worth noting that since any given file will be stored on a particular disk, the full specification for a file is:

<drive:name.extension>

For example:

a:CLASS.SAV (i.e. drive:name.extension),

indicating an SPSS FOR WINDOWS save file in drive a:.

Remember that each file that you create must have a unique name – if not, the computer cannot differentiate between files.

You can create files yourself in a number of different ways. It is possible to enter text or data files directly in DOS or WINDOWS using the editor facilities. However, for the purposes of this text, you will more usually be creating files for analysis in SPSS. For those using SPSS/PC+ we will be doing this using a **data entry** facility called QED which is part of SPSS/PC+. In SPSS FOR WINDOWS, data can be entered directly into a spreadsheet or 'data window'. You will be shown how to do this later on in this chapter.

File handling

The three most important file handling tasks to learn are: listing files, deleting files and copying files.

* File handling in DOS

Listing files

In order to see what files are on your floppy disk, the command

    C:\> dir_a:

should be used. This will report to you the details of the files that are stored on your disk in a:.

Deleting files

In order to get rid of a file that you no longer want the 'del' command should be used. An example should demonstrate the general principle:

    C:\> del_a:class.dat

In other words, delete from my disk in a: the file called class.dat.

Copying files

As explained earlier, at some stage you will be required to copy files stored on disk C: on to your own disk. The following command structure should be used:

    C:\> copy_trial.sys_a:trial.sys

In other words, copy on to my disk a: a file called trial.sys which is currently stored on C: (the default drive, which the computer assumes if it is not specified).

File handling in WINDOWS

Listing files

In order to see what files are on your floppy disk, double-click the 'Winfile' icon from the program manager window to access the 'File Manager' window. Then select drive a: by clicking the disk-drive box labelled 'a' from the row of disk-drive boxes shown at the top of the window, to display the files in a:. Return to the program manager by clicking the top left-hand corner of the 'File Manager' window and selecting 'Close' from the drop-down menu.

Deleting files

In order to get rid of a file that you no longer want, from the 'File Manager' window (see above for how to access this) just click the file you want to delete and select the item 'Delete' from the drop-down 'File' menu on the menu bar. (The computer will usually helpfully check with you that you do in fact want to delete that file!) Return to the program manager as above.

Copying files

As explained earlier, at some stage you will be required to copy files stored on disk C: on to your own disk. WINDOWS really comes into its own here!

In the 'File Manager' window (see 'Listing files' above for how to access this) click and keep your finger down on the mouse button to select the file you want to copy. Then 'drag' the file (keeping your finger down on the mouse button) by moving the pointer of the mouse up to the disk-drive box labelled a: in the line of such boxes along the top of the window. Then release your finger from the button. If you have done this correctly then the computer will prompt you to make sure that you really want to copy that file to that disk. Return to the program manager as above.

File directories

All files are stored within file directories. Files in the main or 'default' directory are what get listed automatically when you do not specify which directory you want the computer to list (just as with default drives). Where there are a large number of files to be stored, however, it is often helpful to store some of them in 'sub-directories'. Thus you will find that all the SPSS/PC+ files are most likely stored in a sub-directory called spsspc (or possibly simply spss – the names of sub-directories are locally variable). Likewise SPSS FOR WINDOWS files are most likely stored in a sub-directory called spsswin (or possibly just spss). The following section shows how you switch from the main directory into the appropriate sub-directories in order to access your SPSS files.

Switching directories

Disk C: contains a number of different programs (stored as files in sub-directories) that you will be using. The most important of these are SPSS/PC+ or SPSS FOR WINDOWS. These programs are likely to be stored on appropriately named sub-directories, usually spsspc or spsswin. So, to check that the relevant files are on the sub-directories of disk C:, do the following.

* **In DOS**

Type:

   C:\> cd_spsspc

or just

   C:\>cd_spss

'cd' is short for 'change directory'; you are changing from the main (default) directory in order to look at the files available in the SPSS suite of programs within the relevant SPSS sub-directories. The next DOS prompt should then read C:\SPSSPC> or C:\SPSS> to remind you that you are looking within the relevant SPSS sub-directory. Type

   dir/w

at the prompt to display the available files. You should be able to see a large number of files, all of which are associated with SPSS.

\# **In WINDOWS**

First get yourself into the 'File Manager' window. (You should by now be able to do this; the file manager is used for all the file handling tasks shown in this chapter. If you have forgotten, refer to the section on file handling in WINDOWS above.)

   The 'File Manager' window is divided into two halves. On the right-hand side you can see files, but the left-hand side of the window shows directories and sub-directories (the sub-directory icons look like folders). In order to see the files contained in any particular sub-directory you need to click the appropriate icon for the sub-directory that you want, and the files displayed in the right-hand side of the window will then be the files in that sub-directory. So, click the spsswin (or spss) sub-directory icon. You should now be able to see the files associated with SPSS in the right-hand side of the window.

The next section, on SPSS, will introduce you to the key features of the SPSS package and show you how you can actually access or 'run' either SPSS/PC+ or SPSS FOR WINDOWS, before going on to describe how data are actually fed into the computer for analysis.

   First, though, we provide a quick reference guide to the syntax of some of the most important DOS commands.

Quick reference guide to DOS commands

You can use this guide to remind yourself of what has already been said about DOS commands so far in this chapter.

In all cases the full command is given but the capital letters shown are sufficient for the computer to accept the command. (It is not important in DOS whether you use capital or lower-case letters.) 'Filespecifications' refers to the file location, file name and file extension, e.g. a:xxxxx.xxx.

DIR_filespecifications	Give directory of all files which match filespecifications.
COPY_old-filespecs_ new-filespecs	Make a copy of 'oldfile' called 'newfile'.
DEL _ filespecs	Delete all files which match file-specifications.
TYPE _filespecs	Type out the contents of file on the screen.
PRINT _ filespecs	Print contents of file on a line printer. (This command may vary locally where particular printers need to be identified.)

SPSS

In this section you will learn the basics of SPSS, the Statistical Package for Social Sciences, which is the most widely-used statistical analysis package in the social sciences.[1] You will learn about its command structure, and about the way in which data can be stored in special **data files** (called 'system files' in SPSS/PC+ and 'save files' in SPSS FOR WINDOWS) ready for analysis. This introduction is not intended as a detailed exposition of the use of SPSS. What is intended here is simply a brief elucidation of some of the ideas behind the program which are relevant to subsequent parts of the book, which you can refer back to at any point. Most of the information provided here is drawn from the relevant sections of the *SPSS/PC+ Release 5.0 User's Guide* and the *SPSS FOR WINDOWS Release 6.1 User's Guide* (Norusis/SPSS Inc., 1993 and 1994). Consequently, if you have any problems with SPSS you can always consult the relevant manual, which should be available in your university or college computing service, or from a public library.

SPSS provides an interactive facility for the analysis of social science data. To produce an analysis, it is first necessary to provide data to the computer in the form of an SPSS data file. Such a file not only contains the raw data but also identifies to the computer on which lines and in which columns of the data the different variables are coded (see Chapter 3). It may also be used to give labels to different variable categories, full names to variables and to specify missing value codes, and so on. This file may be created in various ways; here we show you how to create it via the SPSS/PC+ QED facility, or directly into the spreadsheet in the data window of SPSS FOR WINDOWS.

Running SPSS on the computer

* Getting into SPSS/PC+ from DOS

Type:

C:\> cd_spss or C:\> cd_spsspc	(to change directory to spsspc sub-directory)
C:\SPSS> spsspc	(enters SPSS/PC+ program)

* Exiting SPSS/PC+

Select the 'Finish' command from the bottom of the main menu by moving the cursor down to highlight it, and paste it into the scratch pad by pressing ENTER [↵]. Then run the command by pressing the [F10] key followed again by ENTER [↵]. This will return you to the DOS prompt.

Getting into SPSS FOR WINDOWS from WINDOWS

Select and double-click the SPSS FOR WINDOWS icon in the program manager window.

Exiting SPSS FOR WINDOWS

Click the upper top left corner of the SPSS FOR WINDOWS application window to display the drop-down menu, and select 'close' by clicking it. The program will then prompt you as to whether you want to save any of the files you have used during your session. Click 'yes' or 'no' as appropriate, the application will close, and you will find yourself back in the WINDOWS program manager.

SPSS commands

We communicate with SPSS through SPSS commands. In both SPSS/PC+ and SPSS FOR WINDOWS these commands are most easily selected initially via on-screen drop-down menus. In either system, they may also be typed directly on to your screen (in fact, once you become proficient at using SPSS, this is often the quickest route). These commands perform a variety of functions. It is important to make clear the distinction between different types of commands that you give to SPSS in the process of data definition, modification and analysis.

First, there are commands for defining and modifying data. These are non-procedure commands, i.e. they do not tell SPSS what you want to do with your data in terms of analysis but only about how to prepare and define data for analysis. Then there are commands which do define analytical procedures such as frequencies, cross-tabulations and regression analysis. These are known as procedure commands, because they involve instructing the computer to actually undertake some analysis of data.

Every command has its own unique identifying word or words, e.g. RECODE, FREQUENCIES, CROSSTABS, and you can select the command that you require from the appropriate menu. Detailed instructions such as the name of a file to analyse, the variables to be changed or included in an analysis, the labels to be given to variable categories, etc. follow the command, as sub-commands. In SPSS/PC+ these are selected from sub-menus associated with specific commands. In SPSS FOR WINDOWS they are accessed from 'dialog boxes' associated with specific commands. For instance, here is an example of a command you will encounter:

FREQUENCIES VARIABLES=VOTE /STATISTICS=ALL.

FREQUENCIES is a command asking for a specific analysis (a procedure command). VARIABLES=VOTE /STATISTICS=ALL are the sub-commands telling SPSS which variable is to be analysed, and what accompanying statistics are required, i.e. it provides the detailed instruction for the FREQUENCIES command.

Note that SPSS command lines appear with a full stop at the end. This indicates to SPSS where to begin and end the execution of a command. In both SPSS/PC+ and SPSS FOR WINDOWS it is created automatically when you use the select and paste facility (SPSS/PC+) or the dialog boxes (SPSS FOR WINDOWS) (see below for selecting and running SPSS commands).

Selecting and running SPSS commands

* In SPSS/PC+

In SPSS/PC+ the basic idea is to select commands and sub-commands from on-screen menus. You highlight the command or sub-command that you want, and then 'paste' it on to the lower portion of your screen by simply pressing the ENTER [↵] key.

You can get practice at this process of selecting and pasting by going through the 'orientation' sub-menu on the main menu that automatically appears on your screen when you access SPSS/PC+. The orientation

sub-menu will also show you how to 'execute' a command that you have
selected and pasted in order to actually run it. (Note that pasting a
command on to the lower portion of the screen, known as the 'scratch
pad', is not itself sufficient to execute the command! In order to actually
run a command that is in your scratch pad you need to press the [F10]
key, followed by the ENTER key [↵].)

In SPSS FOR WINDOWS

In SPSS FOR WINDOWS you select the initial command from drop-down
menus. These menus are attached to the items listed in the menu bar
which runs along the top of the main window in SPSS FOR WINDOWS (the
'application window'). So, for instance, if you wanted to do a FRE-
QUENCIES analysis (which is a statistical procedure) you would select
the 'Statistics' drop-down menu by clicking the 'Statistics' item in the
menu bar. From the drop-down menu you then select 'Summarize' by
clicking it. Another drop-down menu appears from which you can select
FREQUENCIES. This automatically accesses the FREQUENCIES
'dialog box', which enables you to specify the analysis you want. In effect
what you are doing when you use the dialog box is selecting SPSS sub-
commands to attach to your command, as described in the previous
section. Once you have specified your analysis using the dialog box you
can then execute the complete command by simply clicking the 'OK'
button. (You will not be able to access the FREQUENCIES command
in SPSS FOR WINDOWS without first having opened or created a data file
for it to analyse. See the section below on creating data files in SPSS FOR
WINDOWS.)

Note that there is an SPSS 'toolbar' (in SPSS release 6.1) which appears
as a series of buttons running across the top of the windows. Essentially
what these buttons do is to provide shortcuts to specific menu items. You
can discover the function of each button simply by pointing the mouse
pointer at it. At the bottom left of the screen a brief description will
appear telling you what it does.

There is also a teach-yourself SPSS tutorial with release 6.1, which goes
through in easy stages exactly how to use SPSS FOR WINDOWS. It is worth
accessing this tutorial (it should have its own icon in the program
manager window), and working through it at your own pace.

Syntax reference for common SPSS commands

Below we set out simplified syntax for some of the basic commands that
you will come across in this text. (Sub-commands may change between
versions of SPSS. Those listed here refer to Release 6.1.)

For more detail on these and other commands you can refer either to the *SPSS Base System Syntax Reference Manual*, Release 6.1, or to the on-screen help facility of SPSS. For those using SPSS/PC+ this is found in the glossary, accessed via the [F1] key. For those using SPSS FOR WINDOWS help with syntax reference can be found via the drop-down menu attached to the 'Help' item on the menu bar of the main application window, or from the 'Syntax' button on the tool bar.

Non-procedure commands

GET	FILE = 'filespecifications'
RECODE	varA (old values = new value) . . . (old values = new value) . . .
MISSING VALUES	varA (missing values) /varB (missing values)
VARIABLE LABELS	varA 'varlabel' /varB 'varlabel' . . .
VALUE LABELS	varA value1 'label1' value2 'label2' . . ./varB value1 'label1' value2 'label2' . . .
SAVE	OUTFILE = 'filespecifications'

Procedure commands

DESCRIPTIVES VARIABLES = varA varB . . . (or) ALL
/STATISTICS = MEAN* MIN* MAX* STDDEV*
VARIANCE SKEWNESS KURTOSIS
SEMEAN SUM RANGE ALL

* Default statistics

FREQUENCIES VARIABLES = varA varB (or) ALL
/BARCHART
/HISTOGRAM
/STATISTICS = MEAN* MIN* MAX* STDDEV*
MEDIAN MODE VARIANCE
SKEWNESS SESKEW
KURTOSIS SEKURT
SEMEAN SUM RANGE ALL

* Default statistics

CROSSTABS TABLES = varA BY varB BY varC
/CELLS = COUNT (count of cell frequencies)*
ROW (print row % s)
COLUMN (print column % s)
TOTAL (print total % s)
EXPECTED (display expected frequencies)

/STATISTICS = CHISQ (Chi-square)
               PHI (phi for 2 x 2, Cramer's V for
               larger)
               LAMBDA
               GAMMA
               D (Somers' D)
               BTAU
               CTAU

Default with no /CELLS sub-command

PLOT   /FORMAT DEFAULT (prints scatterplot only) or
                  REGRESSION (draws regression line on chart)
                  /PLOT varA WITH varB

SPSS files

Before moving on in the next section to discuss the process of creating a file ready for analysis in SPSS it is important to clarify the different types of files that exist in SPSS. The most significant of these are data files, output files and command syntax files.

* **Files in SPSS/PC+**

- Data files (****.sys)
- Output files (spss.lis)
- Command syntax files (scratch.pad)

* *Data files in SPSS/PC+ (.sys)*

In SPSS/PC+ data files are defined with the file extension '.SYS', and are usually referred to as 'system files'. These are the files which contain all your data and the associated information on variable names, category values and locations. In other words the files you use to do analyses on. They are accessed using the GET command, with the sub-command FILE, e.g:

    GET FILE 'SOCIAL1.SYS'.

They are saved using the command SAVE, this time with the sub-command OUTFILE:

    SAVE OUTFILE 'SOCIAL2.SYS'.

See the section below for how to create data files in SPSS/PC+.

* *Dealing with output in* SPSS/PC+ *(spss.lis files)*

spss.lis is the default name given to your output file (i.e. containing the results of your analyses) in SPSS/PC+. It is automatically created in the SPSS sub-directory of the C: drive every time you enter SPSS/PC+. If you want to examine this file on screen while you are in the middle of an SPSS/PC+ session you press key [F1] and [↵] to access 'Review help' and select 'switch windows' ([F2] key) from the menu of options available. You then need to make sure the 'switch' option at the bottom of the screen is high-lighted and press enter [↵]. The menu disappears and the top half of the screen now shows your output file (spss.lis) in green, which you can scroll through and edit if you choose. To return to the menu, simply reverse the process; press [F2] to switch windows, make sure 'switch' is highlighted at the bottom of the screen and press enter [↵].

To print your spss.lis file at any point during your session, you will need to access the DOS prompt from the Main Menu and type:

C:\SPSS> print_spss.lis   (to print your output file – remembering that the print command may be locally different from this)

Having done this return to SPSS/PC+ by using the DOS 'exit' command:

C:\SPSS> exit

You can of course treat the spss.lis file like any other file when you are in DOS; i.e. you can use the standard DOS commands type, print or copy in order respectively to display the file on the screen, print it or copy it.

Note: Remember that new spss.lis files are automatically created when-ever you enter the SPSS/PC+ program from DOS. This means that previous files of the same name are automatically deleted! If you want to make sure that spss.lis files are not deleted then either copy them off the C: drive on to a floppy disk (or another non-default drive) or rename them using the 'copy' command on the C: drive.

* *Keeping and using command syntax files in* SPSS/PC+
(scratch.pad)

The commands that you write into the scratch pad (blue area of the screen) in SPSS/PC+ are automatically saved as a file called scratch.pad in the SPSS sub-directory on the C: drive. This means that if you have written a large number of commands into the scratch pad you can retrieve them en bloc when you next go into SPSS/PC+.

In order to do this, when you exit SPSS/PC+, you must then save scratch.pad either with a different name or on to another drive (e.g. on to a floppy), to prevent it being overwritten when you next re-enter SPSS/PC+. Then when you re-enter SPSS/PC+ you can retrieve it in the following way: press [F1] then enter [↵] to access Review help, then [F3] to insert a file. When you are prompted for the name of the file you want to insert type in the name and location of the saved scratch.pad file containing your commands. After you have done this and pressed [↵], the commands you want will appear in the blue scratch pad area of the screen!

Files in SPSS for windows

- Data files (****.sav)
- Output files (output.lst)
- Command syntax files (syntax.sps)

Data files in SPSS FOR WINDOWS (.sav)

In SPSS FOR WINDOWS data files have the file extension '.SAV', and are therefore referred to either simply as data files or as 'save files'. These are the files which contain all your data and the associated information on variable names, category values and locations. In other words, the files you use to do analyses on. They can be accessed using the 'open' command from the drop-down 'File' menu or from the 'folder' button on the toolbar. Similarly they are saved via the 'save' command on the same menu.

See the section below for how to create data files in SPSS FOR WINDOWS.

Dealing with SPSS FOR WINDOWS output (output.lst) files

The output resulting from any analysis that you do in SPSS FOR WINDOWS will appear in an output window, which takes the file extension .lst when you save it at the end of your analyses. Whilst in SPSS FOR WINDOWS you can therefore move between the data window and the output window by clicking the relevant window with your mouse. You are thus able to examine and edit your output at any point during your session.

An output window called '!Output1' will normally appear automatically whenever you go into SPSS FOR WINDOWS, and the results of any analysis that you do will automatically go into this window. You save the output window by selecting the 'Save SPSS Output' item on the drop-down File menu, and you will then be prompted for a name to give the file (use the file extension .lst). You can also print the output file at any point in your session by selecting the 'Print' item from the drop-down File menu or by clicking the print button on the toolbar.

It is possible at any time to open a new output window. Simply click 'New' in the drop-down File menu and select 'SPSS Output' from the sub-menu. The new output window will automatically appear. However, you also now have to indicate that this new output window is the one in which you want the results of any new analyses to appear. To do this you have to move the exclamation mark (!) (which appears before any window which is currently in use) from the old output window, !Output1, to the new one, Output2. With the new output window on the screen all you have to do is click the 'exclamation mark' button on the tool-bar. You will find that the window which had just been called 'Output2' is now called '!Output2', signalling that this is now the current output window.

Dealing with SPSS FOR WINDOWS command syntax files (syntax.sps)

In SPSS FOR WINDOWS you have the option when running analyses of writing out your SPSS commands in a syntax window (file extension .sps) and then running them directly by clicking the 'Run' button on the tool-bar (indicated by a forward-pointing arrow). (The alternative is to use the 'dialog boxes' accessed via the 'Statistics' drop-down menu on the menu bar at the top of the screen – see the section above on running commands in SPSS FOR WINDOWS.) If, at the end of your session, you then save the commands that you have written into the syntax window, you will be able to re-access them and use them again in a subsequent session. A syntax window called !Syntax1 should automatically appear whenever you enter SPSS FOR WINDOWS, and you can move between it and the other windows (e.g. data and output windows) by simply clicking the relevant window.

To save the contents of the syntax window you just click the 'Save SPSS Syntax' item on the drop-down file menu and give a file name when prompted. Use the file extension .sps.

In order to re-access, in a subsequent session, the sequence of commands saved in an .sps file you first need to get the appropriate syntax file. Do this by selecting the item 'Open' on the drop-down File menu (or the 'folder' button on the toolbar) and specifying that you want to open a syntax file. Select the file you want from the list shown in the box (remember to identify if necessary the drive in which the file is stored) and click the 'OK' button. The command syntax file that you want should then appear in its own syntax window, ready for use.

As with the output file (.lst) you can also print .sps files at any point during the session.

For beginners with SPSS, it may be easier to start doing your analyses using the dialog boxes. However, syntax windows become particularly useful when you have acquired a good knowledge of the syntax of basic SPSS commands for two reasons. First it is usually quicker to type commands than to open dialog boxes, and, secondly, the full command syntax provides rather more flexibility than the more limited options available in the dialog boxes. More experienced analysts will often therefore prefer to use syntax windows.

Note: You can always paste the commands that a dialog box uses into the syntax window by clicking the 'Paste' button on the dialog box. This is a good way to start to learn more about SPSS command syntax.

Creating SPSS data files

As discussed above, data files are those which contain both your data and a set of instructions which name the variables, locate them in the data, provide labels, etc. in a format which is readable by SPSS. Once the data file is created it can be repeatedly accessed for analysis so that you don't need to re-define your raw data every time you analyse them. All you have to remember is that you need to re-save as a new data file any such file in which you have made modifications to the original data, if you want to make those modifications permanent. For example, if you change a variable's codes in an existing data file and you wish to make that re-coding permanent, you will need to re-save the data file as a new data file. Once generated, the new data file may be accessed in exactly the same way for further analysis or modification.

Entering the data

We have now got to the point where we are in a position to enter some data into the computer in order to create an SPSS data file. What we do is to use a specially prepared sub-set of data which we can proceed to analyse in Part III. Since we will only be using this sub-set as an example, and you will have to go through the tedious process of entering it into the computer, we have restricted its size to 20 cases and three variables.

Demo.dat

As its name indicates DEMO is a demonstration data set. It contains data on three variables for each of 20 cases and we will use it here to demonstrate the creation of SPSS data files. In Part III we will use it to illustrate the first techniques of analysis. There are 20 cases, and the three variables are: (1) age; (2) sex; and (3) vote. The questions we will ultimately be asking of this data concern the relationship between variables (1) and (2) and variable (3).

Below is a print-out or 'hard copy' of the raw data for the data file we will create. As they stand, these numbers are relatively meaningless, although the blank columns obviously serve to separate one set of numbers from the next. You have probably guessed, however, that the numbers in the first two columns (count each space as a single column) indicate the individual cases. Similarly, it is not hard to deduce that columns 4 and 5 represent the cases' ages. Column 7 is probably the variable 'sex', since it only has two categories, and column 9 must be vote, represented as a three-category variable. There are no missing data.

```
01 24 1 3
02 41 2 1
03 58 2 1
04 23 1 2
05 61 1 3
06 19 2 2
07 64 2 1
08 56 2 2
09 38 1 1
10 44 1 2
11 24 2 1
12 18 1 3
13 56 1 3
14 22 2 3
15 33 1 1
16 42 1 3
17 27 2 2
18 44 1 1
19 22 2 2
20 47 2 1
```

Variable codes are:

Sex   1 = female
        2 = male

Vote   1 = Conservative
        2 = Labour
        3 = Other

Now we could just create a file containing only this raw data. However, the computer is not as clever as you are, and it hasn't been given the information which you have about the variables. It could not analyse the data as it stands because it doesn't know what the numbers in the columns refer to. Therefore it needs to be given 'data definition' information as well in order to create a data file which it can analyse. Once created, this data file is accessed each time we wish to do any further computer analysis on the DEMO data. This is because it will contain all the information which SPSS needs to identify the variables (such as the names of the variables) and how to interpret the numbers as category codes.

When you come to enter your data in the way shown below, name your variables:

1 AGE
2 SEX
3 VOTE

and give them variable labels, where appropriate, as follows: VOTE 'vote at last election'. (The other variable names are self-explanatory, and therefore do not require labels.) Once you have entered all the information into the computer and created (saved) the resulting data file you will be in a position to analyse it in SPSS, since the program will now know from the data file what the raw data are about and how to interpret them.

* **Creating data files in SPSS/PC+**

The easiest way to create system files for SPSS/PC+ to analyse is to enter your data via QED. You can select, paste and run QED from the SPSS/PC+ 'READ OR WRITE DATA' menu.

Like SPSS/PC+, QED is a menu-driven program which is quite simple to use. When you enter it, you are presented with two menus. For the meantime you are only interested in the Main Menu. On all QED menus, the key [F1] asks for help, which, if pressed, displays the menus in help mode, which will show you the commands associated with each key. To get into QED, then, you need to do the following:

1 From disk C: get into the SPSS sub-directory:
    C:\> cd_spss [↵]
2 From the SPSS sub-directory, enter the SPSS/PC+ program:
    C:\SPSS_spsspc [↵]
3 Select and paste QED from the READ OR WRITE DATA menu.
4 Activate QED by running it from SPSS/PC+:
    [F10] [↵]

Once in the QED Main Menu, to create a new system file press the shift key [⇑] and the F7 key together. Then, when requested, type the new system file name, including the name of the disk on which you want it to be stored, e.g. a:DEMO.SYS. Give the file the file extension .sys

Next you will need to define the variables in your file. QED holds a 'dictionary' which will contain the names and definitions of all the variables in your file(s) when you have fed them in. To enter the dictionary press [⇑] [F4] from the Main Menu. Yet another menu will appear!

First you need to define variables so press [F2], and DE will display an easy-to-use Variable definition window. Enter your variable names and variable labels (optional) where indicated. The next four items all have 'default' values displayed. If these are acceptable press the ENTER key. If not, type the correct value. Note the following points in relation to the Variables definition window:

1 Non-numeric variables are known as 'string'. The up and down arrow

cursor keys move you between numeric and string options. All the variables in these data are numeric (i.e. they are numbers rather than letters).

2 Leave 'Display Mode Edit' as it is.

3 The variables here take up either one or two columns in the 'variable length' item. There are no decimal places.

4 If there are any missing data you can fill in any missing value codes for the variable at 'Missing'. However, there are none here.

When you have finished typing in the definition for each variable press [Ctrl] [F10] to go on to the next one. The [ESC] key pressed twice takes you back to the Main Menu.

The next stage is to save the system file. To do this press [⇑] [F3] to save a file. You will then be asked what the name of the file to be saved is. Since you have already named the file all you have to do is press the ENTER key a couple of times and it will save your new file for you as an SPSS/PC+ system file.

Having got a file defined, you now need to put some data into it. This is done case by case in QED by entering the raw data in rows and columns called spreadsheets.

To enter your data, then, type [⇑] [F5] from the Main Menu to get into the Data Menu. Press [Spacebar] to enter data in the spreadsheet. The variables you have defined will appear in a line across the top of the screen. All you need to do now is to type in your data, remembering to press [↵] after each value. You can use the cursor arrows

to move around the raw data as you enter it, correcting errors if necessary by using the backspace key. You will not need to type the identification numbers of the individual cases, as this will be done automatically for you as you go in the left-hand column of the spreadsheet. When you start to enter the data for the last case you will first need to type [F6] to indicate that there are no more cases to add. After the last value for the final case has been entered [ENTER] and [Esc] will take you back to the Main Menu.

Do not forget to SAVE the file you have created with the data in it: press [⇑] [F3] from the Main Menu. Press [ENTER] when it gives you the file name (unless you want to change it), then type 'yes' when you are asked if you want to replace the existing file, and [ENTER] again where you are prompted about compressing the file. The file will now be saved for you on disk a: ready for access and analysis in SPSS/PC+. To return to SPSS/PC+ from QED simply press [⇑] [F10] from the Main Menu.

Creating data files in SPSS FOR WINDOWS

In SPSS FOR WINDOWS the simplest way to create save files is to enter the data directly into a data file spreadsheet which is available automatically whenever you go into the SPSS FOR WINDOWS program. This spreadsheet, called 'Newdata' is initially empty, and will disappear if you access an already existing data file for analysis (see Chapter 6 on analysing data in SPSS FOR WINDOWS). But if you are going to create your own data file for future use, then all you have to do is to start filling in the cells of the spreadsheet with your own data – in this case with the DEMO.DAT data.

To do this, you simply locate your cursor in the top left-hand cell of the spreadsheet by clicking it with your mouse, and begin entering the data line by line exactly as it appears on p. 71. You will not need to type the identification numbers of the individual cases, as this is done automatically in the left-hand column of the spreadsheet. Use the tab key [→] to enter data and move from one column to the next, and the enter key [↵] to enter data and move down to the next row. You can use the cursor arrow keys to simply move around the spreadsheet. When you have finished entering the data for the 20 cases, the next task is to name the variables, and to enter their value labels. This procedure becomes slightly more complicated, and involves using the 'Define Variable' box.

First, click the cell above the first column of the data, which at the moment only contains the number Var00001. The entire column should now be highlighted. Then click the drop-down 'Data' menu at the top of the screen and select the item 'Define Variable'. The Define Variable box should now appear. In the area called 'variable name' type 'age'. You do not need to provide a variable label because the variable name 'age' is self-explanatory. Nor, with this variable, do you need to specify any value labels for its categories. So all you have to do now is to click the 'OK' button, and you will find that the number Var00001 in the cell above the first column of the data has been replaced with the variable name 'age'. Then proceed to name the other variables in the same way. Note the following points:

1 Enter a variable label for the variable 'vote', as indicated on p. 71, by clicking the 'labels' button on the Define Variable box and typing in the variable label in the Define Labels box. Then click the 'Continue' button to return to the Define Variable box.

2 The variables 'sex' and 'vote' require value labels. Select the labels button on the Define Variable box. Enter the category values and their labels (as specified on p. 71) in the area provided in the value labels area of the Define Labels box, clicking the Add button to record each of your labels once you have typed them. Return to the Define Variable box by clicking 'Continue'.

3 If there are any missing data you can fill in the missing value codes for the variable concerned by pressing the 'Missing Values' button on the Define Variable box. However, there are none here.

Having entered your data, Define Variable and value label information, the next thing to do is to save the file as an SPSS FOR WINDOWS data file, with the file extension .SAV. To do this just select the 'Save Data' item on the drop-down file menu, and when the 'Newdata: Save Data As' box appears fill in the appropriate file location and name (i.e. decide which drive you want the file to be saved on to, and with what name). Use the file extension .SAV.

You have now, hopefully, created and saved your own SPSS data file, containing both the raw data and the data definition instructions, ready for analysis in SPSS. Part III goes on to discuss how we go about this, returning initially to recap some of the basic principles involved in data analysis. Finally, though, we provide a quick reference guide to some computing terms that you may come across, and be confused by!

Glossary of computing terms

This glossary provides an introduction to some of the computing terms that you will come across. Two of the most common terms you are likely to hear are hardware and software. Hardware refers to the computer and its accessories or peripheral devices, i.e. the actual machines and the bits that go into them. Software refers to the instructions which determine the operation of the hardware, i.e. to computer languages in which programs are written, programs themselves and suites of programs called packages.

Hardware terms

bit   the smallest unit of information stored. Bit means binary digit and because computers operate in a binary system it assumes a two-value, 0/1, on/off form.

byte   a combination of bits.

CD ROM   a laser-read disk; the computing equivalent of the CD with much greater storage capacity than the conventional 'hard' disk.

disk   an information storage device. A disk is a two-way device which can provide information to, and receive it from, the computer. Disks come either as 'hard' (a platter of magnetic material rather like a cylindrical record) 'floppy' (a thin bendable portable diskette with more limited storage capacity) or 'floppy/cassette' (a more robust version of the floppy, with greater capacity). Magnetic tapes are an alternative, but slower and heavier, means of storing information.

mainframe   large number-crunching computer.

micro or PC   desk-top or portable computer with more limited processing capacity.

printer   prints output ('hard copy') from the computer.

VDU screen   'Visual Display Unit' screen attached to a computer on which you type what you communicate with the computer.

word   a combination of bytes.

workstation   a more powerful version of a PC, providing multi-user facilities.

Software terms

compiler/interpreter/assembler   the means by which programming language is translated into the binary machine language of 0/1.

input   any of the ways in which information can be put into the computer.

machine language   this is the built-in binary language understood by the computer.

operating system   the system by which resources are allocated, users defined, files created and manipulated (i.e. which generally does the computer's 'housekeeping').

output   any of the ways in which information can be sent from computer to user.

package   (e.g. SPSS, WORD, EXCEL, etc.). A suite of programs put together into a single 'package' with a simplified set of instructions for the user to give to the computer.

program   a set of instructions written in a programming language by which the user can tell the computer to perform certain tasks.

programming languages   these are computing languages (e.g. C+, BASIC, FORTRAN) which the computer can translate into its machine language so that it can execute its operations.

Other terms

database   a large set of files.

file   an organized set of information stored on tape or disk.

record   some unit of information, e.g. the information for a single individual in a survey.

run   the process of submitting data and instructions to a computer, the subsequent execution of the task and retrieval of results.

Note

1 For further details about SPSS products please contact:
SPSS UK Ltd
SPSS House
5 London Street
Chertsey
Surrey KT16 8AP

Key concepts

Make sure you have understood the following key concepts:

- SPSS

- MS-DOS

- floppy/hard disks

- files

- SPSS data files

- data entry

Part III

Descriptive data analysis in social research

5 | From computer to analysis: describing single variables

Aims

- To calculate and interpret frequency distributions for single variables.

- To describe measures of central tendency appropriate for different levels of measurement of variables.

- To understand simple indices of dispersion for different levels of measurement of variables.

- To describe the properties of the normal distribution.

Having learnt in Chapter 4 about the first steps in communicating with a computer, and how to set up SPSS data files ready for analysis we now return to discuss in greater detail some of the principles of data analysis introduced in Chapter 2. We will show how to display data in various graphical forms, and how to interpret and calculate simple summary measures of variance and central tendency, before turning in Chapter 6 to combine the information contained in the previous two chapters in order to perform a simple analysis on the system file we have already set up. First, however, we need to recall some basic principles of data analysis.

As we saw in Chapter 2, data analysis is basically concerned with *explaining variance*, that is with explaining why there is variability in a population or sample with regard to a particular characteristic of some theoretical importance. Despite the practical emphasis of Chapter 4, it cannot be emphasized enough that the whole process of data collection and analysis in the social sciences must always be theoretically informed. The questions we ask of data should relate to the theoretical problems in which we are interested. The data themselves take the form of a series of variables, i.e. theoretically derived measures of certain characteristics of the population or sample under consideration. No matter how complicated the technique being used, the basic process of data analysis can be thought of as one of *partitioning variance* – which is the process that we described at the end of Part I when we were attempting to account for variations in voting behaviour as an indicator of political ideology.

In this sense all data techniques involve summarizing data. We begin with raw data but we have to process that raw data in order to summarize it, i.e. we have to simplify complexity, which is in any case the joint task of theorizing and analysing. In other words each stage in the process of analysis involves the 'loss' of some information but a 'gain' (hopefully) in our ability to understand social processes. As we shall see, data analysis involves these kinds of trades-off, if we are to summarize complex patterns over large numbers of cases.

An illustration will help. Once we have created our system file, we could ask the computer to produce the following arrays by instructing it to list variable by variable the category *codes* for each case in our sample, i.e. the numbers corresponding to the categories for every individual in the survey, e.g.:

Sex

       12211222112112112122

Vote

       31123212121333132121

These arrays, however, tell us very little indeed. They are just two lists of numbers. Imagine what such an array from a data set of 1000 cases and 500 variables would look like. It would be meaningless. We cannot use the data in this form, so we have to find a way to summarize them. One way we could do this would be to count the number of occurrences of each category. For these variables we would obtain the following.

For sex:

Category	Number of occurrences
1 Female	10
2 Male	10

For vote:

Category	Number of occurrences
1 Conservative	8
2 Labour	6
3 Other	6

This is much easier to understand than the array because we can now see a relationship between the categories and the number of occurrences. Instead of a series of numbers we now have a count of how often each number occurs – we have what is called a **frequency distribution**. From this we can quickly see that more people in this small sample vote Conservative than for any other party. If we were to revert to our guessing game, and guess the party which an individual, picked out at random from the sample, voted for at the last election, we would have to guess Conservative, with an 8/20 chance of being right. In this case, then, 'Conservative' represents a sort of average – the best guess we can make of an individual's vote where that vote is unknown. What we are really interested in, though, is why some people vote Conservative and others vote for other parties, i.e. in explaining the *variation* in the variable 'vote'. We therefore need to think in terms of explaining this variation in respect of the variation in another variable. In the example we are using we can do this by matching the categories of the 'vote' variable with the categories of the 'sex' variable, to determine whether people's voting behaviour is affected by their sex. We are back here to the familiar $X \rightarrow Y$ equation, which we have interpreted as 'a change in the value of X (the independent variable) is associated with a change in the value of Y (the dependent variable)'. It should be fairly clear that in this case 'vote' is the dependent variable – we could hardly hypothesize that voting behaviour might influence sex!

If we examine the two variables in conjunction, we can see that there is a pattern in the data: women are more likely to vote Other and men are more likely to vote Conservative.

Sex = F	Vote (Y)	Sex = M	Vote (Y)
1	1	2	1
1	1	2	1
1	1	2	1
1	2	2	1
1	2	2	1
1	3	2	2
1	3	2	2
1	3	2	2
1	3	2	2
1	3	2	3

Now, if all men voted Conservative and all women voted Labour or Other, then we would have a paradigm case for the *explanation* of Y by X. If we put *this* result in a table, we would obtain:

Vote (Y)	Sex (X)		Total
	Male	Female	
Conservative	10	0	10
Labour/Other	0	10	10
Total	10	10	20

Needless to say, things never work out so neatly in real research. However, these examples have allowed some important points of principle to be reiterated. Data are of little use in an array. They must be summarized in some way. We can do this in simple ways to begin with by finding summary measures and simple forms of presentation for single variables. We can then go beyond this to look at the influence of one variable on another, in *bivariate analysis*; and from there to *multivariate analysis*. But no matter how complicated the analysis becomes, our aim is to describe and explain variance.

In what follows, we examine various ways of presenting data and describing variance via **descriptive statistics**. Descriptive statistics are concerned with the interpretation and summarization of *frequency distributions* (the number of cases in the categories of a variable) and *percentage distributions* (the percentage of cases in the categories of a variable). As we have already seen, such distributions may involve analysing only one variable (univariate), or two variables (bivariate) or three or more variables (multivariate) in conjunction. The kinds of statistics we can use for summarization and interpretation will depend on the level at which the variables are measured.

It is descriptive statistics which concern us here. In Part IV we will consider *inferential statistics*. The purpose of inferential statistics is to make generalizations from a limited body of data such as a sample to the whole population from which the sample was drawn. They allow us to determine the extent to which relationships appearing in our sample are also likely to appear in the population concerned, on the basis of mathematical probability theory.

Univariate descriptive statistics

We begin the discussion of data analysis, then, by examining the simplest ways of presenting and describing data for single variables. This section will deal with the following:

- univariate frequency distributions
- univariate percentage distributions

- univariate cumulative distributions
- various forms of graphic representation
- measures of central tendency – the mean, median and mode
- measures of dispersion – variance and standard deviation.

The purpose of these techniques will become more apparent with their application to substantive examples involving familiar variables. At the same time, issues discussed in the abstract earlier, especially those concerning levels of measurement, should become clearer.

Frequency distributions

We start by looking at how we can measure and present the way in which single variables are distributed within a group of sampled individuals. Suppose we were conducting a piece of research in which marital status was an important variable. Let us say we had decided we could measure this variable in terms of responses to a closed or structured question in a survey of the following kind:

Question: What is your marital status? Are you:

Married	1
Living as married	2
Single	3
Widowed	4
Separated	5
Divorced	6

One way in which we could examine answers to this question would be to look at the actual observations. Say 30 people had answered this question. We could copy down their actual answers, as in Table 5.1.

These are our observations, but in this form they are of very little use for analysis. The observations need to be turned into data. We noted previously that we could do this in terms of a data array, i.e. replace the observations with the numerical category codes from the original question, hence 1 = Married; 2 = Living as married; 3 = Single; etc. However, we

Table 5.1 Marital status of 30 individuals

Married	Divorced	Single	Living as married
Single	Married	Married	Single
Living as married	Widowed	Divorced	Divorced
Married	Refused	Married	Married
Separated	Married	Separated	Living as married
Married	Married	Married	Single
Married	Married	Widowed	Married
Divorced	Divorced		

Table 5.2 Frequency distribution of marital status in Table 5.1

Marital status X_i	Number or frequency f_i
Married	13
Living as married	3
Single	4
Widowed	2
Separated	2
Divorced	5
Missing	1
Total	30

also saw that such data arrays were not very useful either, because any pattern which might exist in the data is difficult to see. If we recall our discussion of variables, there is a simple solution to the summary of the marital status data. Apart from a name and a verbal definition, a variable has a set of mutually exclusive categories and a procedure for sorting cases into categories which is inclusive of all responses. All that needs to be done is to find a way of indicating how many cases fall into each category. The most obvious way to do this would be simply to count the number in each category. The presentation of univariate data in which the number of cases in each category of a variable are counted is known as a *univariate frequency distribution*. In effect this is a table with only one variable within it, as in Table 5.2, which shows the different categories of the marital status variable, together with the frequency (the number of times) each category occurs over the 30 cases. Note that, because one person refused to answer the question, we require a seventh category for *missing data* since all cases must be assigned to a category (the rule of total inclusiveness). Also Table 5.2, contains two symbols at the head of each column, X_i and f_i. These are pronounced 'X subscript i' and 'f subscript i' because the i comes below the symbol to which it is related. As before, X simply indicates a variable; f means frequency and i refers to the ith category. In our example, therefore, i refers to any of the marital status categories. If you were asked 'what is f_i when $X_i = $ married?', you would look at Table 5.2 and answer '13'.

What Table 5.2 gives us, then, is a more helpful way of summarizing the observations from Table 5.1. We can now see a pattern in the data. Most people are not married, but those married do represent the largest category, followed by the divorced, single, living as married and widowed and separated, respectively. However, what is most obvious is the relatively large number in one category – the married. If we chose, we could add some of the categories together because of their obvious similarities. A slightly different pattern would then emerge, as in Table 5.3. This re-categorization helps to emphasize the fact that most of the 30 people in

Table 5.3 Re-categorization of marital status in Table 5.2

Marital status X_i	Frequency f_i
Married/Living as married	16
Single	4
Widowed	2
Separated/Divorced	7
Missing	1
Total	30

the sample are living in a relationship with someone else. Suppose, however, that the 30 people in our sample had been drawn from a housing estate with 600 residents. Let us say that we also know that the overall distribution of marital status in the estate is as indicated in Table 5.4.

Table 5.4 Marital status in housing estate

Marital status X_i	Frequency f_i
Married/Living as married	340
Single	80
Widowed	40
Separated/Divorced	140
Total	600

If we wanted to know how accurate the distribution of marital status in our sample was in terms of the distribution in the estate from which it was drawn, it would not be easy to do so by comparing Tables 5.3 and 5.4 because of their different numbers or frequencies. What we require is some way of *standardizing* the data in the two tables. This is done by constructing a *univariate percentage distribution* (sometimes called a *relative frequency distribution*). Each frequency is converted into a percentage by dividing it by the total number of cases in the table and then multiplying by 100. Thus in Table 5.3, the percentage of married/living as married is:

$$\frac{16}{30} \times 100 = 53.3\%$$

If we do this for all the frequencies in both tables we obtain the figures in Table 5.5. By comparing the percentages in each category we can now see that the sample and the whole estate have very similar distributions of marital status. (The figures in parentheses show the percentages when

Table 5.5 Comparison of data in Tables 5.3 and 5.4

Marital status	% Table 5.3	% Table 5.4
Married/Living as married	53.3 (55.2)	56.7
Single	13.3 (13.8)	13.3
Widowed	6.7 (6.9)	6.7
Separated/Divorced	23.3 (24.1)	23.3
Missing	3.3	0.0
Total	99.9 (100)	100.0

we remove missing data from consideration, as we often do in such analyses. These figures have therefore been calculated on the basis of a total of 29 cases instead of 30.)

So far we have only examined frequency distributions for a nominal level variable. However, variables measured on ordinal or interval/ratio scales can be treated similarly. In the case of interval/ratio scales, we would normally produce *grouped* frequency or percentage distributions. The reason for this is fairly obvious. Many interval-level variables (and from now on interval assumes ratio, too) have a wide range and many values within a sample. For example, the 30 people asked about marital status might also have been asked their ages. This could have produced 30 different answers. If we had then proceeded to create a separate category in our age variable for each answer given, we would have produced a most unhelpful frequency distribution with one case in each category. Instead, we would be more likely to count frequencies within age bands or groups. Suppose in our sample there was one person who was 20, another who was 21, and three more who were respectively, 22, 23 and 24. Instead of presenting the data as

Age	Frequency
20	1
21	1
22	1
23	1
24	1

we could present it as

Age	Frequency
20–24	5

Table 5.6 Frequency distribution of age groups (1)

Age group (X_i)	Frequency (f_i)	%
20–24	5	16.7
25–29	7	23.3
30–39	8	26.7
40–49	5	16.7
50–59	3	10.0
60–69	2	6.7
Total	30	100.1

Of course in the process we lose some information. All we now know is that five people were aged between 20–24. We no longer know (or at any rate show) what the raw data revealed. However, we do gain in conciseness of information. Rather than knowing that 30 people all had different ages, we could show that they fell into age groups as in Table 5.6. Note that the age groups do not overlap. The reason for this is the need for mutually exclusive categories. If, say, we had categories of 25–30, 30–35, 35–40, where would we put someone who was 30 or 35? It is not clear which category they should go in, so there is an opportunity for error to creep in. Note also that the age groups are not equal. The last four categories contain 10-year groups; the first two contain groups of 5 years. These latter categories could have been constructed differently to come into line with the rest of the table, viz.:

Age group	Frequency
20–29	12

The way in which group intervals are chosen depends on what you want to demonstrate with the data and that will usually depend on theory. However, if other things are equal, intervals would probably initially be selected which offered the best way of describing the pattern in a variable. Remember, it is always possible to change how the data are presented by re-categorization into new group intervals. The age group data

Table 5.7 Frequency distribution of age groups (2)

Age group (X_i)	Frequency (f_i)	%
Under 40	20	66.7
40 or over	10	33.3
Total	30	100.0

Table 5.8 Cumulative frequency distribution for age-group data

Age group (X_i)	Frequency (f_i)	%	Cumulative f_i	Cumulative %
20–24	5	16.7	5	16.7
25–29	7	23.3	12	40.0
30–39	8	26.7	20	66.7
40–49	5	16.7	25	83.4
50–59	3	10.0	28	93.4
60–69	2	6.7	30	100.1
Total	30	100.1	30	100.1

could be presented as in Table 5.7. It is often the case that we categorize variables simply in order to have sufficient cases in each category to do meaningful analysis, as we shall see later. Provided such an exercise is not done with intent to deliberately alter the results, this makes a great deal of sense.

The final type of distribution that is sometimes used is the *cumulative frequency distribution*. Once again this is most likely to be used with interval or ordinal level data. It involves showing the number or percentage of observations that are less (or more) than a particular value as in Table 5.8. Here frequencies and percentage frequencies are cumulated up to 30 (the number in the sample) and 100 per cent respectively. It is easy to see that, for instance, 20 people or 66.7 per cent of the sample are 39 or under.

A more visual way of presenting the information in a frequency distribution is via graphs or diagrams. There are a variety of types of graphical or diagrammatic displays available but here we demonstrate only two of these – the **bar chart** and the **histogram**. The bar chart is most

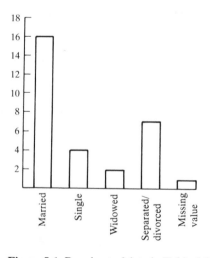

Figure 5.1 Bar chart of data in Table 5.3

appropriately used for nominal level data. Consider again the data in Table 5.3 on marital status. These data could have been presented in a bar chart as in Figure 5.1. Each category of the marital status variable is contained within bars or blocks which are of equal width. However, the height of the bars is proportional to the frequencies of the categories on a scale of 0.25 cm for each person. Hence the block for the category 'single' is 1 cm high (four people) and that for the 'separated and divorced' category is 1.75 cm high (seven people). As can be seen, the differing heights show the relative importance of the categories and we can see that far more people are living in relationships than in any other category of marital status. Because nominal measures are merely classifications which imply difference there is no implied order and hence no scale on the horizontal axis. The bars may be of any width (although all should be of the same width) and are kept separate from one another to emphasize the nominal nature of the measurement.

When we are dealing with interval measures such as the data on age groups in Table 5.8, we might use a *histogram* for a graphical display. Blocks are raised in a similar way to that described for bar charts but the width of each block is made proportional to the size of the age-group interval. Where intervals and therefore block widths are unequal this will be reflected by adjusting the height of each block until its area is proportional to its relative frequency. The best way to conceptualize this is in terms of 'building-bricks' of a set volume representing each individual. Where interval sizes (and thus block widths) are unequal, therefore, the height of the blocks has to be adjusted in order to compensate for the different numbers of bricks required to fill the block width before the 'building-up' of the blocks can begin. So for an interval twice as wide as another, but containing the same frequency, the block would only be half as high (but

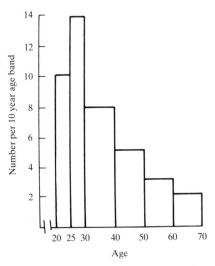

Figure 5.2 Histogram of age-group data

twice as wide). The blocks in a histogram are not separated but contiguous (Figure 5.2). In the case of the age-group data, since the first two age groups contain only half the number of years as the following four (five years instead of ten), the widths of their bars on the histogram are only half as wide. In order to compensate for this (in other words, to make the *proportional* frequencies equivalent), the number of cases in the first two groups are multiplied by two to standardize the proportional frequencies with those of the other age-groups (i.e. at ten years).

You should be able to see that this process of describing the frequency distributions of variables represents the first step in the data analysis process – it is how we initially determine the breakdown of the variables within the sample. Whenever you are faced with a new set of data, then, your first aim should be to try to discover this. Chapter 6 will show you how to achieve it using SPSS.

We now turn to the next step in the description of single variables; measuring their central point, or the central tendency around which they are distributed.

Measures of central tendency

The **central tendency** *of a distribution refers to the place in the distribution of category values where a particular distribution is centred.* There are three main measures of central tendency, and, as we shall see, which one we use depends largely upon the level at which a variable is being measured. The three measures are: (1) the *(arithmetic) mean*; (2) the *median*; and (3) the *mode*. We will take each in turn.

The (arithmetic) mean ($\bar{X}$)

The mean is perhaps the most familiar of all measures of central tendency. It is what is generally referred to as the 'average', as, for example, in a cricketer's batting average. It is quite simply the sum of all values of each observation of a variable divided by the total number of observations; in formula it is denoted by $\bar{X}$ (pronounced 'X bar'). The following is the formula for the mean:

$$\bar{X} = \frac{\sum X_i}{N}$$

$\sum$ (pronounced 'sigma') is the summation sign. It means we should add together whatever is listed after it, and so here it means 'add up all the individual values on X'. N is just the shorthand way of writing 'total number of observations'. Thus, for a cricketer's batting average, X_i refers to his or her scores in individual innings and N to the total number of innings. However, what if, as will often be the case, we want the mean for a frequency distribution? Here we have to take into account the frequencies for each category of the variable, as in Table 5.9. Weekly income provides us with our score categories, X_i. Number of employees denotes the frequency of cases in each score category, f_i. To work out the mean we must obviously take into account f_i as well as X_i. Hence, for frequency distributions

$$\bar{X} = \frac{\Sigma X_i f_i}{N}$$

We can therefore add a third column to our data in Table 5.9 to represent $X_i f_i$ (Table 5.10).

Table 5.9 Weekly income of clerical employees in Widgets plc

Income (X_i) (£)	Number of employees (f_i)
80	7
90	12
100	16
110	22
120	10
130	15
140	25
150	13
175	8
200	5
Total	133

Table 5.10 Addition of $X_i f_i$ to columns of Table 5.9

Income (X_i)	Number of employees (f_i)	($X_i f_i$)
80	7	560
90	12	1080
100	16	1600
110	22	2420
120	10	1200
130	15	1950
140	25	3500
150	13	1950
175	8	1400
200	5	1000
	$N = 133$	$\Sigma X_i f_i = 16\,660$

$$\bar{X} = \frac{\Sigma X_i f_i}{N} = \frac{16\ 660}{133} = £125$$

The arithmetic mean is a measure of central tendency which requires variables to be measured at interval level.

The median (Md)

The median is literally the middle position – the value below which (and above which) half the values in a distribution fall. For a simple set of observations, say a sample of five students in respect of the number of essays handed in by the end of term, we might have the results

4, 1, 2, 0, 1

The median is the midpoint of the scores in ascending or descending order, e.g.

0, 1, 1, 2, 4; therefore Md = 1

Where there are many scores, however, we would need a formula to calculate the median. If we regard N as the number of cases, and N is *odd* (as in the example above), Md is the value of the middle score. This would be the Kth score in the ranked array of scores where

$$K = \frac{N+1}{2}$$

But what if we have an *even* number of scores? Say we had only four students, viz.

0, 1, 2, 4

Here we would take the value half-way between the two middle values, i.e. half-way between 1 and 2, or 1.5. In formula we want the point on the scale between the Kth and $K + 1$ scores where this time:

$$K = \frac{N}{2}$$

And what if we have a grouped distribution for an ordinal level variable as in Table 5.11(a)? Here we would need to first obtain *cumulative* percentage frequencies so that we can pinpoint the median group, as in Table 5.11(b). Remembering that the median is the midway point in a distribution, the median group in Table 5.11(b) would be lower middle class, since the 50 per cent point occurs somewhere in that group. In other words in this case the median falls in a large group of responses, so that the number of responses above and below the category lower middle class are not exactly equal.

Table 5.11(a) Class identification

Class identification	%
Working class	40
Lower middle class	35
Upper middle class	25
Total	100

Table 5.11(b) Class identification

Class identification	%	Cumulative %
Working class	40	40
Lower middle class	35	75
Upper middle class	25	100

The median is a measure of central tendency which requires variables to be measured at least at ordinal *level.*

The mode (Mo)

The mode is the value of the score which most frequently occurs in a collection of scores. For example in Table 5.3 the modal category would be 'married/living as married'. In Table 5.12, the mode is Labour. (In fact, relative to the other percentages, Labour and Conservative are very similar, and the distribution could well be regarded as having two modes or as being *bi-modal*.) If we take the following exam marks

55, 46, 63, 67, 58, 52, 59, 63, 65, 70, 63, 55

then the mode is 63, because it occurs most frequently. *The mode is the only measure of central tendency for nominal level variables. If the variable is ordinal or interval we lose much information if we only use the mode.*

Table 5.12 Party political preference of students

Party	%
Labour	47
Conservative	39
Liberal-Democrat	6
Other	4
None	4
Total	100

Given that the median and the mode can be used as measures of central tendency for ordinal measures, and that mean, median and mode can be used for interval measures, how do we decide which one is the most appropriate measure to use for a particular distribution? Other things being equal we would normally use the mean for interval measures and the median for ordinal measures, because they convey the most information we can obtain. However, other things are not always equal. Consider the following distributions of annual income:

A	B
£8 000	£8 000
£10 000	£10 000
£15 000	£15 000
£20 000	£20 000
£22 000	£100 000
Median = £15 000	Median = £15 000
Mean = £15 000	Mean = £30 600

The median is the same for both distributions but the mean is vastly different. This is because extreme scores have a disproportionate effect on the mean, as in distribution B. In this case, although the data is interval level, the median is more 'typical' than the mean. It is, therefore, a better measure for these data. The more skewed the distribution of an interval variable, the more preferable is the median to the mean – and data on incomes are often skewed in this way.

Measures of dispersion

So far we have concentrated on three simple measures of central tendency. However, as argued earlier, what we are actually interested in is *variation*. We want to account for differences between people (or other 'things' like countries) on a particular variable: we wish to analyse *variance*. Measures of central tendency are useful starting points for univariate analysis but they cannot reveal everything about a particular distribution. Where we are dealing with interval variables we can examine not only the measures of central tendency (and principally, of course, the mean) but we can also examine how *dispersed* our scores are around the mean; that is we can also provide a **measure of dispersion**. *Variance*[1] is a measure of dispersion for interval variables which tells us how dispersed cases are about the mean. The smaller the variance, the closer the cases are to the mean; the greater the variance, the more widely the cases are scattered. What we are therefore actually doing is examining the difference between each actual value and the mean of a variable, or, notationally:

$$(X_i - \bar{X})$$

The obvious thing to do to find the variance is, then, to sum the distances of each value from the mean. However, for some values of X the difference will be positive (where the value is greater than the mean) and for others negative (where the value is less than the mean). Since the mean is the central point, positive and negative differences added together will cancel out, and the summed result will always be zero. To avoid this, we first *square* the individual differences, i.e. $(X_i - \bar{X})^2$. (Remember that the square of a negative number is always positive.) The sum of these squared differences is called the *variation*. We then obtain the variance by taking the average of the variation, i.e. dividing it by the number in the sample. Thus, the formula for the variance is:

$$\frac{\Sigma(X_i - \bar{X})^2}{N}$$

In calculating the variance, though, what we have not done is to remove the effect of squaring the $(X_i - \bar{X})$ differences. We do this by taking the square root of the variance, and by so doing we produce the standard descriptive measure of dispersion, the *standard deviation*, which is represented in formula by s or more properly $s(X)$, pronounced 's of X'.

Let us take an example to illustrate what we have said. Imagine we have two groups of five trainees who are each administered a test for which the maximum mark is 20. The distribution of scores for trainees in each group is shown in Table 5.13.

Table 5.13 Scores in test for two trainee groups

Trainees in Group 1		Trainees in Group 2	
A	20	F	12
B	15	G	11
C	10	H	10
D	5	I	9
E	0	J	8

If we take the mean for Group 1

$$\bar{X} = \frac{\Sigma X_i}{N} = \frac{20 + 15 + 10 + 5 + 0}{5} = 10$$

It so happens in Table 5.13 that not only is the mean score for both groups the same, but so is the median (work it out!). Yet obviously the spread of scores is very different in each group. This is where a measure of dispersion helps since it tells us how dispersed or spread the scores are about the mean. Let us therefore derive the variance and standard deviation for each group. For Group 1:

X_i	$\bar{X}$	$(X_i - \bar{X})$	$(X_i - \bar{X})^2$
20	10	10	100
15	10	5	25
10	10	0	0
5	10	-5	25
0	10	-10	100
			$250 = \Sigma(X_i - \bar{X})^2$

The number of scores or cases is 5, i.e. $N = 5$. Hence:

$$\text{Variance of } X = \frac{250}{5} = 50$$

and the standard deviation of $X = \sqrt{50} = 7.07$

Doing the same exercise for Group 2 we have:

X_i	$\bar{X}$	$(X_i - \bar{X})$	$(X_i - \bar{X})^2$
12	10	2	4
11	10	1	1
10	10	0	0
9	10	-1	1
8	10	-2	4
			$10 = \Sigma(X_i - \bar{X})^2$

$$V(X) = \frac{10}{5} = 2$$

$$s(X) = \sqrt{2} = 1.414$$

The standard deviation for Group 2, where the distribution is much more closely clustered around the mean, is much smaller than for Group 1 where scores are more dispersed. Without seeing the actual distributions we could get quite a good idea about them by comparing their means and standard deviations.

Table 5.14 Income in £ p.a. of two groups

Group A	Group B
9 800	5 000
9 900	7 500
10 000	10 000
10 100	12 500
10 200	15 000

Finally, let us take another example which compares the income of two groups as in Table 5.14. If you calculate the mean and the median for each group you will obtain the same result, i.e. £10000, but what about the variance and standard deviation? For Group A,

X_i	$\bar{X}$	$(X_i - \bar{X})^2$
9 800	10 000	40 000
9 900	10 000	10 000
10 000	10 000	0
10 100	10 000	10 000
10 200	10 000	40 000
		$100\ 000 = \Sigma(X_i - \bar{X})^2$

$$V(X) = \frac{100\ 000}{5} = £20\ 000$$

$$s(X) = \sqrt{20\ 000} = £141$$

For Group B,

X_i	$\bar{X}$	$(X_i - \bar{X})^2$
5 000	10 000	25 000 000
7 500	10 000	6 250 000
10 000	10 000	0
12 500	10 000	6 250 000
15 000	10 000	25 000 000
		$62\ 500\ 000 = \Sigma(X_i - \bar{X})^2$

$$V(X) = \frac{62\ 500\ 000}{5} = £12\ 500\ 000$$

$$s(X) = \sqrt{12\ 500\ 000} = £3536$$

We can see from the above examples why the standard deviation makes more intuitive sense as a measure of dispersion than the variance, since the former produces a result in terms of a figure much closer to those with which we began.

We have seen that measures of dispersion such as the standard deviation and variance show us how widely dispersed scores are around the mean. The mean is the average score of an interval level variable but individual scores vary with respect to that average. We have already noted that one of the principal tasks of data analysis is to explain the variation from an average score. Measures of dispersion are a first step in this process since they show just how varied or dispersed cases are. The smaller the variance or standard deviation, the closer cases are to the average score; and the larger the variance or standard deviation, the more scattered they are.

We would normally use the information derived from measures of central tendency and dispersion to inform further stages in data analysis. For example, if we discover there is little or no variation in a variable (i.e. it is very nearly a constant) there would be nothing to explain. However, if there is reasonable variation, we can begin to follow the general procedures explained earlier for accounting for it. For example, we would use the information provided by the mean and the standard deviation to inform us in the categorizing of an interval level variable for use in further analysis. We might, for instance, decide to collapse the data above and below the mean and at one or two standard deviations from the mean on either side. This procedure would not necessarily give us exactly what we want in terms of our initial hypotheses, but it would ensure reasonable numbers of cases in each category. As always we need to come up with a workable balance between theory and practicability. Before moving on, however, we show how to deal with the slightly more complex calculations required where data are presented in the form of frequency distributions.

Measures of dispersion for frequency distributions

Obviously where frequency distributions for interval level variables are concerned we need to take account not only of the X_i but also the f_i (as for the calculation of a mean from a frequency distribution). Below is an example where we calculate the mean, variance and standard deviation of an interval level variable in a neat and simple way. Refer again to Table 5.9, showing the distribution of weekly income in Widgets plc (p. 93). In that table, weekly income provided us with our score categories (X_i) and number of employees with the frequency of cases in each score category (f_i). We need to add two columns to the data in Table 5.9 to produce information necessary to calculate the mean and the variance. Since the mean is

$$\frac{\sum X_i f_i}{N}$$

we need a column for $X_i f_i$, as in Table 5.9, but we also need to calculate $f_i X_i^2$ in order to work out the variance. We do the calculation in the following manner:

X_i	f_i	$X_i f_i$		$f_i X_i^2$
80	7	560	$(7 \times 80^2) =$	44 800
90	12	1080	$(12 \times 90^2) =$	97 200
100	16	1600	$(16 \times 100^2) =$	160 000
110	22	2420	$(22 \times 110^2) =$	266 200
120	10	1200	$(10 \times 120^2) =$	144 000
130	15	1950	$(15 \times 130^2) =$	253 500
140	25	3500	$(25 \times 140^2) =$	490 000
150	13	1950	$(13 \times 150^2) =$	292 500
175	8	1400	$(8 \times 175^2) =$	245 000
200	5	1000	$(5 \times 200^2) =$	200 000
$N = 133$		$\sum X_i f_i = 16\ 660$		$\sum f_i X_i^2 = 2\ 193\ 200$

$$\bar{X} = \frac{16\ 660}{133} = £125$$

In the quick formula for the calculation of the variance from a frequency distribution (i.e. avoiding having to calculate $(X_i - X)^2$ for every observation):

$$\text{Variance } (X) = \frac{\sum f_i X_i^2}{N} - (\bar{X})^2$$

$$= \frac{2\ 193\ 200}{133} - (125)^2$$

$$= 16\ 490.23 - 15\ 625 = 865.23$$

$$S(X) = \sqrt{V(X)} = \sqrt{865.23} = £29.41$$

Don't worry if you don't really understand the formula. It has two things going for it: (1) it can quite easily be calculated on a calculator if necessary and (2) it works! In general, though, you will not have to plough through these calculations yourself, since the computer will do them in microseconds.

The form of distributions

Thus far we have examined two features of distributions, the central tendency or typical value of a distribution and the ways in which we can measure variation from the central tendency. There is a third feature of a distribution which must now be examined and that is its *form* or shape. We have already seen something about the form a distribution can take. For example, histograms and bar charts, precisely because they are graphic techniques, show something about the shape of a distribution. The histogram of age group data above showed a *unimodal distribution*, that is it has a peak for the age group 25–29. Similarly, when discussing whether the mean or median was the best measure of central tendency for an interval variable, we saw that, where there are some extreme scores, the median might be the best measure. Again this was a reference to the form of a distribution: we said it was skewed.

At this stage, however, it is necessary to be more precise. Just as there are different measures of central tendency and dispersion, so there are different forms of distribution. Equally there are summary measures for the form of distribution, just as we have seen there are summary measures of central tendency and dispersion. In fact there are three principal features of the form of a distribution in terms of, first, the number of *modes* it has; second, its *symmetry*; and finally, its *kurtosis*. We can examine each briefly in turn.

Number of modes

Figure 5.3 shows examples of unimodal, bimodal and multimodal distributions. As can be seen, these terms refer to the number of peaks there are in a distribution. Put in more familiar terms, this is a reference to whether one category of a variable clearly predominates in terms of frequencies (a unimodal distribution); or whether two categories have equal or nearly equal frequencies (a bimodal distribution); or whether there are three or more equal or nearly equal categories in terms of frequencies (a multimodal distribution).

Figure 5.3 Varieties of modal distributions

Symmetry

Figure 5.4 demonstrates three aspects of the symmetry of distributions. We can see that while the middle distribution is symmetrical, those on either side are skewed. A symmetrical distribution is one where the mean, median and mode all occur at the same point on the curve at its highest point. If we divide the distribution at that point we would have two identical halves which would be mirror images of each other.

Figure 5.4 The symmetry of distributions

A skewed distribution is one which has a trailing of frequencies in one direction towards extreme scores. If it skews to the right it is said to be positively skewed; if it skews to the left it is said to be negatively skewed. It is precisely when an interval variable is highly skewed (as is often the case with income) that we would prefer to use the median to the mean.

Kurtosis

Kurtosis is a feature of symmetrical distributions, as can be seen in Figure 5.5. It refers to whether the frequencies tend to pile up closely around the centre of the distribution, are more evenly distributed or widely distributed. Where there is piling up we speak of a *leptokurtic* distribution; where there is relatively even distribution, the term *mesokurtic* is used; and where the distribution is relatively flat, we refer to it as *platykurtic*.

However, we do not need to draw the shape of a distribution to find out about it. Just as we can summarize measures of central tendency and

Figure 5.5 Kurtosis

dispersion in terms of a summary index, so it is with the form of a distribution. Clearly one way in which we can interpret the form of a distribution has already been discussed implicitly. If we know that the mean and median of an interval variable are substantially different, we know, as in our income example on page 96, that the distribution is skewed. In this case we had a positively skewed distribution because the extreme score in income distribution B (£100 000) was high. Had the extreme score been low we would have had a negatively skewed distribution.

Nevertheless we do also have summary measures for the skewness and kurtosis of distributions. SPSS refers to these statistics simply as skewness and kurtosis. Where skewness is zero there is a symmetrical distribution, where negative it is negatively skewed, and where positive, positively skewed. The size of the skewness statistic indicates how skewed a distribution is. Kurtosis has a value of zero for a mesokurtic distribution, with negative values representing a flatter (platykurtic) distribution, and positive values a more pointed (leptokurtic) distribution.

The normal distribution

There is an extremely important form of symmetrical distribution in statistics which is known as the **normal distribution**. We shall encounter it again when we discuss statistical inference but it is also necessary to mention it briefly at this point. This is because it brings out the importance of the standard deviation and introduces us to *standardized* or *z-scores* which are widely used in inferential statistics.

The normal distribution, a hypothetical mathematical curve, is displayed in Figure 5.6. Like all symmetrical distributions, the mean, median

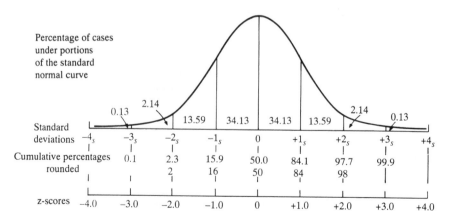

Figure 5.6 The normal distribution
Source: Loether and McTavish (1974).

and mode coincide. It is unimodal and mesokurtic. Without detailing the full statistical properties of the normal distribution, suffice it to say that as a mathematical curve it is a function of the mean and standard deviation. We can see from the shape of the normal distribution that there are few extremely low or high scores, with most scores tending towards the mean. Because it is an idealized model the curve never touches the horizontal axis but approaches it over an infinite distance.

Why is the normal distribution so important? At this stage we will only discuss its importance in relation to the calculation of standard deviations and z-scores. Notice in Figure 5.6 that the standard deviation at the mid-point or mean is 0. To the left we have between –1 and –4 standard deviations and to the right we have between +1 and +4 standard deviations. Similarly we have z-scores (bottom row) which range from –4 through 0 to +4. Consider now some of our earlier data on incomes. We discovered that the mean income for two groups of people was £10 000 in each case but that the standard deviation for Group A was £141 and for Group B £3535. We could equally well call £141 for Group A *one standard deviation from the mean;* or, for Group B, £3535 is *one standard deviation from the mean.* For the two groups, therefore, two standard deviations from the mean is equal to £141 × 2 = £282 and £3535 × 2 = £7070 respectively; and so on. In other words it is possible to convert from our original scale where we measured in pounds, to one where we measure in terms of standard deviations. As we shall see this can prove extremely useful because we can then make comparisons between individual scores on different variables. This is the significance of the word 'standard' in standard deviation – it enables us to derive a *standardized* scale for comparing variability.

In relation to the mathematical properties of the normal curve we can also see from Figure 5.6 that a certain proportion of all cases fall under the curve within one standard deviation in either direction from the mean (34.13 × 2, or approximately 68 per cent); and that approximately 95 per cent of cases fall within two standard deviations from the mean (68 per cent + (13.59 × 2)). If our data are normally distributed, therefore, about 95 per cent of cases lie within two standard deviations from the mean and about 68 per cent lie within one standard deviation. But how can we use all this information? Again the answer lies in the ability to standardize between variables.

Suppose you obtained a mark of 56 per cent in an examination where the marks overall formed a normal distribution. You want to know how your mark compares with that of others. If you were told that the mean mark was 52 per cent, you would know that you had done better than average – but how much better relative to others? If, however, you were told that the standard deviation was 4 and then looked at Figure 5.6, your mark of 56 per cent represents one standard deviation above the mean and that would put you 84 per cent up the distribution, i.e. in the top fifth of your group (see cumulative percentages under the curve); 84 per cent of your fellow students scored less than you, and 16 per cent more. However, suppose in another subject you had obtained a mark of 60 per cent. Does that mean you are doing better relative to others in this subject than in the one where you only obtained 56 per cent? On a straight comparison of marks it might seem so, but we are not comparing like with like. How can we equate a mark of 56 per cent in, say, Quantitative Data Analysis with 60 per cent in, say, Sociological Theory when the two distributions of marks overall might be rather different? This is where standardized or z-scores are useful.

We have, in fact, already calculated the z-score for Quantitative Data Analysis since

$$z = \frac{X_i - \bar{X}}{S}$$

i.e for Quantitative Data Analysis

$$z = \frac{56 - 52}{4} = \frac{4}{4} = 1.0$$

i.e. our mark of 56 per cent was 1 standard deviation above the mean. Suppose that for Sociological Theory the mean mark was 60 per cent and the standard deviation was 8. Then

$$z = \frac{60 - 60}{8} = \frac{0}{8} = 0.0$$

In other words, your mark is the mean for the distribution of scores in Sociological Theory. Therefore, you have a lower z-score in Sociological Theory than in Quantitative Data Analysis, even though you have a higher absolute mark (60 per cent compared to 56 per cent). Even though the Sociological Theory mark is higher, the standard score in Quantitative Data Analysis is relatively speaking better when compared to other people. In Quantitative Data Analysis you would be in the top fifth but in Sociological Theory only half-way up the distribution of all marks. This is because your mark falls 84 per cent up the cumulative percentage distribution under the curve for Quantitative Data Analysis, but only at the mean value (i.e. 50 per cent up the curve) for Sociological Theory.

Remember that all of this only applies to normally shaped distributions because of their particular mathematical properties. Because our income data, for example, are not normally distributed but positively skewed for Group B, it would not make sense to calculate z-scores. We will return to the importance and use of z-scores and other properties of the normal distribution in Part IV.

Conclusion

In this discussion of univariate descriptive statistics we have seen a number of ways in which we can present and describe the data for a single variable. Different techniques apply to data according to the level at which we are measuring (see Table 5.15). As always, the most powerful techniques apply to data which are measured at the interval level. We have also discussed three aspects of distributions – central tendency, dispersion and form. In cases where we have interval variables we would present data via frequency or percentage distributions and histograms. We would use the mean as a measure of central tendency provided that we had a reasonably symmetrical distribution. If the distribution was highly skewed we might prefer the median. We would measure symmetry using skewness. We would measure dispersion with variance or, more usefully, standard deviation. With ordinal variables we use frequency or percentage distributions and cumulative distributions. The median is the most useful and appropriate measure of central tendency and we could use bar charts for graphic display. Finally, nominal variables can be presented via frequency or percentage distributions and bar charts. The mode is the only measure of central tendency. In terms of form we would be interested in the number of modes.

Table 5.15 Summary of commonly used univariate descriptive statistics

Level of measurement	Interval	Ordinal	Nominal
Measure of form	Kurtosis	Skewness	Modality
Measure of central tendency	Mean or median	Median	Mode
Measure of dispersion	Variance and standard deviation	Quartile deviation*	Index of dispersion*
Graphic presentation	Histogram	Bar chart	Bar chart
Tabular presentation	Frequency, % and cumulative distributions	Frequency, % and cumulative distributions	Frequency and % distributions

* These measures are rarely referred to. Those wishing to pursue these statistics further are referred to Loether and McTavish (1974).

We are now in a position to use SPSS to produce some of these descriptive statistics using the SPSS data file which we created in Chapter 4.

Note

1 In this text we refer to all forms of data analysis as being concerned with the 'analysis of variance'. In this instance we are discussing one particular measure which happens to be called 'variance'.

Key concepts

Make sure you have understood the following key concepts:

- frequency distributions
- descriptive statistics
- bar charts/histograms
- central tendency
- measures of dispersion
- normal distribution

Multiple choice questions

1 Is the distribution of the interval-level variable below

  (i)   positively skewed?

  (ii) negatively skewed?

  (iii) mesokurtic?

2 What level of measurement of variable are the following measures of central tendency appropriate for?:

  (i)   median

  (ii) mode

  (iii) mean

3 The standard deviation measures:

(i)   the range of a variable;

(ii) the central tendency of a variable;

(iii) the dispersion of scores around a variable mean.

4 From the diagram of the normal distribution below:

(i)   What percentage of cases are to be found between +1 and −1 standard deviation?

(ii) If your z-score for this test is 2, how well have you done relative to others in the class?

(iii) What information do you need to calculate a z-score?

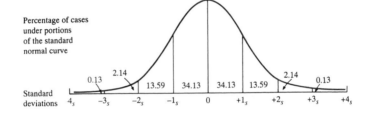

Percentage of cases under portions of the standard normal curve

Standard deviations

6 Univariate descriptive statistics using SPSS

Aims

- To introduce the principles of analysis using SPSS.
- To describe the logical sequence of SPSS commands.
- To understand how to produce univariate descriptive statistics using SPSS.

We already have a data file (called DEMO.SYS in SPSS/PC+, and DEMO.SAV in SPSS FOR WINDOWS) containing some data and its definitions. This chapter describes how to start analysing it in SPSS, putting together the information contained in Chapters 4 and 5 concerning data entry and data analysis on a computer. It is assumed that you will already be familiar with the content of both chapters. The analyses performed here are all univariate in character; in other words they all involve the description of single variables. This stage of analysis is vital in helping the analyst to get a feel for the variables being used, and should never be foregone even when we get around to thinking about more complex and interesting analyses in subsequent chapters.

First let us recap a little of what was said in Chapter 4 concerning the structure of commands in SPSS before moving on to describe how you actually perform (run) an analysis to produce univariate descriptive statistics. Analysis in SPSS works via commands known as *procedure commands* because they specify which of the SPSS analytic procedures (e.g. **FREQUENCIES**, PLOT, CROSSTABS) are to be performed on the data. Every actual analysis of your data therefore starts with a procedure command, and is further specified by sub-commands, e.g.

FREQUENCIES   VARIABLES VOTE CLASS.

Once run, this command would activate the SPSS frequencies procedure and produce frequency distributions for the variables VOTE and CLASS. There are many other sub-commands associated with particular procedures. For example, with the CROSSTABS /CELL sub-command you can choose whether you wish percentages to be calculated down the columns, across the rows or both. Similarly, there is a /STATISTICS sub-command associated with various procedures which allows you to choose between a number of available statistics which might help you describe your data, or make statistical inferences from it. For further information on the structure of specific SPSS commands and associated sub-commands refer either to the on-screen help system (see Chapter 4), the quick syntax reference guide on p. 64–5 or to the *SPSS Base System Syntax Reference Guide*, Release 6.1 (Nornsis SPSS Inc., 1994).

Selection of commands

* To select commands for doing an analysis in SPSS/PC+

There are, in fact, two ways of entering commands on to the scratch pad in SPSS/PC+, of which we have so far only shown you the first:

1 The appropriate command is pasted into the scratch pad from the on-screen menus and executed by pressing [F10] [↵].
2 Alternatively, you can type out the commands directly on to the scratch pad using 'edit mode' ([Alt] [E]) and then execute them in the same way by pressing [F10] [↵]. (If you choose to work this way, remember to type the full stop at the end of each command line!)

From the Main Menu all the procedure (i.e. analysis) commands are found by selecting the 'Analyze Data' menu. The procedure commands used in this chapter (FREQUENCIES, DESCRIPTIVES) are found in the 'Descriptive statistics' item of this menu. When you select a procedure command in this way, the command is pasted on to the screen and the appropriate command menu appears listing all the available sub-commands for that procedure. Remember to look at the examples that are given in the right-hand box next to the command menu. These show you exactly how the commands and sub-commands should be constructed for that procedure. You can then start to construct them yourself by selecting and pasting the sub-commands that you need.

To select commands for doing an analysis in SPSS FOR WINDOWS

There are, in fact, two ways of selecting commands in SPSS FOR WINDOWS, of which we have so far shown you only the first:

1 To use the dialog boxes for analysing data you click the 'Statistics' item on the Menu Bar. To find the procedures used in this chapter select the 'Summarize' item on this menu. Then select 'Frequencies', and when the Frequencies dialog box appears you select (by highlighting) the variables you want frequencies for from the list of variables in the data file (which appears automatically). You then specify the sub-commands that you want by clicking the appropriate button on the dialog box and entering the desired specifications in the relevant spaces of the new sub-command dialog boxes which will appear. When you have finished, you click the 'Continue' button to return to the main dialog box, and then 'OK' to run the analysis. (You will not be able to access the FRE-QUENCIES command in SPSS FOR WINDOWS without first opening a data file – see below.)

2 You can also type the commands you want directly into the !Syntax window. (If you choose to work this way, remember to add the full stop at the end of each command line!) To run the commands that you have typed into the !Syntax window, first select (i.e. highlight) all those you want to run and then click the 'Run' button on the tool-bar at the top of the screen (indicated by a forward-pointing arrow). The advantage of typing the commands out directly like this is that you can save the contents of the Syntax window as a file for future use (see Chapter 4). In order to achieve the same thing using the dialog boxes you first have to paste the commands you have used into the Syntax window by clicking the 'Paste' button on the dialog box.

Analysing the demo data

SPSS has two procedures for summarizing the distribution of single variables – FREQUENCIES and **DESCRIPTIVES**. DESCRIPTIVES provides a range of summary statistics of central tendency and variation for interval-level variables. FREQUENCIES produces frequency, percentage and cumulative percentage distributions and should be used for nominal and ordinal-level variables. With FREQUENCIES we can also produce a bar chart and all the summary measures which DESCRIPTIVES provides. Each procedure has sub-commands associated with it which specify the details of the analysis.

We are now in a position to ask SPSS to produce frequencies for the variables on the demo data file (DEMO.SYS or DEMO.SAV). The logical steps that we need to follow are:

1 Entering SPSS
2 Accessing the appropriate data file
3 Locating and running the FREQUENCIES command:

FREQUENCIES   VARIABLES ALL.

Table 6.1 Frequency distributions for DEMO variables: computer output

AGE

Value Label	Value	Frequency	Percent	Valid Percent	Cum percent
	18	1	5.0	5.0	5.0
	19	1	5.0	5.0	10.0
	22	2	10.0	10.0	20.0
	23	1	5.0	5.0	25.0
	24	2	10.0	10.0	35.0
	27	1	5.0	5.0	40.0
	33	1	5.0	5.0	45.0
	38	1	5.0	5.0	50.0
	41	1	5.0	5.0	55.0
	42	1	5.0	5.0	60.0
	44	2	10.0	10.0	70.0
	47	1	5.0	5.0	75.0
	56	2	10.0	10.0	85.0
	58	1	5.0	5.0	90.0
	61	1	5.0	5.0	95.0
	64	1	5.0	5.0	100.0
	Total	20	100.0	100.0	

Valid cases   20   Missing cases   0

SEX

Value Label	Value	Frequency	Percent	Valid Percent	Cum Percent
Female	1	10	50.0	50.0	50.0
Male	2	10	50.0	50.0	100.0
	Total	20	100.0	100.0	

Valid cases   20   Missing cases   0

VOTE   vote at last election

Value Label	Value	Frequency	Percent	Valid Percent	Cum Percent
Conservative	1	8	40.0	40.0	40.0
Labour	2	6	30.0	30.0	70.0
Other	3	6	30.0	30.0	100.0

The section above has already shown you how do to this in both SPSS/PC+ and SPSS FOR WINDOWS. However, the most important thing at this point is that you grasp the basic stages that need to be followed, which remain the same whichever analytic procedure you are using. These stages are explained in greater detail below, *so try to read through the text first before beginning your analysis.*

If we were to successfully follow the above steps using the appropriate commands and sub-commands we would produce the frequency distributions shown in Table 6.1 for the variables in the demo data file (we have displayed the output much as it would appear on your printed copy of the output file – this should give you practice at interpreting it!).

For the variables SEX and VOTE we get useful summaries of the numbers in each category, the percentage in each category, and the cumulated percentage frequencies as described in Chapter 5. However, in the case of AGE (an interval-level variable) we can see very little in the way of a pattern because most of the individual ages contain only one case. Since our purpose in data analysis is to summarize and search for patterns, this procedure for AGE is of little use to us. First, therefore, we must group the interval-level raw data into categories.

We do this by use of a *data modification command* called **RECODE** which creates new categories for variables. These commands allow you to transform or modify your data. For example, you might decide to take a variable with four categories and reduce the categories to two. You would do this with the RECODE command. Or you can RECODE a continuous variable such as age or income into a categoric variable, as in this case.

One way we could do this for AGE would be to split the variable above and below some age which we think might provide some variance in the dependent variable VOTE. This decision therefore must be taken at least partly at the theoretical level. For instance, we might hypothesize that age 40 represented an age above which people might be more conservative in their approach to life, and thus more likely to vote Conservative. However, we also have to consider practical issues, since there must be adequate numbers for analysis in each category that we create. This consideration may require a compromise between the theoretical and the practical, and is another instance of the way in which we must constantly be moving mentally between theory and methodology.

We could, therefore, locate the RECODE command and enter:

RECODE AGE (LO THRU 39 = 1) (40 THRU HI = 2).
VALUE LABELS AGE 1 '<40' 2 '40+'.

* SPSS/PC+

In SPSS/PC+, the RECODE command is found from the 'Modify data or files' Menu on the Main Menu. VALUE LABELS is found from the 'Read or write data' Menu under 'Labels and formatting'. Alternatively, type the commands directly into the scratch pad using edit mode ([Alt][E]), which is probably quicker.

 # SPSS FOR WINDOWS

In SPSS FOR WINDOWS you can use the menus and dialog boxes, but it is probably quicker and simpler to type data modification commands directly into the !Syntax window in order to run them. If you want to explore the menus, click the 'Transform' item on the Menu Bar and select 'Recode'. Select the 'Into Same Variable' option and a dialog box will appear which enables you to recode your variable. You need to specify the name of the variable you want to recode and then the old and new (i.e. recoded) values of the variable.

The recode shown above would produce a dichotomous variable with 10 cases in each category. We might, however, prefer to produce a poly-tomous variable which takes into account possible differences between those in their thirties and those younger than that. We could, then, specify:

RECODE AGE (LO THRU 29 = 1) (30 THRU 39 = 2)
    (40 THRU HI = 3).
VALUE LABELS AGE 1 '<30' 2 '30–39' 3 '40+'.

It is very important that, whenever you recode a variable, you then produce another FREQUENCIES table showing the new variable to reassure you that you have recoded it correctly. This is one of the most common sources of error in data analysis, so check each recode thoroughly before attempting to analyse the new variable further. If you want to retain your unrecoded variables as well as the recoded versions for future analysis you can do this by recoding your original variable into a different variable with a new name (see below). In this way both the old (original) variable and the new (recoded) variable will be available in your data file. It is a good idea to do this, since recoding always results in a certain loss of information about the original data.

Recoding into a different variable

* **SPSS/PC+**

To recode into a different variable in SPSS/PC+, you use a **COMPUTE** command first to create a new variable with the same values as the old variable, and then you recode the new variable, as in the example shown below. COMPUTE is found in the 'Modify data or files' Menu.

* **SPSS FOR WINDOWS**

To recode into a different variable in SPSS FOR WINDOWS, you can recode directly from one variable into a new one using the same RECODE command by adding INTO <newvar> at the end of the command (see example below). Alternatively, you can use the dialog boxes to achieve the same thing – see the section on using the SPSS FOR WINDOWS dialog boxes below.

A full set of commands, then, for producing univariate statistics from these data might look like this:

1 GET FILE 'a: DEMO.SYS.'   (*or* DEMO.SAV.)
2 DESCRIPTIVES VARIABLES AGE/STATISTICS ALL.
3 COMPUTE XAGE = AGE.
  RECODE AGE (LO THRU 39 = 1)(40 THRU HI = 2). } (SPSS/PC+)
  or
  RECODE AGE (LO THRU 39 = 1) (40 THRU HI = 2)] (SPSS FOR
    INTO XAGE.   } WINDOWS)
4 VALUE LABELS XAGE 1 '<40' 2 '40+'.
5 FREQUENCIES VARIABLES XAGE SEX VOTE/
    HBAR/STATISTICS ALL.
6 SAVE OUTFILE 'a: DEMO1.SYS.'   (*or* DEMO1.SAV.)

The **GET** command specifies the data file to be analysed. Next the DESCRIPTIVES command requests an analysis of the interval-level variable AGE with all statistics. The RECODE of AGE into the new ordinal-level variable XAGE is performed next, followed by VALUE LABELS to assign labels to the newly created XAGE variable categories. FREQUENCIES is then used to produce frequency distributions and bar charts for all the categoric variables. Note that the sub-command /STATISTICS ALL is included. This is a mistake (but a deliberate one!), the significance of which will be shown below. Finally, the new data file containing all the original variables (including the unrecoded interval-level variable AGE and the new categoric variable XAGE) is **SAVEd** for future analysis on disk a:.

Using the dialog boxes in SPSS FOR WINDOWS

The commands listed above are those that you would type in to the !Syntax window. If you choose instead to use the menus and dialog boxes then you should follow the steps below:

1 Open the data file DEMO.SAV using the drop-down File menu.
2 Select the DESCRIPTIVES procedure from the 'Summarize' item on the drop-down Statistics menu, and complete the dialog boxes by selecting variable 'age' and then all statistics (mark each with an X by clicking) from the associated 'Options' sub-command dialog box.
3 The RECODE command is found from the drop-down Transform menu. You need to select the 'Into Different Variables' option and fill in the old ('input') and new ('output') variable names and the old and new values as appropriate from the respective dialog boxes, referring to the commands shown above. (It is recommended that you type data modification commands such as these directly into the !Syntax window; it turns out to be much quicker!)

4 Select FREQUENCIES from the 'Summarize' item on the drop-down Statistics menu, select (highlight) the variables to be analysed, and complete the sub-command dialog boxes appropriately.
5 Finally, save the new data file using the drop-down File menu.

The output resulting from these analyses is shown below (Table 6.2). First we have the information produced by DESCRIPTIVES for the variable AGE. We can see the statistics which SPSS produces via the DESCRIP-TIVES procedure. Most of these statistics are now familiar. However, we have not previously mentioned range (the minimum value subtracted from the maximum value of a variable – hence minimum and maximum values also), S.E. Mean or standard error of the mean (which we will encounter when we discuss inference), and sum which is another name for sigma (Σ). The mean age for this sample is 38, the standard deviation is 15.33, kurtosis is –1.36 and skewness is 0.248. The skewness value indicates a very slight skew to the right and the kurtosis value indicates a platykurtic distribution, although with a sample of only 20, not too much should be made of this! The output then gives frequency, percentage and cumulative percentage distributions, plus bar charts for the recoded variables, resulting from the FREQUENCIES command. Note that the bar charts are followed by some slightly odd statistics. Here we have the deliberate mistake. When we ask for statistics for categoric variables we must remember that SPSS will calculate its statistics using the *category codes* rather than the actual data! Here, for example, the mean, median and standard deviation for XAGE have been calculated on the basis of the values of the new category codes, not the unrecoded data. They are, therefore, meaningless as they stand beyond telling us that, say, the mean lies somewhere within the range of code 1, i.e. ages 1 to 39! Asking for ALL statistics is therefore pointless for a categoric variable.

Univariate analysis is an important first step in the process of data analysis and much can be gleaned from it. However, the real excitement of data analysis begins when we start to relate one variable to another. The first stage of this involves examining how bivariate tables are constructed and it is to this that we turn in Chapter 7. First, however, we recap some of the essential points about analysing data using SPSS.

The order of commands in SPSS

Obviously it is necessary to enter your SPSS commands in a logical order. For instance, before you can begin analysis you must either already have an SPSS data file available on disk for analysis, or you must create one first, as you were shown with DEMO.DAT in Chapter 4. You need to access an SPSS data file for analysis in SPSS *whenever* you want either to modify data or to analyse them, or both. Then, if you are going to modify

Table 6.2 Univariate statistics for DEMO variables: computer output

Variable AGE

Mean	38.150	S.E. Mean	3.428
Std Dev	15.332	Variance	235.082
Kurtosis	−1.355	S.E. Kurt	.992
Skewness	.248	S.E. Skew	.512
Range	46.000	Minimum	18
Maximum	64	Sum	763.000

Valid Observations –   20   Missing Observations –   0

XAGE

Value Label	Value	Frequency	Percent	Valid Percent	Cum Percent
<40	1.00	10	50.0	50.0	50.0
40+	2.00	10	50.0	50.0	100.0
	Total	20	100.0	100.0	

```
   1.   <40    ...........................................................................
   2.   40+    ...........................................................................
              U ----------- U ------------ U ------------- U ----------- U ----------
              0            2             4              6      8          10
```

Mean	1.500	Std err	.115	Median	1.500
Mode	1.000	Std dev	.513	Variance	.263
Kurtosis	−2.235	S E Kurt	.992	Skewness	.000
S E Skew	.512	Range	1.000	Minimum	1.000
Maximum	2.000	Sum	30.000		

* Multiple modes exist. The smallest value is shown.

Valid cases   20   Missing cases   0

SEX

Value Label	Value	Frequency	Percent	Valid Percent	Cum Percent
Female	1	10	50.0	50.0	50.0
Male	2	10	50.0	50.0	100.0
	Total	20	100.0	100.0	

```
   10    1    ...........................................................................
   10    2    ...........................................................................
              U ----------- U ------------ U ------------- U ----------- U ----------
              0            2             4              6      8          10
```

Mean	1.500	Std err	.115	Median	1.500
Mode	1.000	Std dev	.513	Variance	.263
Kurtosis	−2.235	S E Kurt	.992	Skewness	.000
S E Skew	.512	Range	1.000	Minimum	1.000
Maximum	2.000	Sum	30.000		

* Multiple modes exist. The smallest value is shown.

Valid cases   20   Missing cases   0

Table 6.2 Continued

VOTE   vote at last election

Value Label	Value	Frequency	Percent	Valid Percent	Cum Percent
Conservative	1	8	40.0	40.0	40.0
Labour	2	6	30.0	30.0	70.0
Other	3	6	30.0	30.0	100.0
	Total	20	100.0	100.0	

```
   8    1    .................................................................
   6    2    .........................................................
   6    3    ...................................................
            U ----------- U ------------ U ------------- U ----------- U ----------
            0           2            4             6           8           10
```

Mean	1.900	Std err	.191	Median	2.000
Mode	1.000	Std dev	.852	Variance	.726
Kurtosis	−1.617	S E Kurt	.992	Skewness	.204
S E Skew	.512	Range	2.000	Minimum	1.000
Maximum	3.000	Sum	38.000		

the data before analysing them, the data modification commands (e.g. RECODE) should be selected and run before selecting and running the procedure commands which produce the analyses (e.g. FREQUEN-CIES, CROSSTABS).

As a simple example of the ordering of commands, let's say we have an SPSS data file like DEMO.SYS or DEMO.SAV already created and available on disk. To modify a variable on this file and produce an analysis we might use these commands:

1 GET
2 RECODE
3 CROSSTABS
4 SAVE

(CROSSTABS is the command you will be using to produce cross-tabulations of two or more variables. For the moment, though, we are simply using it as an example of an SPSS analysis.) Each command is selected and then run in SPSS. *Note that only the commands are shown here* – the subcommands you use will depend respectively on:

1 The name and location of the SPSS data file to be accessed.
2 The name of the variable to be recoded and the detail of the recode.
3 The names of the variables to be cross-tabulated.
4 The name and location of the new data file to be saved (if required) containing the new recode.

Here is a hypothetical example:

```
GET FILE 'a:SOCIAL.SAV.'
RECODE INCOME (5200 THRU 9999 = 1) (10000 THRU HI =
    2).
VALUE LABELS INCOME 1 '<10000' 2 '10000+'.
CROSSTABS TABLES = INCOME BY SEX /CELLS = COUNT
    ROW COLUMN.
SAVE OUTFILE 'a:SOC1.SAV.'
```

Here the data file selected for analysis is an SPSS FOR WINDOWS system file SOCIAL.SAV on disk a:. The continuous variable INCOME is recoded into two groups; those with incomes between £5200 and £9999 per year, and those with incomes of £10 000 and above. The VALUE LABELS command comes after the RECODE command in order to identify the two groups produced by the recode on INCOME. (These labels subsequently appear by the relevant categories of the new recoded INCOME variable on any output.)

An analysis is then performed using CROSSTABS to produce a 2 × 2 table of income by sex. The /CELLS sub-command is used to specify inclusion of both row and column percentages. The recoded income variable is then saved (together with the other information in the original data file) in a new SPSS FOR WINDOWS data file called SOC1.SAV, again on disk a:. The output file containing the analysis appears both on your screen as you do the analysis and in an 'output file' called SPSS.LIS in SPSS/PC+, and in the '!Output' window in SPSS FOR WINDOWS. You can print the output file from DOS or directly from SPSS FOR WINDOWS. Refer back to the section on 'dealing with output' in Chapter 4 if you can't remember how to do this.

We have included a simple exercise below which will give you practice at accomplishing much of what has been discussed in this chapter.

Key concepts

Make sure you have understood the following key concepts:

- SPSS accessing and saving of data files:

  GET

  SAVE

- SPSS analysis procedures:

  FREQUENCIES

  DESCRIPTIVES

- SPSS data modification commands:

  RECODE

  COMPUTE

Exercise 1: Creation and analysis of a data file

For this exercise you must first invent your own data. Alternatively, if you have access to some real data of a sufficiently manageable size, you could take the opportunity here to do some analysis on it. The exercise consists in entering the data into an SPSS data file, exactly as you did with DEMO.DAT in Chapter 4, then using SPSS to produce univariate descriptive statistics for your variables. You should find all the information you need to do this in what has been covered so far in the text. As in all research, one of the most important things is to know where to go to look something up!

The file

Create an SPSS data file which contains:

- Twenty cases (or more if you have your own data).
- At least three variables, one dependent and two independent. So when you construct this file you will need to think in terms of two variables (a dependent and an independent) which could plausibly be related, and a third which might alter or explain that relationship in more detail. If you are unsure about this, go back to Chapter 2 on the logic of data analysis before you attempt the exercise.

Think in advance about this file: what your hypothesis is, what the variables are, how you think they might be measured, what problems of measurement might be involved with them, etc., since this will constitute the introduction to your write-up.

The analysis

Using SPSS produce:

• Frequency distributions and/or descriptive statistics for your variables
• Barcharts where appropriate
• Appropriate measures of central tendency and dispersion

In order to do this, you may require a RECODE command, and should then include VALUE LABELS.

Finally, print out a copy of your output file, and comment briefly in your report on the relevant statistics.

Completing the exercise

You should therefore end up with:

• A statement of your hypothesis, detailing the expected relationship between the variables.
• A introductory note of explanation about the file: what the variables are, how you think they might be measured, what problems of measurement might be involved with them, etc.
• The output file from your analysis, and a discussion of results.

This represents a simplified version of what you would be expected to produce if you were undertaking a piece of data analysis as a research project.

7 Bivariate analysis for categoric variables: measures of association

---

Aims

- To set up and correctly interpret cross-tabulated data.
- To discuss the different *aspects* of association between cross-tabulated variables, i.e. existence, strength, direction and nature.
- To discuss the principles behind standardized measures of association.
- To understand simple measures of association for different levels of measurement of variables.

Having looked at the description and analysis of single variables (a crucial first step in any piece of quantitative research), we now move on to the really interesting task of looking at the way in which variables interact. It is here that we begin the process of *explaining* the variance that we have described in single variables.

The idea of **bivariate analysis** will already be familiar from earlier discussions (see Chapter 2). When we investigate whether variable X is related to variable Y, we are asking about the nature of a bivariate relationship. The usual way to examine such a relationship is in the context of a table which includes both variables. Generally such a table is called a **cross-tabulation** or sometimes a *contingency table*. A bivariate cross-tabulation or contingency table is simply a table of joint frequencies for two variables classified into categories. In this chapter we are going to examine this type of bivariate analysis. Chapter 8 introduces techniques of bivariate analysis for interval-level data. In a similar format to the previous discussion of univariate analysis, we shall look first at how to create contingency tables, and then develop ideas about how we can examine the existence, nature and strength of relationships between variables. Just as it is possible to summarize aspects of a univariate frequency distribution in terms of certain statistical measures, so it is with bivariate relationships, and we describe and discuss some of these measures later on in the chapter.

Creating and examining tables

In the British Class Survey, one of the things which was investigated was the extent to which people's perception of their class location was related to their actual location according to several different class classifications. The sample were asked:

'Suppose you had to say which class you belonged to, which would you say?'

Responses were categorized for these purposes into middle class and working class (hardly anyone admits to being upper class!). Actual class location was derived by the researchers according to a range of criteria depending on the class classification used, and including such variables as occupation, previous occupation, status within the workplace, whether a person was a supervisor or not, autonomy over work tasks, etc.

The following tables show the overall distribution of class identification from the sample, cross-classified by the Registrar General's Social Class classification (which, as we noted earlier, is the official British government definition). For simplicity of presentation we have divided this classification into two groups of classes, manual and non-manual (as is frequently done in government publications). Table 7.1 shows the univariate distribution of class identification for everyone in the British Class Survey who was assigned a class location according to the Registrar General's classification (again you will recall that, as with all occupationally based class classifications, a relatively large proportion of a random sample cannot be assigned, because they are out of work, retired, disabled, students, housepersons, etc.).

Obviously Table 7.1 does not allow us to say anything about the relationship between class identification and class location, because it is

Table 7.1 Class identification of the sample

	f_i	%
Middle class	526	43.7
Working class	677	56.3
Total	1203	100.0

Table 7.2 Class identification for the non-manual group

Class	f_i	%
Middle class	372	60.9
Working class	239	39.1
Total	611	100.0

Table 7.3 Class identification for the manual group

Class	f_i	%
Middle class	154	26.0
Working class	438	74.0
Total	592	100.0

a univariate distribution of the dependent variable only. The independent variable does not appear in the table. What we are interested in, however, is to what extent people's class identification is associated with their actual class location. The first step in examining this relationship is to compare the separate distribution of class identification for each group of classes from the Registrar General's classification, as in Tables 7.2 and 7.3. From these tables it is evident that while most of the non-manual group identify as middle class, and most of the manual group identify as working class, there are still substantial proportions who identify in a way that we might not have expected. However, it would be much easier to see the relationship (and much more efficient in terms of paper!) if we had all the information from Tables 7.1, 7.2 and 7.3 in one combined table relating the dependent and independent variables. This is precisely what a cross-tabulation or contingency table does, as in Table 7.4.

Table 7.4 combines the previous three tables. The first two columns of the table are from Table 7.2; the next two columns are from Table 7.3; and the final two columns are from Table 7.1. Here we have a two-variable table made up of three sub-tables placed side by side. Of course, the number of such sub-tables which make up any bivariate table depends upon the number of categories of the independent variable. In our example, class location has two categories plus an overall total, making three sub-tables in all, which can be put together into a single bivariate cross-tabulation.

In Table 7.4 we can see the overall distribution of class identification in the final two columns of the table. In the other columns we see that distribution broken down between the categories of the independent

Table 7.4 Class identification by social class location (Registrar General's definition)

Class identification	Class location					
	Non-manual		Manual		Total	
	f_i	%	f_i	%	f_i	%
Middle class	372	60.9	154	26.0	526	43.7
Working class	239	39.1	438	74.0	677	56.3
Total	611	100.0	592	100.0	1203	100.0

variable, class location. We can see how the distribution of the dependent variable changes, according to the category of the independent variable. A table in this format can be produced in SPSS by specifying the CROSSTABS procedure, with TABLES = dep var BY indep var and /CELLS = COLUMN to display column percentages (see syntax of SPSS commands on pp. 64–75). To be sure you understand it, you should try and write a brief description of the relationship between the dependent and independent variables revealed by Table 7.4.

As we proceed with this analysis we would want, of course, to explore in more detail the nature of the relationship between class identification and class location. That is, we would wish to elaborate and specify the relationship in the manner already discussed in Part I. While the data we have in Table 7.4 show a relationship between the two variables such that class identification varies by class location, we can nevertheless imagine that other variables might affect the degree and strength of the relationship. For the moment, however, we will concentrate on bivariate relationships in order to demonstrate the basic principles of contingency table analysis. We do this with reference to tables which contain two variables, each with two categories (two *dichotomous* variables), one variable being the independent and the other the dependent variable, as in our example. First, how do we set up and examine such tables?

Note: In what follows you will see one way of creating and examining tables which many researchers find useful. It is that recommended by Davis (1971: 35) and Loether and McTavish (1974: 175). However, not all researchers follow the same rules. You should never assume anything about the way published data are presented and that includes the 'rules' which are set out here. There is no substitute for the close scrutiny of tables produced by other people!

Table 7.5 is an abstraction of Table 7.4. To refer to terms which are by now familiar, the table includes two variables X and Y. The categories of

Table 7.5 Nomenclature for a 2×2 Table

| | Variable X | | |
Variable Y	c_1	c_2	Total
r_1	Frequency A	Frequency B	Marginal frequency r_1
r_2	Frequency C	Frequency D	Marginal frequency r_2
	Marginal frequency c_1	Marginal frequency c_2	N (Total of all cases in table)

variable X are labelled c_1 and c_2 for column 1 and column 2, and those of variable Y are labelled r_1 and r_2, for row 1 and row 2.

Conventionally, variable X (the independent variable) lies in what is known as the *heading* of the table and variable Y (the dependent variable) in the *stub*. The table is referred to as a 2×2 or fourfold table because the two categories of each variable give two rows by two columns yielding in total four *cells* (labelled Frequency A, Frequency B, Frequency C and Frequency D) at which rows and columns intersect. Taken together the four cells are referred to as the *body* of the table. Of course tables can have any number of rows (r) and columns (c) depending on the number of categories per variable. In general terms, therefore, we refer to $r \times c$ tables where the number of cells is equal to the number of rows multiplied by the number of columns. For example, Table 7.4 has four cells (a 2×2 table), each containing a frequency and a percentage.

When we add together the frequencies in each cell in a particular row or column we obtain the total **marginal frequency** for that category of the variable concerned. For example, in row 1 of Table 7.4 there are 372 non-manual and 154 manual respondents who identify as middle class. This yields a total marginal frequency of 526 individuals in this category of the variable 'class identification'. In Table 7.5 the equivalent is labelled 'Marginal frequency' r_1 because it is the frequency in the *margin* of the table for category 1 of variable Y. All such frequencies of the categories of variables are labelled as marginals because they appear in the margins of the tables. The marginals of a table actually constitute the *univariate distributions*. You can confirm this by a comparison of Table 7.1 and Table 7.4. The univariate distribution of class identification shown in Table 7.1 corresponds to the row marginal frequencies for Table 7.4.

There is one part of Table 7.5 which has not been mentioned so far and that is the bottom right-hand corner labelled N. This gives us the total number of all cases in the table. Hence we have the following:

Frequency A + Frequency B = Marginal frequency r_1;
Frequency C + Frequency D = Marginal frequency r_2;
Marginal frequency r_1 + Marginal frequency r_2 = N

and, therefore, A + B + C + D = N. Also:

Frequency A + Frequency C = Marginal frequency c_1;
Frequency B + Frequency D = Marginal frequency c_2;
Marginal frequency c_1 + Marginal frequency c_2 = N

and, therefore, A + C + B + D = N.

These conditions must hold for any 2×2 table (and so, of course, must equivalent statements for any $r \times c$ table).

Finally, we should note some conventions associated with table layout. First, a table should always have a title which lists the dependent and independent variable and gives sufficient information for someone to read the table without having to consult the author's explanation in the text. In the same way both heading and stub should be clearly labelled with variable and category names. Second, it is conventional to place the independent variable in the heading of a table and the dependent variable in the stub (hence the placement of variables X and Y in Table 7.5). Last, there are two rules where percentages are used in tables. One is that we should always indicate the marginal frequency on which percentages are based even if we do not give individual frequencies in the cells. The other is that percentages should always be computed in the direction of the independent variable. Hence each category of the independent variable should sum to 100 per cent. Thus, in percentage form, and including full labelling, Table 7.4 would appear as Table 7.6.

In Table 7.6 the percentages sum to 100 per cent in the columns because it follows the convention of placing the independent variable in the heading. However, it is important to realize that this convention is not always followed. Never assume that a table has been constructed in the way described here: always look and see. The computation of percentages in the direction of the independent variable is, however, more than

Table 7.6 Class identification by social class location (Registrar General's definition), British Class Survey, 1984

Class identification	Class location		
	Non-manual (N = 611) %	Manual (N = 592) %	Total (N = 1203) %
Middle class	60.9	26.0	43.7 (N = 526)
Working class	39.1	74.0	56.3 (N = 677)
Total	100.0	100.0	100.0

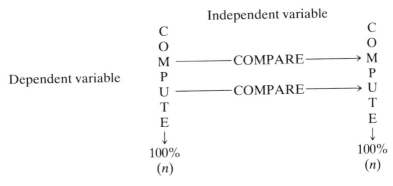

Figure 7.1 Model for analysing percentaged tables

just a convention. It is vital to correct analysis. We can see this by examining Table 7.6. Assume we have a hypothesis which states that respondents whose actual class location is manual are more likely to define themselves as middle class than those whose class location is non-manual are to define themselves as working class. We need to show the distribution of class identification *within* the different class location groups in order to test this hypothesis. This can only be achieved by standardizing (through percentaging) for the different numbers in the manual and non-manual groups. In other words, we percentage down the columns of the independent variable, allowing comparisons of percentages to be made across rows. There appears to be no support for our initial hypothesis, since a lower proportion identifying as middle class (26 per cent) is found among the manual group than among the non-manual group identifying as working class (39 per cent). Back to the theoretical drawing-board!

The model for analysis which we used, therefore, is as indicated in Figure 7.1.

In the case of a 2 × 2 table it is, of course, relatively easy to see what is going on. However, the larger a table is, and especially where there are more than two variables involved, the more difficult it becomes to pick out the important features of a relationship from a table. The solution to this problem, just as it was with univariate data, is to use summary statistics, i.e. create overall indices which summarize for us the aspect of the distributions which we are most interested in examining. This, therefore, takes us on to the idea of *association*.

Association

Let us begin by briefly stating what we mean by an association between variables. The usual way to think of a relationship, as we have attempted to explain previously, is in terms of *co-variation* – the extent to which a change in one variable is accompanied by a change in another variable.

If, therefore, two variables change or vary together (either in the same or opposite directions) we say they co-vary and are associated or related $(X \to Y)$. Hence a perfect positive relationship is one in which an increase in the independent variable is always accompanied by an increase in the dependent variable; a perfect negative relationship is one where an increase in the independent variable is always accompanied by a decrease in the dependent variable. No relationship exists where the dependent variable is as likely to increase, decrease or stay the same when the independent variable changes.

This idea of no relationship (or *statistical independence*) is the beginning point for statistical analysis. A relationship is said to exist between two variables if the data do not meet the definition of statistical independence. (And just a reminder here: we are talking about associations or correlations and *not* causes – measures of association do not reveal causal mechanisms, although they may aid us in looking for them. Explanation must depend on initial theorizing and detailed examination of data.)

So, basically, the statistician's reasoning on association or correlation goes in four steps:

1 By definition, our data either show a relationship, however weak, or they do not.
2 Let us calculate what the data in a table *would* look like if X and Y are not related.
3 Then we compare our actual data with our calculated table showing no relationship.
4 If actual differs from calculated, we conclude that X and Y are associated.

We will return to this idea below in more detail. What we must do first is to run through those characteristics of an association between variables which can be singled out for summary, in much the same way that we singled out central tendency and variation as two summary characteristics for univariate distributions.

There are basically four such characteristics to think about when examining a bivariate association:

1 Whether or not an association *exists*.
2 The *strength* or *degree* of that association.
3 The *direction* of the association.
4 The *nature* of the association.

Let us take each in turn. You will see that we have done a lot of the hard work already in our previous discussion.

We can say a relationship *exists* if, after computing percentages in the appropriate direction in a table, there is *any* difference in the percentage distribution of the dependent variable between the categories of the

Table 7.7

Variable Y	Variable X		Total
	c_1	c_2	
r_1	20	40	60
r_2	5	35	40
Total	25	75	100

Table 7.8

Variable Y	Variable X		Total
	c_1	c_2	
r_1	a	b	60
r_2	c	d	40
Total	25	75	100

independent variable. Remember, we do this by percentaging in the direction of the independent variable and comparing across.

In Table 7.6 we saw that 60.9 per cent of the non-manual group identified as middle class compared to 26.0 per cent of the manual group, a difference of 34.9 per cent. Clearly, there is a relationship; and the value for the difference we have calculated here even has a name: it is referred to as epsilon or ϵ. Despite its name this is really just what we calculate intuitively in our minds when comparing the distribution of a dependent variable among the categories of an independent variable. Obviously, this calculation is only a very rough and ready guide to an association.

Another way to test for the existence of an association is to do what we have just discussed – set up a **model of no association**. Let us see how this is done. First look at Table 7.7 containing some hypothetical data. Table 7.8 shows only the marginal frequencies from Table 7.7. The question then becomes, what would the pattern of frequencies be for cells a, b, c, d, if there is no association between X and Y? If there is no association in the tables, then the ratio of r_1 cell frequencies should be the same throughout as it is in the overall distribution of Y itself, i.e. 60 : 100, or 0.6. In Table 7.8 therefore, we would expect 0.6 of the 25 cases in the c_1 category of X to be in cell a. And we would expect the same proportion of the 75 cases in the c_2 category of X to be in cell b. In other words we assume that the same percentages apply to each column as in the univariate marginal percentages for the dependent variable, which is just another way of saying that the distribution of the dependent variable is

Table 7.9 Expected frequencies with no association

Variable Y	Variable X				Total
	c_1	%	c_2	%	
r_1	15	60	45	60	60
r_2	10	40	30	40	40
Total	25	100	75	100	100

the same for all categories of the independent variable. We could then produce our table of *expected* frequencies by doing the necessary calculations as in Table 7.9. The cells of this table contain the expected frequencies. The column percentages are included to show that under this model the distribution of the dependent variables is the same for each category of the independent variable. The simple formula for calculating expected frequencies is:

$$fe_{ij} = \frac{(n_i)(n_j)}{N}$$

where fe_{ij} refers to the expected cell frequency (fe) for the cell in the ith row and jth column of the table; n_i is the total for the ith row and n_j is the total for the jth column; N is the total number of cases. (The algebraic abstraction of referring to the 'ith' and 'jth' row and columns is necessary for a *generalized* formula, since not all tables will be simple 2 × 2 cross-tabulations as this is. The algebraic notation allows extension to tables of any dimension.) Hence, for our example, if we want to know what the expected frequency would be in the cell where row 2 and column 1 intersect it is calculated as:

$$\frac{40 \times 25}{100} = \frac{1000}{100} = 10$$

In other words we have calculated the value of cell c in Table 7.9 by multiplying the marginal totals for row 2 and column 1 and dividing them by N.

So we now have our expected Table 7.9 (expected, that is, given no association between X and Y) to compare with our actual observed Table 7.7. We make the comparison by subtracting expected frequencies from observed frequencies for each cell, i.e.

$$fo - fe$$

We call the result delta, denoted Δ. If any Δ values are not zero (in other words, if observed and expected frequencies vary) then we have at least some relation. But how strong is the association we have discovered? Δ (like ϵ) is not a standardized measure. It only tells us that there is an association when its value is not zero. Since tables almost never show a Δ of zero this is not that helpful. Generally the smaller Δ, the less likely that there is any real association, but what we ideally need are measures which show the *degree* of association in a more precise way than either Δ or ϵ provide. This is the subject of the next section on *standardized measures of association*.

First, however, to conclude this discussion of the examination of an association, we summarize ϵ and Δ via a real example, shown in Table 7.10. The first question to ask is whether there is any association between the variables. Having percentaged down in the direction of the independent variable, we make comparisons across rows. There is clearly an association. If we computed Δ, we would find large differences between observed and expected frequencies. We then move on to make some assessment of the *strength* or *degree of association*. If social class has a simple relationship with educational qualifications, then we should find the largest ϵ between the manual and professional/intermediate categories of social class for the high and low categories of educational qualifications, i.e. we compare first the upper left and upper right cells of the table and observe an ϵ of $(53.3 - 1.4) = 51.9$; then we compare bottom left and bottom right cells and see that $\epsilon = (61.5 - 16.8) = 44.7$. These are substantial values for ϵ, but they are not equal to 100 per cent, the largest value ϵ could take.

Since we have an example here of two ordinal variables, it makes sense to discuss the *direction of association*. We do this by comparing across rows and noting the highest cell value for each row. Counting from left to right across the rows in Table 7.10 we would therefore note cell c in the first row (third cell); in the second row we would note cell e (second cell); and in the third row we would note cell g (first cell). We then draw an imaginary line through these cells to represent the major diagonal line along which cases tend to concentrate. In this case the line extends from bottom left to top right, i.e. the higher the educational level the higher the social class – an example of a positive direction of association.

Table 7.10 Qualification level by Registrar General's social class, British Class Survey 1984

Index of qualification	Manual (%) (637)	Skilled non-manual (%) (294)	Professional/ intermediate (%) (375)	Total (%) (1306)
High	1.4	8.2	53.3	17.8 (233)
Medium	37.0	59.5	29.9	40.0 (523)
Low	61.5	32.3	16.8	42.1 (550)
Total	99.9	100.0	100.0	99.9

Assuming we have set up our tables with ordinal variables arranged as in Table 7.10 (i.e. low-to-high reading across the categories of the independent variable and high-to-low reading down the categories of the dependent variable) then, if cases concentrate along the diagonal from bottom left to top right, we have a positive relationship; if they concentrate along the diagonal from top left to bottom right, we have a negative relationship. Whatever else we do in terms of analysis we must first describe the direction of the relationship observed at this stage in some detail. Summary measures of association as described later are an *aid* in doing this, but they are not a substitute for the detailed examination and description of tables.

Finally, we can examine the *nature of the association*. This refers to the general *pattern* of data in a bivariate table. We can usually discover this by examining the pattern of percentages in a properly percentaged table. In Table 7.10 the pattern is relatively simple. We find a relatively uniform shift towards higher qualification levels as we move to higher social class groups. Because we have ordinal variables, we call such an association *monotonic* rather than *linear*. To define a relationship or association as linear, we would require defined distances so that we could determine whether there was a constant amount of shift in the values of one variable given a fixed amount of change in the other, and to do this we would require interval-level variables. With ordinal variables we can only say that the value of one variable remained the same or changed in a fixed direction with increases in the other variable. This is, therefore, what we mean by a monotonic nature of association. For nominal variables we cannot talk about the direction of association in the same way because nominal measures lack any kind of order or hierarchy.

Standardized measures of association for nominal and ordinal variables

So far we have been struggling against the problems which arise from the imprecision of measures such as ϵ and Δ which are not standardized. Ideally we would like measures which indicate for us the *existence, strength* and (where appropriate) *direction* of association, as discussed above. Such a measure would vary from minus values (for negative associations), through zero (for no association), to positive values (for positive associations); the larger the value of the measure in either direction from zero, the greater the association would be. Moreover we need such measures to have *fixed limits* – such as between –1.00 and +1.00. Given all these characteristics we would then have a *normed* or **standardized measure of association**. Normed measures would allow us to make valid comparisons between different tables in the same way that percentages allow us to compare different distributions. This would obviously help us in interpreting our data when assessing the relative effect of different independent variables upon particular dependent variables. We would want, therefore, a scale such as this:

	-1.00		0		$+1.00$
Strength of association =	Strong	weak		weak	Strong
Direction of association =		negative		positive	

There are, in fact, a wide variety of such measures available and different researchers have their own prejudices about which are the most appropriate to use. Much will depend on the purpose of the research; but in addition different measures of association are appropriate for different levels of measurement. Here we will deal only with measures appropriate to nominal and ordinal level variables. For interval level variables powerful measures based on regression analysis are available and these are discussed in Chapter 8.

Below we illustrate the principles behind calculating one or two examples of such measures. SPSS will provide a range of these on the CROSSTABS procedure, many of which will often turn out to be very similar to each other if you ask for the STATISTICS ALL sub-command. Some texts provide rather complicated tables of which measures to use under what conditions, and these are referenced later in this chapter. Remember that there are two important things to be borne in mind when you are calculating any statistic:

1 Where a number of different statistics are available it is best to stick to those you understand well.
2 Any statistic is merely an aid to interpretation, and should never be regarded as the end point of analysis.

However correct you are in precisely which statistic you use in social research, any accuracy you might gain by this is almost certainly trivial compared to the problems of operationalization, representativeness and various forms of bias. A statistic, then, should be regarded simply as one of many guides to the interpretation of data of which you should be aware. Bearing this in mind, of course, one should try to use the most appropriate statistic for the circumstances.

Measures for 2 × 2 tables

We noted earlier, when discussing direction of association, the way in which cases in a table tend to fall along one diagonal when association is strong. The way we can define perfect association is, therefore, one where *all* cases pile up along one diagonal. In a 2 × 2 table this would mean that two diagonal cells would have frequencies and two would not. For 2 × 2 tables with this definition of perfect association, an appropriate measure of association would be the *phi coefficient* (ϕ). Phi is a measure of the degree of diagonal concentration and has values between -1.0 and $+1.0$. A measure of 1.00, either positive or negative, would therefore mean that all cases are concentrated in one diagonal of the table. For a table constructed in the form:

	X		Total
	c_1	c_2	
$Y \begin{cases} r_1 \\ r_2 \end{cases}$	a	b	a + b
	c	d	c + d
Total	a + c	b + d	N

ϕ can be calculated quite simply as:

$$\sqrt{\frac{ad - bc}{(a + b)(c + d)(b + d)(a + c)}}$$

This is a simple measure for simple tables of the 2×2 variety. Where larger tables are involved, an equivalent statistic is *Cramer's V*, and SPSS will calculate the appropriate version automatically. These measures do not require us to make any distinction between the independent and dependent variables, that is they are *symmetric* measures of association. However, some measures of association do require such a distinction to be made, since they aim to measure the usefulness of an independent variable for predicting values of a dependent variable. We call these *asymmetric* measures of association.

Asymmetric measures of association

There are a number of asymmetric measures of association for use with nominal-level data based on a relatively simple-to-grasp principle which can be used to illustrate the logic of **proportionate reduction of error** (PRE) *measures*. But what do we mean by PRE? PRE measures are simple ratios of the amount of error made in guessing the value of one variable for an individual under two situations: (1) where the only information we have is the distribution of the dependent variable; and (2) where we have additional knowledge about how the dependent variable is distributed among the categories of the independent variable. What a PRE measure does is to state the proportion by which one can reduce

Table 7.11 Housing tenure by region

Tenure	North	Midlands	South	Total
Owner-occupier	200	200	700	1100
Council tenant	250	250	200	700
Private tenant	50	50	100	200
Total	500	500	1000	2000

guessing errors made in (1) by using information from (2). If you think about it, you will see why PRE measures would be useful in social research. For example, our theoretical knowledge might tell us that social class background is related to educational achievement. Put in more quantitative terms, what we are claiming is that knowledge of social class background should enable us to make predictions about educational achievement. If, in fact, all errors of prediction could be eliminated by predicting educational achievement on social class background, we would have a perfect association between the two variables (a value of 1). On the other hand if social class background was not a good predictor of educational achievement, the measure of association will indicate this in a value of 0 (or close to 0). We can see what this means by an examination of the hypothetical data in Table 7.11.

We are dealing here with nominal variables and so what we are interested in for the prediction of individual values is the most typical category of the dependent variable, that is, the *modal* housing tenure. The first step is to make this prediction on the basis of the dependent variable alone, i.e. on the univariate distribution of housing tenure. This we find in the total column of Table 7.11. Our prediction on this basis would be 'owner-occupier', that is, owner-occupation is the modal housing tenure. If we were to guess the housing tenure of any of the 2000 individuals in the table we would have to guess 'owner-occupied' and we would be correct on 1100 occasions and wrong on (2000 – 1100) or 900 occasions. We then move to step two. If we had more information, how many of the 900 'errors' made in the step one prediction could we eliminate? More specifically, if we use the knowledge provided by Table 7.11 of the distribution of the dependent variable, housing tenure, between the categories of the independent variable, region, could we refine our prediction and make fewer errors?

So now we must compare down the columns. For column 1 (North) the modal status is not owner-occupied but council tenant; the same applies for column 2 (Midlands). For column 3 modal status remains the same as that of the univariate distribution of tenure, owner-occupied. Hence for the North and Midlands our guess would be council tenant and in each case we would be right 250 out of 500 times. We, therefore, have:

Within category model frequency	Category of independent variable
250	North
250	Midlands
700	South
1200	

Has the added information about the distribution of tenure within regions increased our predictive power? Clearly it has. We would now be correct 1200 times rather than 1100 times. We have therefore made 100 fewer errors. We can now apply the appropriate formula for calculating a normed asymmetric measure of association.

There are several of these, and which we use will depend upon which statistic is appropriate to our table. Examples of some we *might* calculate are *Goodman and Kruskal's tau* (τ), and *lambda* (λ). Useful tables and advice on which measures are best used in particular circumstances are found in Loether and McTavish (1974: 255–7) and de Vaus (1991: 69 and 194–6). Basically, however, the principle underlying the different formulae is the same, and involves relating the number of predictive errors made knowing only the distribution of the dependent variable to the number made when knowing the bivariate distribution of the dependent by the independent variable, and expressing this as a proportion. So a value for Goodman and Kruskal's τ (for instance) of 0.08 would be interpreted to mean that we have improved our prediction of the value of the dependent variable by knowing its distribution in the categories of the independent variable by 0.08; we have achieved an 8 per cent proportionate reduction in error.

We now move on to normed statistics for ordinal-level variables. These are rather more complicated statistics to compute given the higher level of measurement involved. With ordinal variables we are interested basically in the *ranking* of scores, and many of the measures which are used for ordinal variables are based on the idea of *pairs* of observations. In other words, given some kind of sample, we work out the total possible numbers of pairs of individuals in order to see how far an individual's position *vis-à-vis* another individual is similar or different for each of the two ordinal variables concerned. That is, we want to know whether or not rank ordering of pairs of cases on one variable is useful for predicting rank order on the other variable. If, for example, individual A was higher than individual B on parental social class, we would expect A to be higher than B on educational achievement. If this were true they would represent a *concordant pair*. However if A were higher than B on one variable but lower than B on the other, we would have a *discordant pair*. Another possibility would be for A and B to be equal on the first variable but ranked differently on the second variable; we would then say they were *tied on the first variable*; a fourth possibility would be pairs *tied on the second variable*; and the final case would be pairs *tied on both variables*.

Hence, the first step would be to discover the total number of pairs, using the formula

$$T = \frac{N(N-1)}{2}$$

where N is the sample size and T the total number of unique pairs in a set of N cases. Hence if we had a sample of 90 individuals there would be

$$\frac{90(90-1)}{2} \text{ pairs} = 4005 \text{ pairs}$$

Consequently our five different possible types of pairs will equal 4005 pairs in total for a sample of size 90. Different kinds of pairs are given different symbols, viz.:

N_s = concordant pairs
N_d = discordant pairs
T_x = pairs tied on the first variable but not the second variable
T_y = pairs tied on the second variable but not the first variable
T_{xy} = pairs tied on both variables.

Having used the formula to find T, we then find the number of each type of pair using procedures that there is not the space (nor the necessity) to explain here. Positive association indicates the same rank order for a pair on the second variable as they had on the first; negative association would indicate opposite rank order. If we find more N_s pairs than N_d pairs we would predict same rank order in our guessing game; more N_d pairs would indicate opposite rank order.

An example of a normed measure of association for cross-tabulated ordinal-level variables is *gamma* (γ). The actual formula for the calculation of gamma is:

$$\gamma = \frac{N_s - N_d}{N_s + N_d}$$

Each measure of association calculated on this basis is a PRE measure, indicating the proportionate reduction in error which could be achieved by predicting either same or opposite rank order given knowledge of the overall ranking of pairs based on the bivariate distribution of two variables, as compared to making a random guess about the rank ordering of pairs for two ordinal variables. So if we get a measure of γ of 0.23 we can interpret it (as for any PRE measure) to mean that by knowing about the bivariate distribution of the variables we have reduced our predictive error by 23 per cent. There are a number of such measures available in SPSS for ordinal and nominal level cross-tabulated variables, but they are

based upon similar principles, and at this stage understanding the underlying concepts of measuring association is more useful than a detailed
knowledge of particular statistics.

In order to help you assess whether you have absorbed the information
about analysing cross-tabulations so far, we have included some multiple-
choice questions and another exercise below.

Key concepts

Make sure you have understood the following key concepts:

- bivariate analysis
- cross-tabulation
- marginal frequencies
- model of no association (statistical independence)
- standardized measures of association
- proportionate reduction of error

Multiple choice questions

1 The purpose of calculating standardized measures of association
   is to:

　(i)　compare z-scores

　(ii)　determine the direction of an association

　(iii)　make valid comparisons between measures of association
　　　using different variables

2 An asymmetric measure of association is:

　(i)　one where the direction of the association is negative

　(ii)　used only with ordinal levels of measurement

　(iii)　used for measuring the usefulness of an independent vari-
　　　able for predicting the values of a dependent variable

3 What does PRE stand for:

　(i)　proportionate reduction of error?

　(ii)　percentage of relative error?

　(iii)　proportion of relationship in error?

Exercise 2

This exercise initially involves a similar procedure to that for Exercise 1 on pp. 121–2, except that this time you will have the experience of using real large-scale survey data in order to put into practice some of the considerations involving the analysis of cross-tabulated data discussed so far.

Provided for you in Tables 7.12 and 7.13 (p. 143) is a description of a sub-set of variables from both the British Class Survey and the British Household Panel Survey Wave 1 data. The sample for the British Class Survey was randomly selected from the population of Britain and comprised 1770 persons of working age (see Chapter 1 for further details). The questionnaire is reproduced in Marshall *et al.* (1988), along with further technical details of the survey. The British Household Panel Survey data-set used here comprises respondents randomly selected on a one-per-household basis, from a total of 5532 surveyed households at Wave 1 in 1991. Technical details and the questionnaire are available in Technical Papers 1–3 of the ESRC Research Centre on Micro-Social Change. Both data-sets are available to you as SPSS data files called CLASS.SYS/ CLASS.SAV and BHPS1.SYS/BHPS1.SAV respectively on the floppy disk which comes with the text. Further information about these files is available on this disk, and the Appendix on p. 230 describes how to begin using it. You do not therefore need to create your own SPSS data file this time (as you did for Exercise 1). Otherwise, though, the task is similar. You should follow these steps:

1 From the frequency distributions of the variables in your chosen data file specify an initial *hypothesis* of the type $X \rightarrow Y$, controlling for C, and involving a dependent and *two* independent variables (one for use as the *control* variable). Say why you think the hypothesis is interesting, and what possible problems may arise at the analysis stage relating to the variable definitions (for instance, if the univariate distributions of the variables concerned show that there is a high percentage of missing values on a particular variable, consider why this is so). In order to do this the best idea is to think up an initial $X \rightarrow Y$ hypothesis which interests you. Produce the appropriate univariate distributions, and then cross-tabulate your dependent (Y) with your independent (X) variable using the CROSSTABS command. Study this table, and then consider which other variable in the set available to you you could introduce as a control variable into the analysis. Your thinking should be: 'It would be interesting to see this $X \rightarrow Y$ table broken down by the categories of C.' The purpose of the

control variable is to help you *clarify* the original $X \rightarrow Y$ relationship. You would expect, therefore, that your control variable will be related to your dependent variable, and it might in addition either add a different *dimension* of explanation to that of your initial independent variable (an intervening variable):

$$X \rightarrow Y$$
$$\uparrow$$
$$C$$

or largely *account* for the $X \rightarrow Y$ relationship (an antecedent variable);

$$C \rightarrow X \rightarrow Y$$

Refer to the section of the text on the logic of analysis (Chapter 2) if you are not clear about the principles described here.

2 Introduce your *control* variable into the cross-tabulation, and say how (and why) the control variable affects the relationship between your dependent and first independent variable. Get SPSS to produce appropriate statistics to aid you in this. Remember to RECODE the variables if necessary, and to include row and column percentages as appropriate (refer to appropriate sections of the text if you have forgotten how to do this).

3 Produce a mini-report detailing your hypothesis and discussion of variables, univariate distributions, tables and discussion of results.

Note: you might wish to use the command SELECT IF (from the MODIFY DATA OR FILES menu in SPSS/PC+ or the Data drop-down menu in SPSS FOR WINDOWS), in order to select sub-groups of the sample for analysis.

Table 7.12 Variable descriptions; CLASS.SYS/CLASS.SAV

Variable name	Description
AGER124	Age (continuous variable)
CLASSX	Class (From question on respondent's class identification)
DISIN15	From: 'Do you think the distribution of income and wealth in Britain is a fair one?'
ECACT36A	Economic activity status
EDINDEX	Index of educational achievement
EOWCL12C	Eric Olin Wright's class categories
HOUSE	Housing tenure
INCOME	(pseudo 'continuous' variable, calculated from mid-points of grouped income categories)
JHG397B	John Goldthorpe's social class categories
MAST117A	Marital status
PARTYX	From: 'If there were a General Election tomorrow who would you vote for?'
SC406	Registrar General's social class categories
SEX122A	Sex of respondent
TAX13A	From: 'Would you be prepared to pay more in tax in order to create jobs for the unemployed?'
TAX13B	From: 'Would you be prepared to pay more in tax so that money could be spent on the Welfare State?'
UNION70	Whether a Trade Union member or not

Table 7.13 Variable descriptions; BHPS1.SYS/BHPS1.SAV

Variable name	Description
AHID	Household ID number (DO NOT USE!)
APNO	Person ID number (DO NOT USE!)
AHHWGHT	Weighting variable (DO NOT USE!)
ASEX	Sex of respondent
AAGE	Age (continuous variable)
AOPCLS2	Subjective social class
AJBRGSC	Registrar General's social class categories
AJBGOLD	John Goldthorpe's social class categories
AJBSTAT	Labour force status
ATENURE	Housing tenure
AFIYR	Annual income (continuous variable)
AQFEDHI	Highest educational qualification
AMASTAT	Marital status
AVOTE	Political party supported (amalgamation of vote and party support variables)
AOPFAME	From: 'Having a full-time job is the best way for a woman to be an independent person' (scaled response)
AOPFAMF	From: 'A husband's job is to earn money; a wife's job is to look after the home and family' (scaled response)

Bivariate analysis for interval level variables: regression and correlation

Aims

- To understand the purpose and uses of the regression line in simple linear regression.

- To describe the calculation of a regression line, including a and b coefficients.

- To explain the meaning and importance of the residual variation.

- To understand the principles of correlation analysis, including calculation of r^2.

- To outline the assumptions underpinning regression analysis.

Having discussed in some detail the analysis of bivariate relationships where the data are categoric in nature, we now turn to the primary technique for investigating the relationship between interval-level variables: *regression analysis*. Regression analysis is subsumed under the widely used family of statistical techniques known as *general linear models* or GLMs (see Part V for more details). Regression is a technique which aims at PRE (proportionate reduction in error) in a similar way to other measures we have already encountered. However, regression analysis not only tells us how strongly related a pair of variables are via a measure of correlation; since we are dealing with real, interval-level numbers it can also actually measure the extent of the effect that a change in the independent variable has on the dependent variable. As with other techniques, the general aim is to simplify and summarize complex information in order to ascertain the underlying patterns in the data.

However, the general linear model has an additional property in that the relationship between variables can be expressed in algebraic form – something which makes many people immediately wary! In fact, in certain circumstances mathematical models may be more concise and more easily formulated than verbal concepts. (This is particularly so when we get on to considering multivariate analysis.) However, it is only in economics among the social sciences that there is anything approaching the reliance on mathematical models using interval-level variables which we find in the natural sciences, because, as we said initially when discussing levels of measurement, there are often many fewer interval-level than categoric variables analysed in social research. In the British Class Survey data, for example, there is only one true interval-level variable recorded – age. Income was collected in pre-coded categories due to the notorious reluctance of respondents to disclose details on this subject. For this reason, and to facilitate calculation, the examples we use in this chapter are based upon hypothetical data.

Why learn about regression, then? We deal with this topic in some detail, since an understanding of the principles behind simple bivariate regression (known as '**simple linear regression**') underlie most of the more complex multivariate analyses we will come across later – all of which also fall into the GLM family. These models constitute some of the most important and up-to-date statistical techniques for the analysis of quantitative data, but, as we shall see, they are grounded in concepts which are quite easy to grasp.

We can start by relating regression to what we discussed in Chapter 5. We know that the mean is the arithmetical average for an interval-level variable and that variance and standard deviation measure how dispersed individual cases are about the mean. We also know that one of the major goals of data analysis is 'explaining variance'. Essentially we need to find independent variables which help explain the distance of a case from the mean of a dependent variable. (Once again, which independent variables we should examine in order to do this is, of course, a matter for *theory*.) As we have said before, if we want to predict the value of interval-level variable Y for a particular case, the best average guess we could make *having information only about Y* would be the mean of Y for all cases ($\bar{Y}$). The *variance* of Y gives us an indication of how far out that guess is likely to be. However, if we can find some independent interval-level variable X which is linearly correlated with Y (so that we know how the values of Y change with the values of X), we could then improve our guess or prediction. We could compute a *regression line* to show the relationship between X and Y and predict the value of Y corresponding to the individual's position on X.

For example, if we wished to estimate the annual income of an individual in a sample, but had no information other than the univariate distribution of income for that sample, then on average our best guess would have to be the mean (or median!) income for that sample. However, if we also knew that income increases linearly with age, then knowing the individual's age would enable us to improve our guess about their income. In fact, if we knew the details of the linear relationship of

Table 8.1 Mean wage of unskilled employees and proportion of unskilled employees who are women in small manufacturing companies

Company	Mean wage (Y) (£)	% of women (X)
1	6500	85
2	6700	71
3	6900	43
4	7100	52
5	7400	36
6	7500	21
7	7700	23
8	8000	15
9	8400	17
10	9000	10

X (age) with Y (income), we would be able to make a prediction of their income based only upon knowing their age. The way we establish these details is to do a simple linear regression from our sample data to produce a **regression line** showing the relationship of X and Y. Now the *actual* or *observed* income from the survey data for any individual case may well be different from the income we *predict* in this way, but hopefully it will not be as different as our original prediction, the mean (or median) income for the sample. In other words, regression is a PRE technique. Its accuracy in prediction will depend on the extent of the linear correlation between X and Y. If this is strong, then our prediction about the value of the dependent variable based on the value of the independent variable alone will be close.

But what is a regression line, and how is it computed? For the bivariate regression model we can demonstrate the technique both visually and algebraically. We shall begin with some 'pictures'. Consider the hypothetical data in Table 8.1. An obvious hypothesis would be that the higher the proportion of unskilled women employees, the lower will be the average unskilled wage. Note that in this example we are not dealing with individuals as cases but with companies. The data here probably would not come from a survey of individuals, but could have been provided, say, by the managements of the companies concerned. As far as analysis goes, however, there is no difference in the procedures to be followed. We will, however, need to bear in mind that, if we find some support for our hypothesis, we cannot conclude from this evidence alone that unskilled women employees are *individually* paid less than men. We would, though, have good reason to investigate this proposition further.

We could have presented the above data in an alternative, graphic form by constructing a **scatterplot**. This is achieved by simply pairing the values of X and Y for each company and locating these *coordinates* for X and

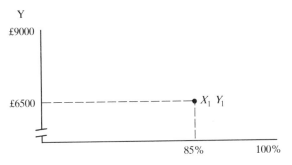

Figure 8.1 Location of coordinates for Company 1 in Table 8.1 (By convention the dependent variable Y is placed on the vertical axis.)

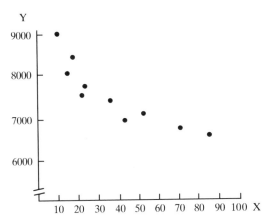

Figure 8.2 Coordinates for data in Table 8.1

Y on a graph or plot. For example, for Company 1 we put a mark on the scatterplot at the point at which the values for mean unskilled wage (£6500) and percentage of unskilled women employees (85 per cent) intersect, as in Figure 8.1. By pairing each of the values of X and Y we can similarly locate all the coordinates for the data in Table 8.1. This is shown in Figure 8.2. We now have the data from Table 8.1 in the form of a scatterplot. Although the points on the scatterplot are somewhat irregular, there is a general downward trend, i.e. a tendency for mean unskilled wages to be lower where there is a greater proportion of unskilled women employees. As with other approaches, regression *cannot* establish whether a causal relationship exists between two variables, but it can determine *how far the known data are consistent with a particular causal proposition*. In this example, we cannot *prove* from the data shown that women are paid lower wages than men, but we can claim that there is a case for investigating the hypothesis further. This is the purpose of regression in social research – it examines the *nature* and *strength* of a relationship between two interval-level variables (or more than two variables in the case of multivariate regression), and allows us to determine whether this relationship accords with what we have hypothesized. In the example we are using we have hypothesized that a higher proportion of unskilled women employees will be associated with a lower mean wage for unskilled employees. We could express this in terms of the kind of arrow diagram we have used before, i.e. $X \rightarrow Y$. In this case X is the proportion of unskilled women employees and Y is the mean wage for unskilled employees. We could equally say $Y = f(X)$, that is, Y is a *function of X* (mean unskilled wage is a function of the proportion of unskilled women employees).

We are now in a position to discuss the bivariate regression model in more detail. Taking our example again, how can we describe the form of relationship revealed by Figure 8.2? One way would be simply to join up all the points or coordinates defined in that scatterplot. The problem with this is that we could not thereby achieve one of the major purposes of data analysis, namely simplification of complex relationships. Regression summarizes the kind of relationship outlined in Figure 8.2 by defining one single line describing the *average* relationship between the variables, but what are the criteria for defining such a line?

Clearly we could draw a line by eye which appears to fit through the overall pattern of the coordinates. However, this would be subjective and arbitrary – different researchers might draw very different lines for the same pattern of dots. We need instead some objective criterion which allows us to derive the best possible straight line for the pattern. Since not all the coordinates will fall exactly on this line, it would seem that the best line would be the one which minimizes the summed distances (deviations) of all the coordinates from the line. It could be thought of as a sort of 'average' line through the coordinates. However, in order to calculate this line mathematically we need to refer to the *squared* deviations rather than simply the deviations themselves. (This trick is similar to that involved in the calculation of the standard deviation, and is necessary because if you take the difference between every individual value for a variable and the mean of that variable, and sum them, the result will be zero. The same consideration applies to the regression line, which is also a kind of average.) The line is then drawn so that the sum of the *squared* deviations from the line is reduced to a minimum. The criterion used in the calculation of the linear model is, therefore, known as the *least squares criterion*. Assuming a linear relationship between the variables, it gives us a straight line positioned and sloped in a manner which ensures that the sum of the squared deviations from the straight line is as small as possible, and smaller than the sum of squared deviations would be from any other straight line which could be drawn.

So, by using the least squares criterion, regression analysis formalizes the process by which a straight line is fitted to a scatterplot. The regression line is the line which minimizes the sum of squared deviations

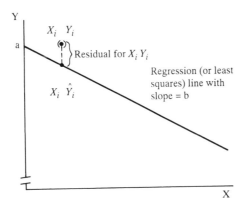

Figure 8.3 Least squares regression line

between itself and the coordinates. The only problem we are left with is whether we are referring to the horizontal or vertical deviations of points on the scatterplot from the regression line, since both could be calculated. As we are predicting from X to Y you might be able to guess that we are concerned here with the *vertical deviations*, i.e. deviations measured along the Y (dependent variable) axis. All of the points we have just made can be summarized diagrammatically. Figure 8.3 should help to see what is meant. As can be seen from the figure the 'deviations' are referred to as *residuals* since they represent the **residual variance** in Y not explained by the average linear relationship with X. Having drawn the line of best fit relating X and Y we can now *predict* values for Y which correspond to the *known* values of X. These points will all lie on the regression line and thus may differ from the observed scores which we originally had in Table 8.1 and plotted on the scatterplot in Figure 8.2. Algebraically (and we shall deal with this in more detail later) we now have two Y values for each X value. We have the observed values of Y with coordinates $X_i Y_i$ and the derived values of Y known as $\hat{Y}$ (Y-hat) with coordinates $X_i \hat{Y}_i$. The difference between Y_i and $\hat{Y}_i$ is therefore just the residuals – for each value of X we have the residual $(Y_i - \hat{Y}_i)$. The regression line was drawn such that $\Sigma(Y_i - \hat{Y}_i)^2$ was at a minimum (the least squares criterion). So we end up with two values for Y; $\hat{Y}$ which is the value of Y we have '*explained*' via the linear regression with X, and Y which is the original observed value.

There are two other important new pieces of information in Figure 8.3. The point at which the regression line meets the Y-axis is known as the *intercept point* and is denoted symbolically by the letter (a); secondly the regression line has a particular *slope* or *gradient* denoted by (b). We shall see how to calculate a and b (the **regression coefficients**) later, and say something more about their importance. For the moment note that, if either b or a are changed, or both, then the line itself changes as illustrated in Figures 8.4–8.6.

Figure 8.4 Two regression lines with the same intercept, a, but different slopes, b_1 and b_2

Figure 8.5 Two regression lines with different intercepts, a_1 and a_2, but the same slope, b

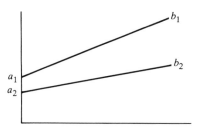

Figure 8.6 Two regression lines with different intercepts and different slopes

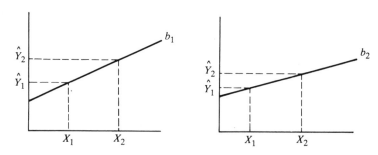

Figure 8.7 The predicted effects upon Y of an identical change in X with regression lines of different slopes

In Figures 8.4 and 8.6 it can also be seen that slope b_1 is steeper than slope b_2. Figure 8.7 summarizes the implications of different slopes. If we increase X by the same amount in each diagram, the steeper regression line (b_1) predicts a greater increase in Y as X increases than the less steep

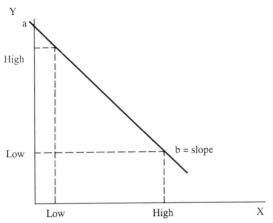

Figure 8.8 Example of an expected pattern for a negative relationship

line (b_2). Note that these examples are of positive relationships, i.e. relationships where a high level of X is associated with a high level of Y and a low level of X with a low level of Y. The relationship between mean wages of unskilled employees and the percentage of unskilled women employees in our example in Figure 8.1 was, on the other hand, a negative one. Figure 8.8 shows such a relationship.

Let us now summarize the information we have about regression lines:

- The regression line summarizes a scatter of data points by minimizing the sum of squared vertical deviations from itself.
- The line has a particular slope, b, and a particular intercept point, a. (As we shall see, in a particular piece of research, a and b take on specific numeric values.)
- The line can describe either a positive relationship such that high levels of one variable are associated with high levels of the other, or a negative relationship (high levels of one variable associated with low levels of the other).
- Once the line has been identified by the a and b parameters (see below for an example) the line can then be used to make *predictions* about the level of Y by making projections from the X-axis up to the line, and then across to the Y-axis, i.e. one can predict the value of the dependent variable knowing only the value of the independent variable – the task that we initially set ourselves.

We can now return to the data in Table 8.1 and see how we can compute the least squares regression line for that data. We first of all take on trust from our friends, the mathematicians, that any straight line can be described as:

$$Y = a + bX$$

where X is conventionally measured along the horizontal axis and Y along the vertical. The quantity a is the Y value where the line intercepts the Y-axis (the intercept); and b is the slope of that line, i.e. the amount by which Y increases for each unit increase of X. The problem is to calculate the estimates of a and b from the data so that the line fits the points on the scatterplot as closely as possible.

We can use the above equation to find the 'least squares' line. Since this is a straight line it cannot give us the actual values of Y-observed which appear in column 2 of Table 8.1. Instead it will give us Y-explained or $\hat{Y}$. We therefore rewrite the equation as:

$$\hat{Y} = a + bX$$

Now, it can be shown mathematically that a and b have the following values:

$$b = \frac{SXY}{SXX}$$

where

$$SXX = \Sigma(X - \bar{X})^2 = \Sigma X^2 - \frac{(\Sigma X)^2}{n}$$

$$SXY = \Sigma(X - \bar{X})(Y - \bar{Y}) = \Sigma XY - \frac{(\Sigma X)(\Sigma Y)}{n}$$

and

$$a = \bar{Y} - b\bar{X}$$

which is the mean of all Y values minus b times the mean of all X values.

Don't panic, these can all be calculated quite simply! What follows shows you exactly how to do it. Of course, hopefully, you will never actually have to do these calculations by hand yourself – but seeing how it *can* be done helps with understanding what the computer will churn out for you.

We can now calculate the value of the coefficients a and b for the equation

$$\hat{Y} = a + bX$$

which represents the straight line relating mean wage for unskilled employees (Y) to the proportion of unskilled employees who are women (X). First the quantitites

$$\Sigma X; \Sigma Y; \Sigma X^2; \Sigma Y^2; \Sigma XY$$

are calculated in Table 8.2.

Table 8.2 The calculation of the a and b coefficients

X	Y	X^2	Y^2	XY
85	6500	7225	42 250 000	552 500
71	6700	5041	44 890 000	475 700
43	6900	1849	47 610 000	296 700
52	7100	2704	50 410 000	369 200
36	7400	1296	54 760 000	266 400
21	7500	441	56 250 000	157 500
23	7700	529	59 290 000	177 100
15	8000	225	64 000 000	120 000
17	8400	289	70 560 000	142 800
10	9000	100	81 000 000	90 000

$\sum X = 373$ $\sum Y = 75\ 200$ $\sum X^2 = 19\ 699$ $\sum Y^2 = 571\ 020\ 000$ $\sum XY = 2\ 647\ 900$

To calculate b:

$\sum X^2 = 19\ 699$

$(\sum X)^2 = (373)^2 = 139\ 129$ (calculate the value in the bracket first)

$$\sum X^2 - \frac{(\sum X)^2}{N} = 19\ 699 - \frac{139\ 129}{10} = 19\ 699 - 13\ 912.9 = 5786.1 = SXX$$

$\sum XY = 2\ 647\ 900$

$$\sum XY - \frac{(\sum X)(\sum Y)}{N} = 2\ 647\ 900 - \frac{28\ 049\ 600}{10}$$

$$= 2\ 647\ 900 - 2\ 804\ 960 = -157\ 060 = SXY$$

$$b = \frac{-157\ 060}{5786} = -27.14 \text{ (negative because the slope is negative)}$$

To calculate a:

$$\bar{Y} = \frac{\sum Y}{N} = 7520$$

$$\bar{X} = \frac{\sum X}{N} = 37.3$$

$a = \bar{Y} - b\bar{X} = 7520 - (-27.14 \times 37.3) = 8532.32$ (two minuses equals a plus!)

Therefore, from

$\hat{Y} = a + bX$ (our original straight-line equation)

$\hat{Y} = 8532.32 + (-27.14X)$

In other words the intercept point for our data from Table 8.1 is £8532.32 and the slope is –27.14. The meaning of the slope parameter is that for every unit increase in X, Y *decreases* by £27.14. Now where does all this get us?

Instead of saying, as we did earlier for our example, that mean unskilled wage = some function of the proportion of unskilled women employees, i.e. $Y = f(X)$, we have effectively replaced f with $a + b$, i.e.

Mean unskilled wage $(Y) =$
$a + b$ (percentage unskilled women employees (X))   (1)

We have shown that for our data

$a = 8532.32$

and

$b = -27.14$

Consequently Equation (1) above can be rewritten as:

Mean unskilled wage =
8532.32 + (−27.14 (percentage unskilled women employees))
$\quad\uparrow\qquad\qquad\uparrow$ (2)
$\quad a\qquad\qquad b$

Given the information in Equation (2), and assuming that we had a larger representative sample, we can now make a prediction about the mean unskilled wage in a company, based only upon knowing that company's proportion of unskilled employees who are women. For instance, supposing we know that 30 per cent of a company's unskilled workforce are women:

Predicted mean unskilled wage = 8532.32 + (−27.14 × 30)
$\qquad\qquad\qquad\qquad\qquad\quad$ = 8532.32 + (−814.2)
$\qquad\qquad\qquad\qquad\qquad\quad$ = £7718 (a plus and a minus equals a minus)

Without the knowledge of the independent variable our best guess of this value would have had to be $\bar{Y}$, i.e. £7520. Using this equation we can of course calculate a predicted mean wage for a company for whom we actually have an *observed* mean wage, viz:

Predicted mean wage in Company 1 =
8532.32 + (−27.14 × 85) = £6225.

This may then be compared with the actual observed mean wage for Company 1 which was £6500. The difference $Y - \hat{Y}$, or in this instance 6500 − 6225, represents the *residual variance*, or the variance in the dependent variable Y *not* explained by the linear relationship with X, i.e. it is the distance on the scatterplot of the point X_iY_i from the regression line. Table 8.3 repeats these calculations for all ten companies from Table 8.1.

Table 8.3 Observed, predicted and residual values for the data from Table 1

Company	% Unskilled women (X)	Observed wage (Y)	Predicted wage ($\hat{Y}$)	$Y - \hat{Y}$ (residuals)
1	85	6500	6225	275
2	71	6700	6605	95
3	43	6900	7365	−465
4	52	7100	7121	−21
5	36	7400	7555	−155
6	21	7500	7962	−462
7	23	7700	7908	−208
8	15	8000	8125	−125
9	17	8400	8071	329
10	10	9000	8261	739

For Company 1
$\hat{Y}_1 = 8532.32 + (-27.14 \times 85)$

Residual $= Y_1 - \hat{Y}_1$
$6500 - 6225 = 275$

For Company 2
$\hat{Y}_2 = 8532.32 + (-27.14 \times 71)$

Residual $= Y_2 - \hat{Y}_2$
$6700 - 6605 = 95$

. . .   .

For Company 10
$\hat{Y}_{10} = 8532.32 + (-27.14 \times 10)$

Residual $= Y_{10} - \hat{Y}_{10}$
$9000 - 8261 = 739$

In order to draw the regression line we have calculated on the scatterplot, we select two points, one at the lower end of the X scale and one at the upper end and calculate the predicted values of $\hat{Y}$ from the regression equation. We then mark and join up these two points on the scatterplot and check that the regression line we have calculated passes through $(\bar{X}, \bar{Y})$.

Example:
For Point 1, if $X = 85$, $\hat{Y} = 8532.32 + (-27.14 \times 85) = £6225$
For Point 2, if $X = 15$, $\hat{Y} = 8532.32 + (-27.14 \times 15) = £8125$
We then mark these $X_i \hat{Y}_i$ points off on our scatterplot and draw the regression line through them.
For Point 1, $X_1 = 85$ and $\hat{Y}_1 = £6225$
For Point 2, $X_2 = 15$ and $\hat{Y}_2 = £8125$
Check that the line passes through the point $\bar{X} = 37.3$, $\bar{Y} = £7520$.

With the drawing of the regression line through our scatter of data points we have now achieved the object of regression analysis. We have used our observations to calculate a line giving us the average linear relationship between an independent variable (X) and a dependent variable (Y) according to the linear regression equation $\hat{Y} = a + bx$. We are able to express that relationship with reference to the two regression coefficients a (the intercept, showing the hypothetical level of Y where

$X = 0$) and b (the slope, giving the increase in Y for a single unit increase in X). This is very useful, but we should remember from the earlier discussion of regression and correlation analyses that, while the regression equation expresses the average increase in Y for a unit increase in X, it does not inform us about the closeness of association between the two variables. In itself, it cannot tell us how great the residual variance is around the line (i.e. how widely the points are scattered). It is possible to calculate a linear regression through *any* set of points, but it only makes sense to do it if the scatterplot shows some sort of linear relationship. If the points on a scatterplot are randomly scattered, or show some pattern which is non-linear, then the residual variation will be very great, and the regression line will be a bad predictor of any particular case's value on Y.

Correlation

Correlation analysis is used to determine how good the regression line is as a predictor of Y. In other words, how closely or widely dispersed the observed values of Y are from the regression line. Like other measures of association it summarizes this information in a standardized value. We can illustrate the principle of correlation by returning to our example.

We know from Table 8.1 that Company 1 *in fact* has an average wage for unskilled employees of £6500, while the prediction from the regression equation is £6255. There is clearly a discrepancy here between the *observed score* (£6500) and the *predicted score* (£6225) and Table 8.3 shows a discrepancy of some sort for all the companies. However, note that the discrepancy is now less than it would have been had we guessed the score only on the basis of $\bar{Y} = £7520$ – once again, PRE has worked! Nevertheless there is a discrepancy between Y-observed and Y-predicted, i.e. between Y and $\hat{Y}$. In consequence the regression equation needs to be rewritten as:

Mean unskilled wage in the ith company =
8532.32 + (–27.14 × percentage unskilled women employees) + e

where e is known as the 'error term'. In general the linear equation is rewritten as

$$Y = a + bX + e$$

We use the extent of these errors over all the cases to measure the degree of residual variance, i.e. the amount of variance we cannot explain by using the regression line for the linear relationship between X and Y as a predictor. Residual variance will, of course, never be greater than total variance. The proportion to which it is less is the proportion of variance explained by the linear regression of X on Y, i.e.

$$r^2 = \frac{\text{total variance} - \text{residual variance}}{\text{total variance}}$$

The proportion of variance explained is called r^2 ('r-squared'). What r^2 shows us is the *proportion* of variation in Y which is explained by the linear relationship between X and Y. In other words it tells us how well the linear model fits the data. The lower limit of r^2 is zero and its upper limit is 1.0. Obviously zero indicates no linear relationship between X and Y and 1.0 would mean that all our data points fell along the regression line (i.e. all the variation in Y is accounted for by the relationship with X). In fact, r^2 is just the squared value of a measure rejoicing in the name of the *Pearson Product – Moment Correlation Coefficient, r*, which is a normed asymmetric measure of association similar to those we have met before, and is calculated as:

$$r = \sqrt{\frac{SXY}{(SXX)\ (SYY)}}$$

where SXY and SXX are calculated as we saw above, and

$$SYY = \Sigma(Y - \bar{Y})^2 = \frac{\Sigma Y^2 - (\Sigma Y)^2}{n}$$

r varies between –1 and +1. If all the (X, Y) pairs lie on a line and the slope is positive (i.e. b is positive) $r = +1$. If all the (X,Y) pairs lie on a negatively sloping line $r = -1$. If $r = 0$ this means that there is no *linear* relationship between X and Y (there may be a non-linear relationship, however, such as a U-shaped curve). Be aware also that a high r or r^2 value does *not* demonstrate a causal relationship between X and Y. All it tells us is that there is a strong linear relationship between the two variables. Inferences concerning causes belong in the realm of theory.

The following points should be noted.

1 A regression analysis of the type we have shown, i.e. a simple linear regression involves a number of assumptions, among them:
   • That the relationship between X and Y is linear (if it is not, there are ways of mathematically transforming the data so that it is).
   • That the distribution of variable Y is normal for any value of variable X. This assumption only applies if we are interested in the *statistical significance* of r (see Part III). It isn't always easy to know if these assumptions are valid, but they may be investigated by plotting the *residuals* on a scatter diagram against X. No pattern should be evident in this plot.
2 A regression line can be used to make projections – imagine a scatterplot of income by age. It is *possible* from the regression line to predict within what limits the income received by an individual of age x will

be at some older age. However, it must be borne in mind that such predictions depend upon the relationship between the dependent and independent variables remaining the *same* for the period over which the projection is made; if this relationship changes, then the prediction will not be valid. Many unfortunate mistakes have been made in this way ...

3 Likewise, it cannot be stressed too often that a correlation is not a cause. In the example above we would need *individual* level data to show that unskilled women are paid less than unskilled men. Even if we had such data we would not get very far in determining *why* this is so, but we would certainly want to know!

Key concepts

Make sure you have understood the following key concepts:

- simple linear regression
- scatterplot
- regression line
- residual variance
- regression coefficients
- correlation analysis

Multiple choice questions

N.B. More than one answer may be correct!

1 Is the equation for a straight line used in the simple linear regression model written as:

    (i) $b + aX$?

    (ii) $aX + bX$?

    (iii) $a + bX$?

    (iv) $aY + bX$?

2 Are *both a* and *b* coefficients:

(i)   correlation coefficients?

(ii) regression coefficients?

(iii) intercepts?

(iv) slopes?

3 What is r^2:

(i)   a (squared) correlation coefficient?

(ii) the residual variance in a regression analysis?

(iii) a (squared) regression coefficient?

(iv) the proportion of variance explained in a regression analysis?

And now try Exercise 3.

Exercise 3

For this exercise you should:

- Create another SPSS data file containing the data shown in Table 8.1.
- Produce the scatterplot showing the relationship between the two variables.
- In SPSS/PC+ produce the regression statistics and correlation coefficient (see below for instructions). Draw the least-squares regression line by hand (i.e. approximately) on to the scatterplot.
- In SPSS FOR WINDOWS make sure that the least-squares regression line is drawn on to the scatterplot by the computer (see below for instructions).

SPSS/PC+

In SPSS/PC+ use the procedure PLOT to produce regression statistics and scatterplots. This can be found in the 'graph data' sub-menu of the Main Menu. You can find the basic SPSS syntax for the PLOT procedure in Chapter 4, but you might also want to use the following sub-commands:

/FORMAT REGRESSION   (to print regression coefficients)
/VSIZE 60   (to change vertical axis length)
/HSIZE 100   (to change horizontal axis length)

SPSS FOR WINDOWS

In SPSS FOR WINDOWS it is necessary to write the syntax for the PLOT procedure directly into the syntax window since there is no dialog box available. You can find the basic SPSS syntax for the PLOT procedure in Chapter 4. When you run the PLOT procedure the scatterplot will appear as an icon at the bottom of your screen called 'Chart Carousel'. Double-click this icon to enter the Chart Carousel window and view the scatterplot. If you include the sub-command:

/FORMAT REGRESSION

in the PLOT procedure the regression line will be shown drawn on to the scatterplot. Print the scatterplot by accessing the Print item of the Files menu for the Chart Carousel window. (There is an SPSS procedure called REGRESSION, which has its own dialog box in SPSS FOR WINDOWS. However, it is designed for multiple regression models and is more advanced than we need at this stage.)

Make sure that the scatterplot has marked on it (i) the regression line and (ii) the position and value of the intercept. Write a few lines showing that you can interpret the regression coefficients a and b, and the correlation coefficient, r, in this example. What does the analysis tell you?

Inferential data analysis in social research

9 From sample to population: the idea of inferential statistics

Aims

- To understand the purpose of statistical significance testing.
- To describe the distribution of repeated sample means, the confidence interval and the null hypothesis.
- To explain and interpret a *t*-test for the difference between two sample means.

The statistics we have dealt with so far are all known as 'descriptive statistics' – that is, they *describe* the relationship between variables. However, one of the most common problems in data analysis occurs when we wish to say something about a larger 'population' based upon a sample of observations taken from that population, and it is with analyses designed to cope with this problem that Part IV of the book is concerned. A 'population' in the context we are referring to means simply the whole group of people we want to say something about; an example might be all mothers, or everyone aged between 20 and 24. Sometimes, the group we are interested in will be sufficiently small or specialized so that we can interview everybody; for example, everyone on a Youth Training Scheme in a small town. In general, though, in social research we will need to use **inferential statistics** to draw conclusions about a population from a sample of interviews. Supposing we wanted to know the mean value of some variable in a population; mean age of mothers, for example. Clearly, we cannot interview all mothers, but we could take a random sample of mothers, and calculate a sample mean. It is unlikely that this sample mean will be exactly the same as the true mean for all mothers, and it is therefore referred to as a 'sample estimate' of the mean. However, by using inferential statistics, it is possible to *infer* the likely range of values of the true population mean. So 'inferential' statistics are an important component of the analyses we would want to carry out on sample survey data. From the 'sample estimates' of measures of central tendency and variability we are able to infer things about the likely range of these measures within the whole population. It is important therefore to be clear about the distinction between the sample estimate and the population values of these estimates.

Conventionally, when inferential statistics are used, Greek letters denote the values of measures for the whole population, while Roman letters denote sample estimates, e.g.:

	Population value	Sample estimate
Mean	μ (mu)	$\bar{x}$
Standard deviation	σ (sigma)	s
Proportion	π (pi)	p

Note that we have switched here to using *lower case* Roman script. This helps to emphasize the fact that from this point on in the text we are using Roman script to denote *sample estimates*, while Greek script is used to denote the *population values*.

Probability distributions

Clearly, what we now need to know is exactly how to make inferences about population values from the sample estimates. If we have a particular sample estimate, for instance the proportion of employed women in the British Class Survey engaged in a particular occupation, we want to be able to infer the likely range of the proportion in that occupation among *all* employed women in the population. To do this, we first have to return to the idea of variable *distributions*.

We have already come across an important distribution for a continuous variable: the *normal distribution* (see Chapter 5). The normal distribution is really a mathematical idealization – called a 'probability distribution' – of some actual population distributions, such as those for the interval-level variables height and weight. The normal distribution is a symmetric, bell-shaped curve, which can be defined mathematically by its mean (μ) and its standard deviation (σ). We saw that, using the normal distribution, it is possible to calculate standardized z-scores via the formula

$$z = \frac{x_i - \bar{x}}{s},$$

or in the new terminology we are using,

$$z = \frac{x_i - \mu}{\sigma} = \frac{(\text{individual value}) - (\text{mean})}{\text{standard deviation}}$$

Since the percentage of the distribution falling above or below any particular z-score can be worked out from the mathematical properties of the normal distribution, it is possible therefore to relate scores in one test to scores in another according to where in the distribution for each test an individual's score fell (as we did in Chapter 5). Now let us turn to how this relates to statistical inference. Suppose we take a random sample from a population and calculate the mean ($\bar{x}$) of an interval-level variable like age or income. Since we have only taken a sample, we know that this value is likely to be somewhat different from the real population mean, due simply to the fact that we have not sampled the whole population, and there is a chance factor involved in who we *do* sample. This chance factor is referred to as *sampling error*. How can we assess the extent of this error?

Intuitively sampling error (i.e. the accuracy of our sample mean as an estimate of the population mean) will depend on two things:

1 The size of the sample.
2 The variability of the variable in the population.

The bigger the sample, the less chance we have of picking for our sample only individuals with extreme values of the variable we are interested in, and the better chance we have of approximating the true population value. In addition, the less variability there is in the population itself, the fewer extreme values there will be to pick for the sample.

Imagine we took a series of samples from the same population, and calculated a mean value ($\bar{x}$) for our variable from each sample. What we would then end up with is a series of sample means which would to a greater or lesser extent approximate the true population mean. We could then plot these sample means as a distribution on a graph. If we have taken sufficiently large samples, most of these means will cluster around the true population mean – but simply by chance there are bound to be a few sample means which are nothing like the true population mean; some will exceed it by a relatively large amount and some will be considerably less than it. In fact it turns out that the shape of our **distribution of repeated sample means** will tend to approximate the shape of the normal distribution (a symmetric, bell-shaped curve) and that this is true even when the distribution of values for the variable in the population is relatively heavily skewed. What we now have is a *distribution of sample means*, which is normal in shape, and has a mean which is equal to the population mean (Figure 9.1).

Just as the normal distribution is defined by its mean and standard deviation, so is the distribution of repeated sample means. The central value of the distribution is simply the population mean (μ), while the standard deviation of the distribution of sample means (called the *standard error* – see below) is given by:

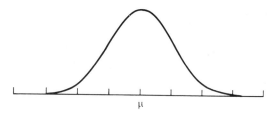

Figure 9.1 Distribution of repeated sample means

$$\frac{\sigma}{\sqrt{n}}$$

σ is just the familiar population standard deviation for the variable concerned (i.e. a measure of population variability), while n is the number of cases in the (repeated) sample. We can see, then, that the *shape* of the distribution as defined by its standard deviation (standard error) depends on:

(i) the size of the sample; and
(ii) the variability of the variable in the population, indicated by the population standard deviation σ.

Note that we are simply restating here what was said previously: sampling error (the accuracy of the sample estimate as a measure of the population value) depends on the size of the sample and the variability of the variable in the population. We call the standard deviation of the distribution of repeated sample means the **standard error of the mean**, or SE ($\bar{x}$), in order to distinguish it from the population standard deviation σ. What SE ($\bar{x}$) actually is, then, is a measure of sampling error. It gives us an indication of how accurate our sample estimate is likely to be as a measure of the true population mean. Where SE ($\bar{x}$) is large, then the mean from any *one* sample is less likely to be a good approximation of the population mean than when SE ($\bar{x}$) is relatively small. How can we use this information?

Since, as we saw, the distribution of sample means approximates to the normal distribution, all the properties of the normal distribution that we described in Chapter 5 can also be applied to the distribution of sample means. For example, we already know that 95 per cent of all values of a continuous, normally distributed variable in a population fall between plus or minus 1.96 standard deviations from the mean (Figure 5.6). In exactly the same way in the distribution of sample means, 95 per cent of repeated sample means will fall between plus or minus 1.96 standard-errors-of-the-mean SE ($\bar{x}$) and the population mean μ. Since we know, then, that 95 per cent of sample means lie within the interval

$$\mu \pm 1.96 \text{ SE } (\bar{x})$$

it follows that there is a 95 per cent chance of getting a sample mean within these limits, if we were to take only *one* sample. (Remember that the distribution of repeated sample means is only a theoretical distribution; in practice we take only one sample of size n and get one value of $\bar{x}$. However, we can treat this value *as if* it were taken from our theoretical distribution of sample means.) In other words, the range between the population mean at the centre of the distribution of repeated sample means and 1.96 times the standard error of the mean in either direction (i.e. lower or higher than the population mean) will contain 95 per cent of all sample means. Since the standard error can quite simply be calculated from the sample data (in the same way that we calculated the standard deviation in Chapter 5) we can actually calculate the range around the population mean within which we expect a sample mean to fall. This is fine as far as it goes, but this is not in fact what we generally want to do. In most cases what we will be interested in is calculating (or inferring) the likely range of the *population* mean from the sample estimate, i.e. the same question, but put the other way round. We take one sample, and want to use it to make inferences about the population mean. Helpfully, the equation works both ways round. An alternative to saying that 95 per cent of sample means will fall between the limits $\mu \pm 1.96$ SE $(\bar{x})$ is to say that there is a 95 per cent chance that the range $\bar{x} \pm 1.96$ SE $(\bar{x})$ will include the real (unknown) population mean μ.

The interval $\bar{x} \pm 1.96$ SE $(\bar{x})$ is called a 95 per cent 'confidence interval', since we can say with 95 per cent confidence that the real population mean lies within the interval plus or minus 1.96 SE $(\bar{x})$ from our sample mean $(\bar{x})$. Since we can calculate both $\bar{x}$ and SE $(\bar{x})$ from our sample data, we have succeeded in the task we initially set ourselves: inferring the likely range of our population mean from the sample estimate. We are now in a position to put into practice some of the theory we have gone through by doing a test of **statistical significance** for the difference between a population mean and a sample mean.

Tests of significance for interval-level variables

Imagine we were investigating the relationship between unemployment and age among men. We take a random sample of 25 unemployed men whose mean age turns out to be 32. Supposing we also know that the mean age of employed men is 40, and that the standard deviation is 6 years (in practice, of course, we are unlikely to know these values). We want to know whether it is possible that the difference between our two mean ages 32 $(\bar{x})$ and 40 (μ) is due only to sampling error. In other words, is it possible that the mean age of unemployed men is really the same as that for employed men, and that we just happen to have chosen a sample with a low mean by chance, or is the mean age of unemployed men really different from that for employed men?

In order to answer this question, we must first advance what is known as a **null hypothesis**, which states that there is no real difference between the sample mean $\bar{x}$ and the population mean μ. In other words, the sample is drawn from a population with mean μ. The null hypothesis is our working hypothesis, which we proceed to test statistically. Here we are following the same process as we described earlier when we were examining cross-tabulations. We asked, what would the cell frequencies be if there were no relationship between the dependent and independent variables? We then proceeded to calculate a set of expected frequencies under the null hypothesis of no relationship, and compared them to our observed frequencies. We do the same sort of thing here. We *assume* that the sample of unemployed men comes from the population of employed men, with a mean age of 40. This implies, of course, that there is no difference between the mean age of unemployed and employed men. We then ask what the chances are of getting a mean age in our sample of unemployed men as low as 32, given that the sample is taken from a population with a mean age of 40? Now, we know that the mean ages of repeated random samples of 25 individuals will be distributed normally (distribution of repeated sample means). Under our null hypothesis the mean of this distribution is 40 (the population mean, or μ), with a standard error of

$$\frac{\sigma}{\sqrt{n}} = \frac{6}{\sqrt{25}} = 1.2 \text{ years}$$

Referring again to the properties of the normal distribution, we know that 95 per cent of sample means lie within the range $\mu \pm 1.96$ SE $(\bar{x})$. Therefore, sample means *outside* this range will occur in only 5 per cent of cases, i.e. with probability of only 0.05. In the case we are dealing with here, the range containing 95 per cent of repeated sample means is:

$$40 \underset{\uparrow}{\pm} 1.96 \times \underset{\uparrow}{1.2} \text{ years} = 40 \pm 2.35 \text{ years} = 37.65 \text{ to } 42.35 \text{ years}$$
$$\text{mean} \qquad \text{SE } (\bar{x})$$

However, the sample mean age for unemployed men which we have derived from our sample (32) lies *outside* the range 37.65–42.35. Therefore we can conclude either:

(i) that by some chance aberration we have picked a sample whose mean is so extreme as to occur in only 5 per cent of repeated samples (i.e. located right out on the extreme ends of the distribution of repeated sample means centred on μ); or

(ii) that our null hypothesis that there is no difference in the mean ages of unemployed and employed men is incorrect.

Of these two possibilities, and in the absence of other information, (i) is less likely, and we conclude that there is in fact a real difference in mean age between these groups. We refer to this difference as *statistically significant*. The probability that we are wrong in drawing this conclusion is less than 0.05. This is so because if the null hypothesis were correct, and there were no real difference between the ages of unemployed and employed men, it is still *possible* that by chance we could have picked a sample with a mean as extreme as this – but the chance of doing so is less than 5 out of 100, or less than 5 per cent. This is usually expressed as $P < 0.05$ ('P less than point zero five'), and we may refer to $\bar{x}$ as 'statistically significantly different from μ at the $P < 0.05$ level'. What we conclude in terms of the original question is that there *is* a statistically significant difference between the mean age for employed and unemployed men. It appears that unemployed men are likely to be significantly younger on average than employed men (compare mean ages). The null hypothesis is therefore rejected. If, however, our sample mean had fallen *inside* the boundaries of the range within which we would expect to find 95 per cent of repeated sample means centred on a population mean age of 40, then we would *not* have had any good statistical evidence to reject the null hypothesis. Indeed, we would expect 95 times out of 100 to find a sample mean within this range if the null hypothesis is correct. We could write this as $P > 0.05$ ('P greater than point zero five'), since the chance that we would be wrong in rejecting the null hypothesis in this case is greater than 5 per cent. The difference between $\bar{x}$ and μ therefore would not be statistically significant.

The 5 per cent level of statistical significance ($P < 0.05$) is conventionally taken as the outermost limit of statistical significance. Any probability of being wrong in rejecting the null hypothesis of greater than 5 per cent is deemed to be sufficient to justify a conclusion of no statistical significance. These rules are essentially arbitrary. It is also quite common to see results expressed in terms of a 1 per cent or even a 0.1 per cent level of statistical significance ($P < 0.01$ and $P < 0.001$ respectively). These are more stringent boundaries for determining statistical significance. The equivalent equation for calculating the range within which we would expect 99 per cent of repeated sample means to fall (i.e. corresponding to the 1 per cent level of statistical significance) is:

$$\mu \pm 2.58 \, \text{SE} \, (\bar{x})$$

Here the normal distribution's 5 per cent boundary of $\pm 1.96 \, \text{SE}(\bar{x})$ is replaced by the 1 per cent boundary, $\pm 2.58 \, \text{SE} \, (\bar{x})$. You can see why this is so by referring to the normal distribution in Figure 5.6 (p. 105). Overall, 5 per cent of the distribution falls outside the limits given by ± 1.96

standard deviations (2.5 per cent above and 2.5 per cent below), while only 1 per cent of the distribution falls outside the limits given by ± 2.58 standard deviations (0.5 per cent above and 0.5 per cent below).

Any case in which there is a statistically significant difference with P <0.01 is conventionally referred to as *highly statistically significant*, since we will be wrong in rejecting the null hypothesis of no difference between μ and $\bar{x}$ in fewer than 1 per cent of samples. Quite often you will also come across significance levels of 0.000 on a computer printout. This means that there is *very* strong evidence for rejecting the null hypothesis. The result is highly statistically significant, since it is less than 0.01, or even than 0.001.

Estimating σ: the 't-distribution'

Another way of arriving at the same result would have been to calculate z-scores in the way that we showed in Chapter 5, substituting SE ($\bar{x}$) for σ in the denominator:

$$z = \frac{\bar{x} - \mu}{\text{SE } (\bar{x})} = \frac{\bar{x} - \mu}{\left(\dfrac{\sigma}{\sqrt{n}} \right)}$$

In this example:

$$z = \frac{32 - 40}{1.2} = -6.67$$

If z is greater than 1.96 (ignore the minus sign) we have a result which is statistically significant at the 5 per cent level ($P < 0.05$), and if it is greater than 2.58 the result is statistically significant at the 1 per cent level ($P < 0.01$). Here we have a result which is much greater than 2.58. We therefore have strong evidence to reject the null hypothesis. We had already arrived at this conclusion by calculating the confidence interval given by $\bar{x} \pm 1.96$ SE ($\bar{x}$), but the method shown here of comparing the z-score with the conventional boundaries of statistical significance is often the simplest way of establishing the significance of a result. Clearly, though, to do this calculation as it stands we need to know the value of both the population mean (μ) and standard deviation (σ). In fact, σ, the population standard deviation, is very often not known, but may be replaced by the standard deviation of the sample, s, since this is our best existing *estimate* of the population standard deviation σ. However, in order to use s as an estimate of σ we can no longer really use normal distribution z-scores, because we have introduced another source of sampling error into the equation (the error involved in estimating σ from s).

We have to use instead another, similar, probability distribution, known as the 'student's *t*-distribution', and calculate *t*-scores instead of *z*-scores to perform a ***t*-test**. Thus:

$$t = \frac{\bar{x} - \mu}{\left(\frac{s}{\sqrt{n}}\right)}$$

This is similar to the calculation for a *z*-score shown above, except that we have replaced σ (the population standard deviation) with *s* (the sample estimate). The *t*-distribution (Figure 9.2) can be thought of as being like the normal distribution, except that in general it has a flatter shape (more platykurtic), which varies according to the size of the sample. As sample size increases the *t*-distribution becomes more similar in shape to the normal distribution. This happens because the larger the sample size the better *s* will be as an estimate of σ, and the closer the *t*-score will be to the *z*-score. If the sample size is small, however, then due to sampling error the value of *s* may not be very close to σ. We take account of this by referring to the sample size when drawing statistical inferences based on the *t*-distribution.

Remember that when we discussed the normal distribution, we saw that 95 per cent of the area under the curve falls within the range μ ± 1.96 σ, while 99 per cent falls within the range μ ± 2.58 σ. These values, used by convention in statistical significance testing, are known as the *critical values* of *z*-scores. They are 'critical' because they are used to determine whether, or by how much, a particular sample mean is statistically significantly different from the population mean. In this instance, however, we are using *s* as an *estimate* of σ, and therefore we need to use more conservative critical values for *t* in order to determine whether a result is statistically significant, since we have introduced a new source of error into the equation. This is why we have described the *t*-distribution as 'flatter' than the normal distribution; it has *wider* critical values (i.e. more conservative). The wider the critical values are the larger the *t*-score has to be in order to infer a statistically significant difference. Because the shape of the *t*-distribution varies according to sample size (approaching the normal distribution where *n* is large), the critical limits of *t* depend on the

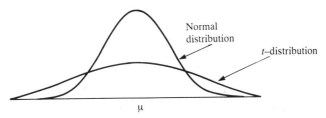

Figure 9.2 The *t*-distribution

Table 9.1 Critical values of t

v	$P = 10\%$	$P = 5\%$	$P = 1\%$	$P = 0.1\%$
1	6.31	12.71	63.66	636.62
2	2.92	4.30	9.93	31.60
3	2.35	3.18	5.84	12.92
4	2.13	2.78	4.60	8.61
5	2.02	2.57	4.03	6.87
6	1.94	2.45	3.71	5.96
7	1.90	2.37	3.50	5.41
8	1.86	2.31	3.36	5.04
9	1.83	2.26	3.25	4.78
10	1.81	2.23	3.17	4.59
11	1.80	2.20	3.11	4.44
12	1.78	2.18	3.06	4.32
13	1.77	2.16	3.01	4.22
14	1.76	2.15	2.98	4.14
15	1.75	2.13	2.95	4.07
16	1.75	2.12	2.92	4.02
17	1.74	2.11	2.90	3.97
18	1.73	2.10	2.88	3.92
19	1.73	2.09	2.86	3.88
20	1.73	2.09	2.85	3.85
21	1.72	2.08	2.83	3.82
22	1.72	2.07	2.82	3.79
23	1.71	2.07	2.81	3.77
24	1.71	2.06	2.80	3.75
25	1.71	2.06	2.79	3.73
26	1.71	2.06	2.78	3.71
27	1.70	2.05	2.77	3.69
28	1.70	2.05	2.76	3.67
29	1.70	2.05	2.76	3.66
30	1.70	2.04	2.75	3.65
40	1.68	2.02	2.70	3.55
50	1.68	2.01	2.68	3.49
60	1.67	2.00	2.66	3.46
70	1.67	1.99	2.65	3.43
80	1.67	1.99	2.64	3.41
90	1.66	1.99	2.63	3.40
100	1.66	1.98	2.63	3.39
00	1.645	1.960	2.576	3.291

sample size, or the *degrees of freedom* associated with our calculation of the t-score (the terminology is not important at this stage, we will come across it again later). Whereas it is quite easy to remember the fixed critical values 1.96 and 2.58 for the normal distribution, it is necessary to look up the critical values of t, which shift according to how many degrees of freedom you have, in a published statistical table. An example of such a table is given in Table 9.1. Study the figures in the table for a moment. The degrees of freedom (in this case, sample size minus one) is denoted by v (pronounced 'nu'). Observe that as the degrees of freedom increase (i.e. as sample size increases and s becomes a better estimate of μ), so the critical values of t get closer to the critical values of z. For example, with a sample size of 16, and thus 15 degrees of freedom, the critical values of t are 2.13 and 2.95 for the 5 per cent and 1 per cent levels of significance as compared to 1.96 and 2.58 for the normal distribution. With a sample size of 30, and thus 29 degrees of freedom, the critical values of the t-distribution at the 5 per cent and 1 per cent levels are 2.05 and 2.76 – nearer to the critical values of the normal distribution. With an infinite sample size ($v = 00$ at the base of the table) the critical values of the t-distribution are identical to those of the normal distribution. Fortunately, the computer will calculate t-scores and levels of statistical significance for you, but it is important to understand how and why t-scores differ from z-scores. In general, the t-distribution should be used for small sample sizes; certainly anything under 50 or so. This is so because sampling error is likely to be greater with small sample sizes. It is therefore prudent to use more conservative critical values in determining statistical significance with smaller sample sizes.

Comparison of sample means

In the examples we have used so far we have been comparing a single sample mean $\bar{x}$, with a population value μ. However, very often what we will want to do is to compare the means of two *samples*, and ask whether it is possible that they were drawn from the same larger population (whose mean is unknown), or whether, in fact, the sample means themselves are statistically significantly different. You might, for instance, want to compare the mean ages of men and women in a particular occupation. Under the null hypothesis both groups come from a single population with a single mean age. You need to establish how likely it is that any difference which you observe from your sample is due purely to sampling error.

In order to cope with this problem, let us first consider two population distributions with means μ_1 and μ_2 and variances σ_1^2 and σ_2^2. In exactly the same way that taking the mean from successive samples gives us a distribution of repeated sample means, if we take repeated samples of size n_1 and n_2 from the two distributions above and calculate $\bar{x}_1 - \bar{x}_2$ each time, we would end up with a distribution of the repeated *differences* between $\bar{x}_1$ and $\bar{x}_2$. Just as the distribution of repeated sample means turned out to be a normal distribution, so does the distribution of repeated differences between two sample means. This is because most $\bar{x}_1 - \bar{x}_2$ differences will be similar to the true $\mu_1 - \mu_2$ difference, but some will be extreme. And if we plot these repeated differences we will end up with a normal distribution curve. The mean of this new distribution $\bar{x}_1 - \bar{x}_2$

Figure 9.3 Two population distributions

will equal $\mu_1 - \mu_2$, while the variance is the sum of the individual variances:

$$\frac{\sigma_1^2}{n_1} + \frac{\sigma_2^2}{n_2}$$

The standard error of the distribution of differences between sample means is just the square root of the two summed variances:

$$SE(\bar{x}_1 - \bar{x}_2) = \sqrt{\frac{\sigma_1^2}{n_1} + \frac{\sigma_2^2}{n_2}}$$

This is just the equivalent measure to SE ($\bar{x}$) for the distribution of repeated sample means. We are now in a position to calculate a z-score in exactly the same way as we did above when comparing a single sample mean with a population mean. First let us state the null hypothesis: we hypothesize that the samples were taken from populations whose means μ_1 and μ_2 are equal. The difference between our actual observed means $\bar{x}_1$ and $\bar{x}_2$ is just due to sampling error. The z-score is calculated using the same basic equation as before, only this time replacing $\bar{x}$ by $\bar{x}_1 - \bar{x}_2$ and μ by $\mu_1 - \mu_2$ (which according to our null hypothesis are equal). So we have:

$$z = \frac{(\bar{x}_1 - \bar{x}_2) - (\mu_1 - \mu_2)}{SE\ (\bar{x}_1 - \bar{x}_2)}$$

Remember

$$SE\ (\bar{x}_1 - \bar{x}_2) = \sqrt{\frac{\sigma_1^2}{n_1} + \frac{\sigma_2^2}{n_2}}$$

and since (according to the null hypothesis), μ_1 and μ_2 are equal $(\mu_1 - \mu_2)$ = 0. This term therefore drops out of the equation. The interpretation of the resulting z-score is exactly the same as for the example with a single sample mean. If the z-score calculated is greater than the appropriate critical values of the normal distribution then we conclude that there is

Age of first child-bearing	Women with educational qualifications	Women with no qualifications
15	3	6
16	13	17
17	17	24
18	20	25
21	18	12
23	6	2
25	1	–
n =	78	86
Σx =	1 443	1 518
$\bar{x}$ =	18.5	17.65
Σx^2 =	27 133	27 088
$(\Sigma x)^2/n$ =	26 695.5	26 794.47
$\Sigma(x - \bar{x})^2 =$		
$\quad \Sigma x^2 - (\Sigma x)^2/n$ =	437.5	293.53

$$s = \sqrt{\frac{\Sigma(x - \bar{x})^2}{n - 1}} \quad = \quad 2.38 \qquad\qquad 1.86$$

$$SE(\bar{x}_1 - \bar{x}_2) \quad = \quad \sqrt{\frac{2.38^2}{78} + \frac{1.86^2}{86}} = 0.34$$

$$z = \frac{18.5 - 17.65}{0.34} \quad = 2.5$$

$$P < 0.05 > 0.01$$

a statistically significant difference between the two sample means and that we have reason to reject the null hypothesis of no difference between the population means. The two samples are most likely *not* taken from the same population. (Again, if our sample sizes are small, we may use the *t*-distribution to determine our critical values, and calculate *t*-scores instead of *z*-scores, using a weighted average of the sample variances to obtain a single estimate of the true variance σ^2.)

Let us look at an example to clarify what we have said: In a study of the mean age of first childbearing in a developing country the following distributions were obtained for two samples of women aged 40–44, one group with no educational qualifications and one group with school certificates and above. The null hypothesis is that level of education has no influence on age at first childbearing.

We conclude from the resulting *z*-score that we have some (although not particularly strong) evidence for rejecting the null hypothesis. The *z*-score falls between the critical values of the normal distribution for the

5 per cent (1.96) and 1 per cent (2.58) level. This is written as $P < 0.05 > 0.01$. The two sample mean ages at first childbearing are statistically significantly different at the 5 per cent level, but not at the 1 per cent level. The two samples were *probably* drawn from different populations (i.e. populations whose means are really different). Looking at the sample means, we may conclude that in the population from which these samples were taken, women with no educational qualifications tended to have children at younger ages than women with some qualifications.

Having discussed the principles of inferential statistics, and illustrated their use with respect to interval-level variables, Chapter 10 goes on to discuss inferential statistics for categoric variables before turning to the important subject of the assumptions underlying statistical significance testing.

Principles of statistical significance testing: Summary

- The idea is to make statements about the characteristics of a population from a **sample** taken from that population.
- We want to know whether a difference that we have found between groups in our sample is sufficiently great, given the sample size, to conclude that that difference also exists in the population, i.e. whether the difference is **statistically significant**.
- To do this we first set up a 'null hypothesis', which states that there is *no* difference between the groups in the population: the difference we have found in the sample is simply due to 'sampling error'.
- We test this hypothesis using a test of statistical significance, e.g. Chi-square, *t*-test, etc. These tests assess whether the difference between sample groups is sufficiently great, given the sample size, to assume that this difference also exists in the population.
- We express this assessment in the form of a probability of being wrong in *rejecting* the null hypothesis, i.e. a small probability (*P*-value) of less than 5% means that there probably *is* a real difference between the groups in the population, and that we should reject the null hypothesis (since the probability that we will be wrong in doing so is very small).
- This result (a statistically significant result) is therefore generally written as '$P < 0.05$'.

Note on computing

The SPSS T-TEST procedure can be found in SPSS/PC+ on the 'Comparing Group Means' item of the 'Analyze Data' menu, and in SPSS FOR WINDOWS on the 'Compare Means' item of the Statistics drop-down menu. Read the information and syntax for the T-TEST procedure before continuing (as you should before starting any unfamiliar analysis), but here are a few pointers:

- In general you will be interested in the independent rather than the paired samples test
- T-TEST requires the specification of an interval level dependent variable and the two categories of independent variable to be compared, e.g.

  T-TEST /GROUPS sex (1,2) /VARIABLES income

- Select whether to refer to the 'equal' or 'unequal' values of t by noting the level of statistical significance of Levene's test for the equality of variance, which is shown on the output. If this test is statistically significant, then refer to the 'unequal' value.

Key concepts

Make sure you have understood the following key concepts:

- inferential statistics
- distribution of repeated sample means
- standard error of the mean
- null hypothesis
- statistical significance
- *t*-test

Multiple choice questions

In these questions, one or more answers may be correct.

1 What is the standard deviation of the distribution of repeated sample means referred to as:

   (i)   the standard deviation of the sample?

   (ii) the mean error?

   (iii) the sample error?

   (iv) the standard error of the mean?

2 A z-score greater than 5% critical value of the normal distribution is generally indicated as:

   (i) $P < 5\%$?

   (ii) $P > 5\%$?

   (iii) $5\% > P$?

   (iv) $0.05 < P$?

   (v) $P < 0.05$?

3 The interpretation of the above result would be:

   (i)   the null hypothesis is correct;

   (ii) the result is statistically significant;

   (iii) the null hypothesis is rejected;

   (iv) we have no evidence to reject the null hypothesis;

   (v)   the result is not statistically significant.

4 What test of statistical significance for the difference between two sample means should we use with a small sample size:

   (i) χ^2 test?

   (ii) Kendall's tau?

   (iii) t-test?

   (iv) gamma?

10 Tests of significance for categoric variables

Aims

- To undertake and interpret a test for the difference between two sample proportions.
- To undertake and interpret a χ^2 test.
- To understand the assumptions behind, and limitations of, statistical significance tests.

Up to this point, all the inferential statistics we have discussed have related to continuous, interval-level, variables. This is because it is easier to explain the principles behind significance testing using illustrations from data measured at the highest level of measurement. It is for such data that these tests were originally designed. We now turn to cases where nominal or ordinal level variables are used. The simplest example of a nominal variable is one where only two categories are involved (a **dichotomous variable**); for example the variable sex, composed of two categories, male and female. In fact, we can treat the *proportion* in a single category of a two-category variable as similar to a mean, and this often allows us to apply methods derived from the analysis of means to proportions.

Remember that the *normal* probability distribution, from which we derived our z-scores, applies only to continuous interval-level variables. Where a variable has only two categories, such that if an individual case is not in one of the categories it must be in the other, it is usually what is known as a *binomial variable*. The term 'binomial' refers to *another* type of probability distribution. However, as we show below, we do not actually need to describe this distribution here, since in many instances the familiar normal distribution will do instead. Imagine that we take a random sample of 10 people ($n = 10$). Of these, the number of women, say, is 6 ($r = 6$). The number of men is therefore $n - r$ or 4. The *proportion* of women (p) is defined by $\dfrac{r}{n}$ = 0.6. The estimated variance and standard deviation of r (our sample number of women) is:

variance $(r) = np\,(1-p)$

which in this case would be:

$10 \times 0.6 \times 0.4 = 2.4$

The standard deviation

$(r) = \sqrt{np(1-p)} = 1.5$

We are able to apply these equations to calculate z-scores as for interval-level data by using the so-called **normal approximation to the binomial distribution**. What this means is that for these purposes we can treat a nominal-level binomial variable as if it were an interval-level variable, since under certain conditions the binomial probability distribution can be approximated by the normal distribution. Here's how. In Figure 10.1 the binomial distribution of the number of women resulting from taking repeated samples of size $n = 10$ from a population where the overall proportion of women is 0.6 is shown, with a normal distribution curve superimposed upon it. Note that the curve of the normal distribution follows the shape of the binomial distribution, cutting through the top of each bar at its half-way point. Since the binomial distribution is based on a whole number or count (and is thus presented as a bar chart rather than a curve) it is necessary in the calculation of z-scores to approximate the probability of finding a particular count, say $r = 7$, to the continuous normal distribution curve between 6.5 and 7.5. This is achieved by adding or subtracting 0.5 in the calculation of the z-score. So the binomial probability of finding at least 7 women in a sample of 10 is approximated from

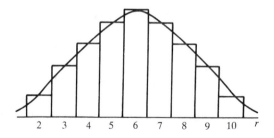

Figure 10.1 Normal approximation to the binomial

the normal distribution by the area under the normal curve from 6.5 to infinity, rather than from 7 to infinity. (This subtracting of 0.5 is known as a 'continuity correction' and will be referred to again.) With this adjustment it is possible to use the properties of the normal distribution to apply to data in the form of binomial proportions. The normal approximation to the binomial distribution works best where the sample size is large, and where p is not too close to either 0 or 1.

Let us apply these considerations to the process of making inferences about a population based on a sample estimate for a binomial variable (i.e. where the data involve proportions rather than means, as they usually do in social research). The procedure here is exactly analogous to that for interval level variables, except that here we are interested in making inferences about π (the population proportion) based on p (the sample estimate) rather than about μ based on $\bar{x}$. In the same way that SE $(\bar{x})$ is the standard deviation of the distribution of repeated sample means, SE (p) is the standard deviation of the distribution of repeated sample proportions, and it is calculated as:

$$\text{SE}(p) = \sqrt{\frac{\pi(1 - \pi)}{n}}$$

where π is the population proportion. For large samples we can usually rely on the normal approximation to the binomial distribution and assume that 95 per cent of repeated sample proportions would be within the limits

$$\pi \pm 1.96 \text{ SE}(p)$$

in exactly the same way that we expect 95 per cent of repeated sample *means* to be within the limits

$$\mu + 1.96 \text{ SE}(\bar{x}).$$

Again, it is generally the case that π, the population proportion, will not be known when we take a sample. In fact, a sample is often used precisely to estimate the value of π. In this case the equation may be reversed, and we can say with 95 per cent confidence that the true population proportion lies within 1.96 SE (p) of our sample proportion, where the standard error of p is *estimated* as

$$\text{SE}(p) = \sqrt{\frac{p(1 - p)}{n}} \quad \text{(because we do not know } \pi\text{)}$$

Significance testing for a proportion

We can now employ exactly the same z-score formulae we used for testing the statistical significance of the difference between the population mean and the sample mean, substituting:

(i)   the population proportion π for the population mean μ;
(ii) the sample proportion p for the sample mean $\bar{x}$; and
(iii) the standard error of p for the standard error of $\bar{x}$, to arrive at:

$$z = \frac{p - \pi \pm \left(\dfrac{1}{2n}\right)}{SE\,(p)} \quad \text{or} \quad \frac{p - \pi \pm \left(\dfrac{1}{2n}\right)}{\sqrt{\dfrac{\pi(1-\pi)}{n}}}$$

$\pm 1/2n$ is the **continuity correction** and is used in order to make the necessary adjustment from the binomial to the normal distribution, as explained above. Since the continuity correction is just the inverse of two times the sample size, the larger the sample size the smaller will be the effect of the continuity correction. This is because the larger the sample size the more closely the binomial distribution is approximated by the normal. The interpretation of the resulting z-score is, of course, exactly the same. Let us see how we can put this into practice with an example.

In a sample of 100 people in a particular occupation 65 said they identified as middle class, while 35 identified as working class. We know that the overall population proportion identifying as middle class was 55 per cent. We ask if it is reasonable to conclude that our sample could have been taken from a population with $\pi = 0.55$ (or is it more likely that a higher proportion of people in this occupation actually identify as middle class?).

The null hypothesis states that: the difference between the proportion in the particular occupation and the proportion in the population identifying as middle class is merely due to sampling error. We calculate:

$$z = \frac{p - \pi - \left(\dfrac{1}{2n}\right)}{\sqrt{\dfrac{\pi(1-\pi)}{n}}}$$

$$= \frac{0.65 - 0.55 - \dfrac{1}{200}}{\sqrt{\dfrac{0.55\,(0.45)}{100}}}$$

$$= \frac{0.0950}{0.0497}$$

$$= 1.91$$

The result is very slightly less than 1.96. Therefore we have no strong evidence against the null hypothesis and cannot convincingly show that it is wrong. The result is said to be not statistically significant. It seems that there is no significant difference between the proportion identifying as middle class in the occupation we are interested in and in the overall population. However, this example illustrates that we must use our judgement in the interpretation of significance tests. Although conventionally speaking we have a non-significant result, we also know that, if the null hypothesis is correct, we would expect to find a difference between the sample and population proportion as large as this is only *just* over 5 per cent of cases. The difference between a 4.99 per cent chance and a 5 per cent chance of being wrong in rejecting the null hypothesis represents the difference between a significant and a non-significant result. Certainly in a case such as this you would want to show the result and point this out. At the least, it requires 'further investigation'!

Now, as before when we were dealing with sample means, let us turn to the more realistic situation where we want to compare two sample proportions, using the weighted average of p_1 and p_2 as the best available estimate that we have of π, the population proportion. Say we are interested in gender segregation in employment. In this instance we take two samples from different occupations, in order to investigate whether the gender distribution is the same in both. In sample 1, $n = 365$ and the number of women (r) is 61. In sample 2, $n = 201$ and $r = 55$. The null hypothesis is that the same proportion of women workers is found in each occupation, i.e. the population proportions π_1 and π_2 are equal. The two sample proportions are:

$$p_1 = 61/365 = 0.1671$$
$$p_2 = 55/201 = 0.2736$$

Clearly there is a difference between these proportions, and what we need to know is; given these sample sizes, is the difference we have found large enough to be statistically significant? Under the null hypothesis the difference $p_1 - p_2$ is merely due to sampling error. Since

$$\text{var} (p_1) = \frac{\pi(1 - \pi)}{365}$$

and

$$\text{var} (p_2) = \frac{\pi(1 - \pi)}{201}$$

$$SE (p_1 - p_2) = \sqrt{\pi(1 - \pi)\left(\frac{1}{365} + \frac{1}{201}\right)}$$

We now need to replace π (which we don't know) by our pooled estimate of p_1 and p_2, which we can just call p.

$$p = \frac{r_1 + r_2}{n_1 + n_2}$$

$$= \frac{61 + 55}{365 + 201}$$

$$= \frac{116}{566}$$

$$= 0.2049$$

Our estimated standard error is therefore:

$$\text{est. SE } (p_1 - p_2) = \sqrt{p(1-p)\left(\frac{1}{365} + \frac{1}{201}\right)}$$

$$= \sqrt{0.205 \times 0.795 \,(0.00771)}$$

$$= \sqrt{0.00126} = 0.0355$$

Having derived our estimated standard error of $p_1 - p_2$ we are now in a position to calculate the familiar z-score according to the following equation for the difference between two sample proportions:

$$z = \frac{(p_1 - p_2) - (\pi_1 - \pi_2)}{\text{SE } (p_1 - p_2)}$$

Remember the null hypothesis that the same proportion of women are employed in both occupations means that π_1 and π_2 are equal, and the difference between p_1 and p_2 is only due to sampling error. Under the null hypothesis $(\pi_1 - \pi_2)$ is therefore 0, and is cancelled out of the equation. Thus

$$z = \frac{0.1671 - 0.2736}{0.0355} = -3.00$$

Since the z-score exceeds the 99 per cent critical value of the normal distribution (± 2.58) the result is highly statistically significant at $P < 0.01$. We conclude that we have good reason to reject the null hypothesis, and that the proportion of women in the two occupations is likely to be really different (with the occupation from which sample 1 was taken having a lower proportion of women than the occupation from which sample 2 was taken; compare p_1 and p_2). These tests are relatively easy to perform, since all you need to know to do the calculations are the relevant proportions, and the sample numbers on which they are based (both of which can be taken straight from a simple cross-tabulation). Since a lot of data in social research is presented in this form, they are also very useful!

Chi-square (χ^2) tests

Up to this point we have considered tests of significance for interval-level variables, and for proportions (based on the normal approximation to the binomial distribution). The χ^2 **test** (from the Greek letter χ or chi, pronounced 'Ky') is used to determine whether a *set of frequencies* is significantly different from those expected under the null hypothesis. The most common usage for such a test in social research will be in the examination of cross-tabulations, and you may ask for the χ^2 test to be performed in the STATISTICS sub-command of the CROSSTABS procedure in SPSS. This is therefore another commonly used and useful inferential statistic in social research.

We are returning here to some concepts that we introduced when we were discussing the analysis of bivariate cross-tabulated data. We described how one could calculate values of epsilon (ϵ), a rough and ready guide to whether or not two cross-tabulated variables were associated, and of delta (Δ), to show to what extent observed cell frequencies differed from a set of expected frequencies, with the expected frequencies calculated by assuming that there was no relationship between the variables. χ^2 is the test of statistical inference which we use to determine whether the difference between the observed and expected frequencies calculated in this way is statistically significant. In other words we ask: is it likely that our sample has been taken from a population where the frequencies expected under the null hypothesis pertain, or is the difference between observed and expected frequencies so great that we must conclude that the sample was not taken from a population with those expected frequencies?

For instance, we could have used the χ^2 test to compare observed and expected frequencies for the example used above; the comparison of the proportion of female workers in two occupations. This information could of course have been shown in the form of a 2×2 contingency table:

Occupation	Women	Men	Total
Occupation 1	61	304	365
Occupation 2	55	146	201
Total	116	450	566

The null hypothesis was that the same proportion of female workers is found in each occupation. The difference between the proportion of women in the two occupations is due purely to sampling error. To test this hypothesis using the χ^2 test, we first have to calculate the cell frequencies we would have *expected* in the table if the null hypothesis were true and there was, in fact, no difference in the distribution of sex by occupation. We then compare the expected frequencies with the actual or observed frequencies and use the critical values of χ^2 to determine the statistical significance of the difference between them. We followed exactly this process in Chapter 7 when we calculated 'Δ values', which were just the observed minus the expected values for each cell. The χ^2 test enables us to draw a statistical *inference* from these Δ values concerning the likely significance of their magnitude (indicating, of course the size of the observed–expected difference in cell frequencies).

How do we go about doing this? First, we calculate the expected values f_e, or more simply, just E. Remember we did this by multiplying the row total by the column total for each cell and then dividing by the overall total. For women in Occupation 1, for example:

$$E = \frac{\text{row total} \times \text{column total}}{\text{overall total}}$$

$$= \frac{116 \times 365}{566}$$

$$= 74.806$$

because the overall rate for female workers, which we would expect to apply to *both* occupations under the null hypothesis, is 116/566 and we are applying this to a total of 365 people in Occupation 1.

For women in Occupation 2 the overall rate is the same, but this time applied to 201 people:

$$\frac{116 \times 201}{566} = 41.194$$

The overall rate for men is 450/566, applied to the numbers in Occupation 1

$$= \frac{450 \times 365}{566}$$

$$= 290.194$$

and to Occupation 2

$$= \frac{450 \times 201}{566}$$

$$= 159.806$$

Having now got our expected values we need to compare them with our observed values (O). We start to do this by calculating Δ values ($O - E$). What we want to end up with is some overall total value of Δ, indicating the extent of the $O - E$ differences over all the cells in the table. However, we cannot simply add up the Δ values we get because we have derived a sort of 'averaged' table in our expected values, so that some Δ values take positive and some negative signs. The sum of all Δ values added together must be equal to zero. We can overcome this problem (as in the calculation of the variance of a distribution) by *squaring* the $O - E$ differences before adding them. The first part of our formula looks like this, then: $(O - E)^2$.

However, we also need to take account of the relative *magnitude* of the difference compared to that of the expected values themselves, since an $O - E$ difference of 7 with an expected frequency of 700 is clearly not so important in proportional terms as when the expected frequency is only 25. These two considerations give us our formula for comparing observed and expected cell frequencies:

$$\frac{(O - E)^2}{E}$$

Squaring $O - E$ means that the Δ values do not sum to zero when you add all the cells together, while dividing by E relates the magnitude of the Δ value to that of the expected frequency for each cell. The value of χ^2 (given by the procedure CROSSTABS if you ask for the CHISQ statistic on the STATISTICS sub-command) is equal to the sum of these:

$$\chi^2 = \Sigma \frac{(O - E)^2}{E}$$

In other words you add together all the individual cell calculations to arrive at the value of χ^2. Let us now apply this formula to our 2×2 table to calculate χ^2:

Occupation		Women	Men
1	O	61	304
	E	74.806	290.194
	$O - E$	-13.806	13.806
	$(O - E)^2/E$	2.548	0.657
2	O	55	146
	E	41.194	159.806
	$O - E$	13.806	-13.806
	$(O - E)^2/E$	4.627	1.193

$$\chi^2 = 2.548 + 0.657 + 4.627 + 1.193 = 9.025$$

We have now arrived at a value for χ^2, which, in terms of where we go from here, we can think of as being similar to a z-score. To assess the statistical significance of this figure, then, we need to find the corresponding critical values of the χ^2 distribution. It is intuitively obvious that as the number of cells increases, the value of χ^2 is also likely to increase (simply because there are more cell numbers to add together to arrive at χ^2). We therefore need to make some allowance for the number of cells in finding our critical values of χ^2. In general the greater the number of cells, the more conservative the critical values of χ^2 must be to take

Table 10.1 Critical values of χ^2

ν	$P = 10\%$	$P = 5\%$	$P = 1\%$	$P = 0.1\%$
1	2.71	3.84	6.63	10.83
2	4.61	5.99	9.21	13.81
3	6.25	7.81	11.34	16.27
4	7.78	9.49	13.28	18.47
5	9.24	11.07	15.09	20.52
6	10.64	12.59	16.81	22.46
7	12.02	14.07	18.48	24.32
8	13.36	15.51	20.09	26.12
9	14.68	16.92	21.67	27.88
10	15.99	18.31	23.21	29.59
11	17.28	19.68	24.73	31.26
12	18.55	21.03	26.22	32.91
13	19.81	22.36	27.69	34.53
14	21.06	23.68	29.14	36.12
15	22.31	25.00	30.58	37.70
16	23.54	26.30	32.00	39.25
17	24.77	27.59	33.41	40.79
18	25.99	28.87	34.81	42.31
19	27.20	30.14	36.19	43.82
20	28.41	31.41	37.57	45.31
21	29.62	32.67	38.93	46.80
22	30.81	33.92	40.29	48.27
23	32.01	35.17	41.64	49.73
24	33.20	36.42	42.98	51.18
25	34.38	37.65	44.31	52.62
26	35.56	38.89	45.64	54.05
27	36.74	40.11	46.96	55.48
28	37.92	41.34	48.28	56.89
29	39.09	42.56	49.59	58.30
30	40.26	43.77	50.89	59.70
40	51.81	55.76	63.69	73.40
50	63.17	67.50	76.15	86.66
60	74.40	79.08	88.38	99.61
70	85.53	90.53	100.4	112.3
80	96.58	101.9	112.3	124.8
90	107.6	113.1	124.1	137.2
100	118.5	124.3	135.8	149.4

account of this. Thus, like the t-distribution, the χ^2-distribution varies according to the *degrees of freedom* (ν). In the same way that we calculated degrees of freedom as $N - 1$ to find the critical values of the t-distribution, we calculate degrees of freedom for the χ^2 distribution as $(r - 1)$ $(c - 1)$, where r = number of rows in the table and c = number of columns.

In this example, since we have a 2×2 table, $r - 1 = 1$ and $c - 1 = 1$, and the degrees of freedom is therefore also 1. This is always the case for a 2×2 table, and it can be shown that for $\nu = 1$ the critical values of the χ^2-distribution are just the square of the critical values of the normal distribution, while χ^2 is just the square of the corresponding z-score. The critical values of the χ^2-distribution are shown in Table 10.1 opposite. You can confirm for yourselves that the critical value of χ^2 at the 5 per cent level of significance and one degree of freedom ($v = 1$) is 3.84, which is just the squared value of the equivalent critical value of the normal distribution, i.e. $1.96^2 = 3.84$. As the degrees of freedom increase, however (i.e. as the number of cells in the table increase) the χ^2 critical values increase correspondingly to take account of the fact that, other things being equal, the larger the number of cells the greater will be the value of the calculated χ^2 (Table 10.1).

The value of χ^2 we have calculated is 9.025 which exceeds the critical value of χ^2 for $v = 1$ at both the 5 per cent (3.84) and the 1 per cent (6.63) level of significance (see table). We therefore have a statistically significant difference between the observed and the expected frequencies, with $P < 0.01$. From the analysis using proportions above we had $z = -3.00$, $P < 0.01$. The result is, as would be expected, the same. There is strong evidence of a difference between the observed and expected frequencies, and the null hypothesis that the same proportion of female workers is found in each occupation is very likely incorrect.

The χ^2 test is extendable to larger $r \times c$ contingency tables in an equivalent way. It must be remembered, though, that, like the other tests of statistical inference we have looked at, the χ^2 test does not tell us anything about the *direction* of a relationship. It cannot inform you that Occupation 1, for example, has a smaller proportion of women than Occupation 2: all it does is allow you to infer a statistically significant difference between them. *You* have to calculate the proportions to show in which direction the relationship lies. Again, these statistics are an aid, but they are *not* a substitute for an examination and discussion of a table.

Notes on computing

1 When you ask for a χ^2 statistic (CHISQ) on the STATISTICS subcommand of the CROSSTABS procedure in SPSS you are given a row of possibly undecipherable notations underneath the relevant crosstabulation. These can be translated as:

Chi-square   type of chi-square calculation. Pearson's chi-square is the one you should refer to here.
Value   value of calculated χ^2.
D.F.   degrees of freedom.
Significance   significance of χ^2 expressed as a probability, i.e. if less than 0.05, this means $P < 0.05$.
Minimum expected frequency   minimum expected cell frequency (see note 2).

Cells with expected frequency <5   number of cells with expected frequency less than 5 (see note 2).

2 The χ^2 test should not be used where very low expected frequencies, 5 or fewer, are involved. In the case of a 2 ×2 table in which there are fewer than 20 cases, SPSS will calculate 'Fisher's exact test' to replace the χ^2 test. Here the probability of getting a sample with frequencies distributed in this way (or in a more extreme way) assuming the null hypothesis to be correct is given as either '1-tailed' or '2-tailed'. All the tests we have referred to so far have been '2-tailed', i.e. they have referred to the proportion under the critical limits of the normal curve at *both* ends of the distribution (Figure 10.2). In general, where we use statistics in social research as a guide in the interpretation of data, it will be the 2-tailed probability that we are interested in. 1-tailed tests are used (commonly in psychological and medical research) where a difference is only of interest if it occurs in a particular *direction*; for instance, if the mean for group A *exceeds* that for group B. In this case a z-score of +1.64 would be considered significant at the 5% level, since this is the value on the normal distribution curve exceeded at *one* end of the tail of the distribution by 5% of repeated sample mean differences. The interpretation of Fisher's exact test in terms of statistical significance is exactly the same as for the χ^2 (i.e. a probability of <0.05 denotes a statistically significant difference).

Part IV has provided a brief introduction to the calculation and interpretation of inferential statistics. Although you will probably always be able to get a computer to calculate the statistics for you, it is important to understand how to interpret the figures that the computer comes up with, and the assumptions that have been made in order to apply a particular test. Some of the more important of these are discussed in the final section.

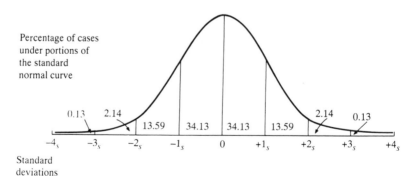

Figure 10.2 Tails of the normal distribution

Assumptions behind inferential statistics

Up to this point, we have discussed the principles behind, and how to calculate, some of the most commonly used simple significance tests. However, a number of important issues still remain to be addressed since the use and interpretation of these tests is, in practice, often quite subjective, and sometimes very controversial. Underlying many of the statistical procedures available to you in SPSS are two major assumptions of which you need to be aware. First, all inferential statistics are based on the *assumption of representativeness*, i.e. that the sample is representative in a quantifiable way of the population from which it has been drawn. We have not gone into the complex question of sample design here. Readers who are interested in pursuing this topic are referred in the first instance to de Vaus (1991) and for more extensive discussions to Cochrane (1977) and Hakim (1987). However, it is important to be aware that, strictly, inferential statistics are only applicable to, and should only be used in conjunction with, particular sorts of sample design.

Essentially there are two types of samples: **scientific** and **non-scientific samples**. Non-scientific samples include those in which cases are selected for their 'typicalness' or availability, and it is not clear how results can be generalized to a wider population. In scientific sampling, the probability of any person in a population being selected as part of a sample is known. This is so because in order to select a scientific sample you first need to have a 'sampling frame', or list of all individuals in the population to be sampled; a well-known example of such a sampling frame, often used in the selection of samples of households, would be a list of addresses from the electoral register or the Postcode Address File. Because of this requirement such sampling techniques are often referred to as 'probability' sampling. Since the probability of inclusion for any individual or household is known, it is possible to generalize, or make inferences about, the wider population from the sample. For example, we saw earlier how to find the probable range within which the true mean value for a population mean μ will fall using the sample estimate $\bar{x}$. We can only make such an inference if we are using a scientifically drawn sample.

There are several different ways in which probability samples may be selected. The purest form upon which most simple inferential statistics are based is the *simple random sample*, in which every person in the population has a known and equal chance of selection for the sample. Simple random samples may be drawn by random number generation on a computer, provided everybody in the population to be sampled is assigned a number in advance (which is why you need to have a sampling frame to begin with). However, due to considerations of cost and convenience scientific samples in actuality are often modifications of a simple random sample, in which individuals in a population have different (although known) probabilities of inclusion. For instance, we may choose to select every fifth person on a list of names (*systematic sampling*), or ensure that we sample different groups in the population in the proportion that they exist in the population (*stratified sampling*), or restrict our sample geographically (*cluster sampling*), or a combination of the above.

The inferential statistics we have discussed here have assumed that a simple random sample is used. The above are all examples of scientific samples, but because they are not simple random samples some of the statistics we have used to make inferences about the population would need modification to take account of this. It is possible to do this mathematically since, as long as we have a scientifically drawn sample, we already know the individual probabilities of inclusion in the sample. More advanced statistical texts than this will go through the mathematical modifications necessary to some of the formulae we have seen in order to accommodate different types of scientific sampling design. However, we *cannot* compute the standard error of the mean for a non-scientific sample, since it would be meaningless as an estimate of the sampling error involved in inferring the likely range of the population mean, because the sample is not representative of the population. (In reality, of course, you will come across examples of tests of significance used with all types of non-scientific sampling designs. Again, it is a question here of subjective judgement as to whether this provides any useful information or not. It should certainly always be made clear that the researcher is aware that such tests are, from a statistical point of view, inapplicable in these circumstances.)

The second major assumption of which you should be aware is the *assumption of an underlying distributional form*. Whereas the χ^2 test only involves making simple assumptions concerning the expected frequencies in different cells (that they are proportional to the marginal frequencies, for example) other inferential statistics involving both interval level and non-interval level data are based on assumptions concerning underlying probability distributions. In the statistics you have been introduced to these have been limited to the normal distribution for interval-level data, and the normal approximation to the binomial distribution for binomial data (i.e. data in the form of dichotomous proportions). These assumptions may be justified on the grounds that even if the distribution of a variable in a population is plainly not normal, the distribution of repeated sample means or proportions often approaches normality. In other words, the methods used are not particularly *sensitive* to non-normality.

There is, however, a branch of statistics designed specifically for use in cases where the assumption of normality seems to be particularly badly violated. (Indeed, some statisticians argue that this is almost *always* the case in social research, and that inferential methods based on probability distributions should only ever be used sparingly and with great caution.) These distribution-free methods are usually referred to as **non-parametric statistics**, since they attempt to avoid reliance on any particular assumptions regarding the form of the underlying distribution or parameters. Instead, many of them make use of techniques for ranking of pairs similar to those used in measures of association for ordinal-level variables such as gamma. These techniques test the null hypothesis that two independent samples come from populations having the *same* distributional form, but do not specify what this form is. They produce statistics similar in interpretation to z-scores. Critical values for the assessment of the statistical significance of these statistics for various sample sizes may be found in published tables.

SPSS has a procedure called NPAR TESTS which enables the calculation of certain of these tests. For instance, a well-known significance test of this type, used for testing the similarity of the distribution of variable x in two random samples n_1 and n_2 (and therefore the non-parametric equivalent to the t-test for comparing two sample means), is the Mann–Whitney U-Test. To run this procedure you would need to use the command:

> NPAR TESTS MANN–WHITNEY
> = dependent var BY independent var (category1, category2)

If you wish to know more about non-parametric statistics it is worth consulting Conover (1980) or Siegel and Castellan (1988). In general, the decision to use non-parametric statistics depends on the likely distributional form of the data, and the preference of the researcher. Because parametric tests are based upon actual values (means and proportions), rather than on the rank order of pairs they utilize more information about the data than non-parametric tests. On the other hand, it is often very hard to know to what extent the assumption of an underlying distributional form (e.g. the assumption of normality) is justified. As long as any of these tests are used as interpretative aids, and not as ends in themselves, it may not, when all is said and done, make a lot of difference.

Limitations of inferential statistics

If this section has introduced doubts in your mind about the value of inferential statistics, that is probably a very good thing. Inferential statistics, although widely available, form only one part of the tools of analysis available to you, and your use of them should be tempered by the recognition of their limitations. It is always best, for example, to use a combination of simple description, measures of association and inferential statistics when describing the relationship between variables.

A common example of the misuse to which inferential statistics are sometimes put is to make a large number of comparisons from the same sample data (for example, to run a series of many t-tests) in order to see which differences between variable means are significant. This kind of inductive analysis cannot be justified on statistical grounds, since if the 5 per cent level is the probability of error judged to be sufficiently small to claim statistical significance, then in a series of 100 tests, we would expect 5 differences between sample means to be statistically significant by chance alone. In other words, in 1 of 20 tests we will reject the null hypothesis of no difference between means incorrectly. We could of course reduce the odds of making this mistake by taking the 1 per cent level as our limit of statistical significance – in which case we would reject the null hypothesis of no difference incorrectly in only 1 out of 100 tests. The point is that we do not know *which* result would be wrong; so the principle of presenting large series of tests like this and making much of statistical significance levels is clearly flawed. Significance testing should always be informed initially by theory and aided by detailed examination of the data, and not just slapped into the computer in a trawl for significant results.

An additional problem with the use of inferential statistics in general is that the larger the sample, the greater the chance of finding a statistically significant difference between sample estimates irrespective of the true population parameters. This mistake is referred to as a **Type I error**; we reject the null hypothesis of no association erroneously and conclude too readily that we have a statistically significant difference. (The opposite of a Type I error, a **Type II error**, occurs when we apply *too* stringent criteria for the determination of statistical significance, and find no evidence to reject the null hypothesis when there *is* really a significant difference.) In general, therefore, the larger the sample, the more conservative should be our arbitrary limit for determining statistical significance (perhaps the 1 per cent instead of the 5 per cent level). For very large samples significance testing using inferential statistics may become meaningless since the chance of obtaining a significant result is so high.

Key concepts

Make sure you have understood the following key concepts:

- dichotomous variable
- normal approximation to the binomial distribution
- continuity correction
- chi-square (χ^2) tests
- scientific/non-scientific samples
- non-parametric statistics
- Type I/Type II errors

Multiple choice questions

In these questions, one or more answer may be correct.

1 What is the formula for χ^2:

(i) $\sum \frac{(O - E)}{O}$?

(ii) $\sum \frac{(O - E)^2}{E}$?

(iii) $\sum \frac{(O - E)^2}{N}$?

(iv) $\sum \frac{(O - E)}{N}$?

(v) $\sum \frac{(O - E)^2}{O}$?

2 What are the assumptions that we need to make when we use parametric inferential statistics?

(i) that we know the population means

(ii) that we have used a random sample

(iii) that the sample is representative of the population

(iv) that we know the form of the underlying population distribution

(v) that we take repeated samples

3 Why do we use inferential statistics?

(i) to perform tests of statistical significance

(ii) to prove our hypothesis

(iii) to test if the normal distribution applies to our sample

(iv) to make claims about population parameters based on a sample

Exercise 4

At this point, you might like to go back to the output you produced for Exercise 2 at the end of Chapter 7 and re-examine it, paying particular attention to the χ-square statistics (re-run your analysis if necessary). Make sure by referring to the text that you understand their meaning, and write a brief report on the analysis incorporating the new information that they give you (i.e. referring to the statistical significance of the results). You should be comparing χ-square values for:

- The original cross-tabulation of the dependent with the independent variable.

- The two (or more) cross-tabulations generated by the introduction of the control variable.

Try to work out whether the introduction of the control variable increases or decreases the value of χ-square, and the implication of this for your conclusions.

What extra contribution do these statistics make to your report?

Part V

Introduction to multivariate analysis

General linear models: multivariate analysis

Aims

- To introduce the concept of general linear models (GLMs).
- To understand the extension of the simple linear regression model to multiple linear regression.
- To introduce multivariate modelling for categoric variables: log-linear analysis.

We have so far introduced you to the basic principles of statistical analysis. You should by now be familiar with some of the most important descriptive and inferential statistics and the levels of measurement of variables for which they are appropriate. Descriptive statistics are those that *describe* the relationship between variables; the simplest forms of these are measures of association, such as Pearson's r for interval level data and Phi or Gamma for nominal and ordinal level data, while the regression equation goes beyond this and allows us to predict, for interval level data, the effect that a change in one variable has on another. Inferential statistics, on the other hand, allow us to make judgements about the likely reliability of our sample *estimates* of means, proportions, etc. with respect to the underlying (but generally unknown) population values. The importance of these latter statistics is based on the assumption that generally we will only be dealing with a *sample* of the population we are interested in; in order to generalize our results, we make use of the properties of certain probability distributions to infer the extent of our likely 'sampling error'. Generally, these two types of statistics are used in conjunction; descriptive statistics to assess the strength of the relationship between variables, and inferential statistics to determine if the relationship is statistically significant given the sample size.

Although we have not explored any very complicated statistical procedures, the basic principles outlined so far should enable you to grasp in a theoretical or intuitive way some of the more complex multivariate techniques that this chapter describes. Some of these techniques are statistically quite difficult to follow and in general you will never be expected to do the computations involved yourselves, so we will concentrate on outlining the basic principles, the sort of data for which they were developed and their relationship to the simpler techniques which we have discussed in more detail in earlier chapters. There will be hardly any equations!

Since this is not a text primarily aimed at those with much experience of data analysis we have tried to keep what follows as simple as possible, and will discuss only a very limited range of the techniques that are available to you on the computer. Some of these techniques are very complicated – in fact quite a few are still in the process of being developed by statisticians – and several of them have computer packages and special texts dedicated entirely to them. Understanding the principles behind the most accessible of them will help you if you wish to explore this area further (see, for example Tabachnick and Fidell (1983); and Gilbert (1981)).

We deal here initially with *multiple linear regression*, which extends beyond, but develops from, Chapter 8 on simple linear regression, and is perhaps one of the most easily grasped multivariate models. It will assist in the understanding of some of the underlying concepts of other models. We then proceed to describe how the principles of multivariate regression – developed for the analysis of interval-level variables – have more recently been extended to the analysis of cross-tabulations, in **log-linear analysis**. This type of model is relatively new, but is rapidly becoming very popular among social researchers precisely because it analyses cross-tabulations, which is the form in which most of our data are presented. Finally, we have included a chapter on longitudinal data, and the primary technique of analysis for longitudinal data: *event-history analysis*. We have included this because there is an increasing recognition that longitudinal data (collected from the same individual or unit over a period of time) are much more likely to provide us with answers concerning causality than are cross-sectional data (collected at only one point in time). It is only relatively recently that the techniques of analysis developed for cross-sectional data have been further developed and applied to longitudinal data. Therefore we discuss both the nature and importance of longitudinal data before introducing the analytic model. First, though, we must return to basic principles.

General linear models

In Chapter 8 on regression and correlation, we mentioned that the technique of simple linear regression was just one example of a group of related techniques known as '**general linear models**' or GLMs. The regression equation:

$$Y = a + bx + e$$

is just one example of a generalized formula which relates a value of a dependent variable (Y) to a systematic component made up of the linear effects of various independent variables (variance *explained*) and a random or error component expressing the variation not accounted for by the relationship between the dependent and independent variables (*residual* variance). In the case of simple linear regression, we were interested in the effect of an independent interval-level variable X on an interval-level dependent variable Y. The relationship between these variables can be displayed quite easily on a scatterplot – in other words, in two-dimensional space. When we move on to a discussion of multivariate techniques, what we imply is the introduction of *more* independent variables into the equation (analogous to the introduction of a control variable to a bivariate cross-tabulation). The **multiple regression** equation for the simultaneous effect of *two* independent variables on a single dependent variable is, for example:

$$Y = a + b_1x_1 + b_2x_2 + e$$

Here you see that we have introduced another 'slope' parameter, b_2, into the equation, expressing the effect of the second independent variable, X_2, on the dependent variable. (The example used here is only an illustration of a more general point; a more extended discussion on multiple regression is provided in the following section.)

Clearly, however, these two slopes *in the same equation* cannot now be represented in the same two-dimensional scatterplot as in the simpler example. We have instead to think in terms of three-dimensional space and conceptualize a plane rather than a two-dimensional slope in order to accommodate the introduction of a second independent variable with its own slope parameter. In other words, we need to conceptualize the simultaneous existence of two slopes, and this can only be done in three dimensions, as a plane rather than a line. Although our cognitive faculties do not permit us to conceptualize beyond three dimensions, mathematically this is a process that can continue *ad infinitum*. Of course, in the real world, sample sizes will very soon prevent us introducing more variables into the analysis but the point is that multivariate statistical analysis involves an extension of the mathematics into multi-dimensional space. As you can imagine, this rapidly becomes very complicated, which is why the widespread usage of many of these techniques is only a very recent phenomenon, dependent upon the development of computing packages able to cope with the calculations involved in a very short time. A good introduction and discussion of various techniques is found in Fox (1984); see also Dobson (1990).

What follows is a simple description of the underlying principles of a few of the most commonly used and important GLMs in social research, beginning with the one that has already been mentioned: multiple regression.

Multivariate analysis for interval-level data: multiple linear regression

Multiple regression is the multivariate technique used to interpret the effect of two or more independent variables on the dependent variable, when all (or the majority) of variables are interval level. It allows the assessment of the effect of each independent variable *when controlling* for the effects of other independent variables. The simple linear regression equation is therefore expanded from

$$Y = a + bx$$

to

$$Y = a + b_1x_1 + b_2x_2 \ldots +b_nx_n$$

where x_1 and x_2 are each interval-level independent variables and b_1 and b_2 are 'partial' slopes or '**partial regression coefficients**'; that is they represent the effect of variables X_1 and X_2 on the predicted value of the dependent variable Y when the effect(s) of the other variable(s) in the equation are controlled for. This procedure is thus analogous to the introduction of a control variable into a bivariate cross-tabulation (see Chapter 7). In addition, because regression analysis involves interval-level variables you can also make predictions from the partial regression coefficients (slopes) concerning the value of Y for any given value of both X_1 and X_2.

However, there is a complication here, because the b values in the expanded equation relate to different independent variables measured in different units, with different variances. Some way of directly comparing their impact is required. This is done by the computation of *standardized* partial regression coefficients, in which each standardized variable is given a mean of 0 and a variance of 1. The standardized partial regression coefficients calculated using these new standardized variables are more or less directly comparable with each other, and indicate the relative importance of each variable in the equation in explaining the variability in the dependent variable.

As an example, suppose we wanted to assess the effects that age had on income over a specified age range. If the scatterplot of the two variables 'income' with 'age' showed the relationship to be broadly linear, the obvious thing to do would be to perform a simple linear regression analysis, but the r^2 that we would arrive at from the correlation is unlikely to be very high. This is so because it is unlikely that a *large* proportion of the variability in income is explained by age alone. Therefore we need to introduce more variables into the regression to see if we can arrive at a better model for predicting income. Some of these variables might be interval level, such as some measure of time spent out of the labour market, while others might be categoric, such as parental social class or level of education. Although regression is basically a technique for interval-level data, categorical (nominal or ordinal) variables can be handled as *independent* variables in the regression equation by the creation of '**dummy variables**', in which each category of the variable in question becomes effectively a single binary variable, for which individuals take the values 1 if they fall into that category and 0 if they do not. An example is

Parental social class	Those with parents in Social Classes I and II	Those with parents in Social Class III
I and II	1	0
III	0	1
IV and V	0	0

Notice that for a three-category variable we only need to construct two dummies (here for Classes I and II, and Class III) – this is because the third category (here IV and V) is specified by default as 0,0.[1]

Including these new variables, the regression equation becomes:

$$Y = a + b_1x_1 + b_2x_2 + b_3x_3 + b_4x_4$$

where the standardized partial regression coefficients are:

b_1 = effect of age
b_2 = effect of time spent out of the labour force
b_3 = effect of parents being in Social Classes I and II
b_4 = effect of parents being in Social Class III

We hope that the introduction of these new variables into the equation will help improve our prediction of Y, income.

In the same way that r^2, the square of the Pearson product–moment correlation coefficient, showed the proportion of the linear variance in the dependent variable which was 'explained' or predicted by the independent variable in simple linear regression, R^2 (the square of the **multiple correlation coefficient**) shows the proportion of the linear variance in the dependent variable that can be explained by *all* of the independent variables acting together. In other words, it tells us how well the multiple linear regression model as a whole actually explains or 'fits' the variation in the dependent variable. It is also possible to calculate *partial correlation coefficients*. These indicate the correlation between an independent variable and the dependent variable when mathematically removing the effect of (controlling for) the other independent variables in the equation.

One of the most important tasks of multivariate analysis is often to find the best and simplest equation (model) for the data. In general in social research you will not expect to find particularly high values of R^2. This is because there are so many things which might contribute to influence a variable such as individual income that we cannot reasonably expect to be able to analyse or even measure more than a few of them. As a rule of thumb (although depending obviously on the individual circumstances) if you come across values of R^2 of over 0.6 or so in a multiple regression equation in social research, you should regard it with some suspicion!

We spent some time at the beginning of Chapter 8 discussing problems of interpretation with simple linear regression. With multiple regression these problems are WRIT LARGE. First we need to consider the issue of sample size. We need to ensure that there are sufficient cases in our sample to justify the addition of extra variables. A model with even four independent variables in general requires many more cases to make interpretation possible than when it contains only two. Secondly, with many independent variables in a model, the problem of providing a coherent explanation of their separate effects on the dependent variable can become very complex. Where a single variable does not contribute very much to the R^2, therefore (in other words, if the partial correlation coefficient is low) it is often better in the interests of simplicity to drop it from the equation. This is the principle of *parsimony*, and it underlies all good multivariate analysis. There are various methods of assessing whether a particular variable should be included in a model. For example, a variable might be added to the regression equation if it contributes a certain value (or more) to the overall R^2; or it may be deleted if it fails to meet a certain minimum contribution to the R^2. If you are using a computer package like SPSS, you simply specify these criteria as subcommands on the REGRESSION procedure and it will do the necessary computational work for you.

Finally, it is important to remember that regression coefficients *in themselves* tell us nothing about causation. They only indicate that certain variables are *associated*. Indeed, all the same strictures and assumptions that were outlined for the simple linear regression model apply here as well, and you should check your data initially for serious violations of these assumptions before embarking on regression analysis. The more complex the analysis, the more detailed such checking should be!

The following points should be noted.

1 SPSS will print the standard error and significance level of regression coefficients. As before, this assumes (a) simple random sampling and (b) a normal distribution of the dependent variable for any point on

the independent variables. However, in addition, there is a further note of caution concerning the simultaneous analysis of multiple variables:

2 The multiple regression equation as stated here assumes that there is no 'interaction' between the categories of the independent variables such as would be the case when, for instance, years of education had a greater impact on young people's income than on old people's. It is possible mathematically to take this interaction factor into account, but the regression results can rapidly reach a point where they become very difficult to interpret. Similarly, where two or more independent variables are very highly correlated themselves, their regression coefficients become unreliable and the effects of the two variables in multiple regression cannot reasonably be separated. Again, judgement must be used in assessing the relative importance of violations of these assumptions. In an exploratory analysis of survey data, they may not be particularly important; for a refined attempt at causal modelling they become much more so.

3 SPSS's procedure for multiple regression analysis is called REGRES-SION. For further details of how to use REGRESSION consult the SPSS/PC+ or SPSS FOR WINDOWS User Guides in conjunction with a more advanced statistics text dealing with regression (e.g. Tabachnick and Fidell, 1983).

Multivariate analysis for categoric variables: log-linear models

We now turn to an extremely important class of models in social research: log-linear models. Although this group of models falls into the same family of models as the multiple regression model (i.e. GLMs), they do not depend on the same assumptions concerning underlying distributional form. In similar manner to the χ^2 statistic, they are based upon the distribution of frequencies across the cells of a cross-tabulation. Consequently, unlike the multiple regression equation which is predominantly for use with interval-level data, log-linear modelling is used for analysing nominal/ordinal level data in the form of cross-tabulations.

You may have seen from the exercises how complicated the interpretation of a contingency table can become when you are dealing with just one dependent variable and two independent variables. Log-linear modelling techniques were developed to cope with the analysis of categorical data in the form of multi-way cross-tabulations. As in multiple regression, log-linear modelling allows the interpretation of the simultaneous effects of a number of independent variables. However, the former technique usually requires an interval-level dependent variable which, for the statistical significance of the coefficients to be assessed, is assumed to be normally distributed with respect to the categories of the independent variables. In log-linear modelling, on the other hand, all the variables are treated as independent, and the dependent variable is the distribution of frequencies in the cells of the resulting cross-tabulation. Thus the number of cases in each cell of an observed multi-way table can be expressed as a function of all the variables in the cross-tabulation. In fact, in log-linear modelling the *natural logarithm* of the cell frequency is used as the 'dependent variable', in order to obtain a linear equation analogous to that used in regression. For a single cell, a, in the table below, therefore, the full log-linear model is expressed as:

$$\log(f_a) = \mu + \lambda_1^i + \lambda_1^j + \lambda_{11}^{ij}$$

Variable i	Variable j	
	1	*2*
1	a	b
2	c	d

You can see that this is basically very similar in form to the multiple regression equation, but here (f_a) is the frequency in cell a; μ is the average of the logs of the frequencies in *all* the cells; λ_1^i is the effect of the first category of variable i; λ_1^j is the effect of the first category of variable j; and λ_{11}^{ij} is the interaction effect of the first category of i with the first category of j.

The parameters μ and λ are *estimated* from the data, in an equivalent way to the estimation of the regression coefficients a and b (see Chapter 8). Where all parameters contributing to the individual cell frequencies are included in the model (as in the above example) the model is known as 'saturated', and the frequencies predicted by the equation will be identical to those observed. For example, to return to the analysis of voting behaviour by sex:

Vote	Women	Men
Conservative	a	b
Labour	c	d
Other	e	f

To arrive at the observed frequency in cell a, we would need to include in our model (according to the equation shown above):

(i)   a measure of the overall average cell frequency, i.e. μ or 'grand mean';

(ii) a measure of the overall ('main') effect of being female, i.e. λ_1^{sex}, based on the marginal frequency of being female;

(iii) a measure of the overall propensity to vote Conservative, i.e. λ_1^{vote}, the main effect of vote, based on the marginal frequency of voting Conservative;

(iv) a measure of the effect of being both female *and* voting Conservative, i.e. λ_{11}, or the interaction effect between the variables.

However, the ultimate aim of log-linear modelling, as with other statistical techniques, is usually to find the simplest (most parsimonious) description of the relationship between variables. This involves the successive elimination of parameters from the model, in an iterative process, to arrive at the model which produces the best 'fit' between the frequencies predicted by the model and the observed frequencies, with the minimum number of parameters. For instance, if the two variables i and j in our example are independent, then no interaction term is required to arrive at a predicted cell frequency for cell a which is identical to the observed frequency. In other words, we may drop the interaction term λ_{11}^{ij} from our model without losing any information, since the observed frequency will then only depend on the marginal totals and not on any interaction between the variables. Similarly, in the interests of arriving at a reasonably intelligible final model expressing the effect of various variables on the observed cell frequencies, we may choose to 'drop' certain variables whose effects are not very important from the model.

By this process we hope eventually to finish with a set of parameters which combine to produce a set of predicted frequencies which fit the observed cell frequencies in the closest and simplest way. The criteria for choosing which parameters to drop or add and which final model to select are (within certain limits) generally up to the researcher, and will depend on the particular exercise being undertaken. In log-linear modelling, the **'goodness-of-fit'** test of the predicted to the observed cell frequencies under a particular model can be based on the familiar χ^2 test. Thus, if the χ^2 value is large, the frequencies predicted by the model being tested do not fit the observed frequencies well; if it is small, then the model produces a good fit to the observed frequencies. The change in the value of χ^2 between two models may then be attributed to the parameters that have been added to, or dropped from, the second model as compared to the first. In this way the simplest model which fits the data adequately can be selected (and hence the most important parameters or variables in the construction of the cross-tabulation may be identified).

An interesting and simple example of the use and interpretation of such models can be found in Marshall *et al.* (1988: 106–7) relating to the British Class Survey data. The data involved constituted a complex three-way cross-tabulation of respondent's class on first entry to employment [F] by their chief childhood supporter's class ('class of origin') [O] controlling for sex [S]. The aim was to investigate patterns of social mobility by sex, where mobility is defined in terms of the relationship between

Table 11.1 Interrelationship between class on entry into employment, class of origin, and sex

Model	Difference		df	χ^2	χ^2/df	P
1 [OS] [OF] [SF]	$\Rightarrow$	OFS	4	2.7	0.7	>0.50
2 [OS] [OF]	$\Rightarrow$	SF	2	194.5	97.3	<0.0005
3 [OS] [SF]	$\Rightarrow$	OF	4	115.3	28.8	<0.0005

Key: O   = Class of origin (chief childhood supporter, Goldthorpe three-category scheme).
    F   = Class of respondent on entry into employment (Goldthorpe three-category scheme).
    S   = Sex.
    $\Rightarrow$ = Attributable to effect of <specified parameter>.
Source: Marshall *et al.* (1988: 107).

class at first entry to employment and class of the chief childhood supporter – in other words a definition of intergenerational mobility. The definition of class used was Goldthorpe's three-category scheme of service class, intermediate class and working class. In order to analyse this rather complex data a series of three log-linear models was used. The results of this analysis are shown in Table 11.1.

The first model, specified as [OS][OF][SF] includes the three two-variable interaction terms possible in a three-variable table, and is equivalent to an equation (in the form we are familiar with) of:

$$\log (f_a) = \mu + \lambda_1^O + \lambda_1^S + \lambda_1^F + \lambda_{11}^{OS} + \lambda_{11}^{OF} + \lambda_{11}^{SF}$$

The only term missing from the full (saturated) model which would reproduce the observed cell frequencies exactly is the three-way interaction term λ_{111}^{OFS}. When this model is 'fitted' to the data, therefore, what we are in fact doing is testing the fit of the cell frequencies predicted under the model against the observed frequencies. If there *is* a statistically significant difference according to the Chi-square test, then that difference can be attributed to the missing parameter, which in this case would be the three-way interaction term. We could then say that this term contributed a statistically significant effect to the model. In fact, if we look along the first row of Table 11.1 we see that the value of Chi-square (χ^2) given is 2.7. With four degrees of freedom (see *df* column) this gives a level of significance of $P > 0.5$ (final column) – a non-significant result. There is *no* statistically significant difference between the observed frequencies and those predicted by the model (i.e. omitting the OFS interaction). We can conclude that the three-way interaction OFS does not contribute significantly to the fit of the frequencies predicted under the model to the observed frequencies, since there is no statistically significant difference between the observed frequencies and those produced omitting the OFS interaction. The interpretation is that the relationship between class of origin and class of entry into employment is *not* significantly different for men and women.

We need now to go on to identify what the important relationships actually are. The next stage, then, is to re-run the analysis dropping the two two-way interaction terms, class of first entry into employment by sex [SF] and class of origin [OF] successively. In this way it is possible, according to the logic outlined above, to determine if there are significant independent effects for class of origin and/or sex on the class of first entry into employment. Looking at the values of P given, which in both cases are < 0.0005, we can conclude that there are *very* significant effects evident in both cases. The two two-way interactions of class of first entry into employment by class of origin and by sex both contribute significantly to a model in which the predicted frequencies fit the observed frequencies well. Neither should therefore be omitted in attempting to arrive at a description of the important relationships evident in the initial cross-tabulation.

In terms of our initial question we can conclude that there is no overall difference evident in the relative mobility transitions between class of origin and class of first entry into employment for men and women. There are, however, significant independent effects of both sex and class of origin on the class of first entry into employment. *Relative* intergenerational mobility may not be influenced by sex, but initial (and subsequent jobs) evidently are.

The following points should be noted:

1 The simplest type of log-linear model has been described here. There are also specific procedures for dealing with ordinal level variables (which can result in a more parsimonious representation of data) and for the case where a dichotomous dependent variable is specified ('logit model'). In addition, various assumptions must be made to cope with cross-tabulations which have impossible combinations of categories in one or more cells.

2 SPSS has two procedures for producing log-linear models: LOGLINEAR and HILOGLINEAR. HILOGLINEAR was developed first to cope with a particular type of model – the hierarchical model – which, if there are interaction terms included in a user-specified model, automatically includes all lower-order terms as well. So in a model containing λ_{11}^{ij}, the terms λ_1^i and λ_1^j will also be included. This procedure may save on computational time but is not particularly flexible. LOGLINEAR provides a more flexible model-building facility, including provision for non-hierarchical models. There are also a number of dedicated statistical packages around, the most well-known of which is GLIM (see Payne, 1987).

3 An excellent introduction to log-linear analysis in social research can be found in Gilbert (1981). See also Upton (1978).

Note

1 In fact, there is a technique called *Analysis of Variance* (ANOVA or MANOVA in SPSS) which is designed for cases where there is an interval-level dependent variable and a majority of categorical independent variables. We do not go into it here because it too belongs in the GLM family, and we are more concerned with introducing you to the underlying principles of multivariate analysis than to the specifics of particular techniques.

Key concepts

Make sure you have understood the following key concepts:

- general linear models (GLMs)
- multiple regression
- partial regression coefficients
- dummy variables
- multiple correlation coefficient
- log-linear analysis
- 'goodness-of-fit' testing

Multiple choice questions

In these questions, one or more answers may be correct.

1 What does GLM stand for:

  (i)   generalized linear multivariate analysis?

  (ii) generalized linear model?

  (iii) generalized logistic model?

2 What is the purpose of dummy variables:

  (i)   to introduce categoric variables into a regression analysis?

  (ii) to perform non-linear regression?

  (iii) to create partial regression coefficients?

3 What does a partial regression coefficient represent:

(i) the overall model fit?

(ii) the correlation between the independent and the dependent variable when controlling for other variables?

(iii) the effect of a change in the independent variable on the dependent variable when controlling for other variables?

4 What is R^2:

(i) the multiple correlation coefficient?

(ii) a partial regression coefficient?

(iii) the sample size squared?

(iv) a measure of goodness of fit of the model?

Longitudinal data: their collection and analysis

Aims

- To describe the distinction between cross-sectional and longitudinal data.

- To undertake and interpret simple cross-wave analysis of longitudinal data.

- To understand the underlying principles of event-history analysis.

Introduction

Social surveys such as the British Class Survey, where a representative sample of the population is interviewed only once, are referred to as *cross-sectional surveys* because they take a slice through time and the various social processes with which they are concerned. Therefore, they provide us with something like a snapshot. When we analyse data from these surveys, we obtain information at the aggregate or *macro level*, for example the proportion of people who belong to a particular class or who would vote for a particular party. What if, however, we wish to answer questions about social processes over time? If we want to know whether there is a permanent underclass as opposed to a constant and steady movement of people in and out of poverty and unemployment over time; or if we want to know how changes in household composition affect the individual welfare of household members, one-off cross-sections are of little use. In this chapter, we are concerned with a form of survey – a panel survey as exemplified by the *British Household Panel Survey (BHPS)* – which is specifically designed to deal with questions such as those we have just posed, i.e. questions about *social change*.

Because most surveys are single snapshots, they cannot tell us much about social change (although we can ask people *retrospective* questions about past states, such as previous occupations; or we can ask about previous events, such as the birth of children or dates of marriage). Regular or *repeated cross-sectional social surveys*, like the General Household Survey, in which the same questions are asked every year of a different sample of the population, are somewhat better tools for the study of change. Nevertheless, as with cross-sections using retrospective questions, they also only permit analysis of net change at the aggregate or macro level (for example, proportion of the population below the poverty line at time t could be compared with the proportion at time $t - 1$). In order to study change at the *individual* or **micro level**, however, it is necessary to employ a *longitudinal design* and, therefore, a *prospective method* such as a *panel survey* in which the *same* individuals are interviewed repeatedly across time. The longitudinal data provided by a panel survey then allows researchers not only to examine the proportion of the population at different times in states such as poverty but to examine flows into and out of these states, thus opening up a wider range of possibilities in terms of causal analyses and inferences. In other words, longitudinal data tell us about change at the individual or micro level; cross-sections tell us only about populations at one point in time.

The UK is particularly well provided for in terms of **longitudinal studies**. Among the best known are various *cohort studies* such as the National Child Development Study (NCDS) in which a sample has been followed from birth. The NCDS cohort is composed of people born in March 1958 who were last re-interviewed in 1991. (Cohorts do not need to be taken at birth, of course. The term 'cohort' is a reference to a group of people with some common characteristic or experience. We could, thus, imagine a cohort of unemployed people; or a cohort of students entering higher education in a particular year.) More recently, the Economic and Social Research Council and the University of Essex have established the BHPS – composed of some 10 000 individuals (drawn from a representative sample of households across Great Britain) who are being interviewed annually through the 1990s.

Why longitudinal data?

Why do we need longitudinal data? There are three main reasons which we will describe and illustrate. First, longitudinal data are precisely concerned with the behaviour of individuals over time. For this reason, they are well suited to the statistical analysis of change and of dynamic behaviour more generally. While it is true that cross-sections can introduce retrospective elements in order to study change, nevertheless the quality of retrospective data decreases the further back in time respondents are asked to remember. Moreover, the ways in which individuals interpret their own past behaviour are coloured by subsequent events. So if we are interested in measuring attitude change, there is no reliable way of obtaining data relating to people's views at some point in the past. Without (probably unreliable) retrospective elements, however, cross-sectional data produce little of help to the analyst of social change.

Second, as noted in the introduction, panel data make it possible to examine *transitions between states* in a way not possible where only cross-sectional data are available. In particular, because they are data on the same individuals over time (micro data), panel data permit the analysis of gross change at the individual level. Thus it is possible to make a deeper, diachronic (across time) analysis of the incidence of conditions and events such as poverty and unemployment. In turn such events can be examined for dynamic links with other factors.

Third, longitudinal data allow analysts to control for certain **unobserved determinants of behaviour**, in particular those unobserved factors which vary across individuals but remain the same across time for any given individual. For example, we know that individuals unemployed at time t have a higher probability of being unemployed at time $t + 1$. Is this because there is something about unemployment that increases the likelihood that the unemployed will remain in that state (for example, demoralization)? Or is there something about the unemployed themselves which puts them and keeps them in that state? We need longitudinal data to begin to tackle such questions.

We can illustrate some of the points we have made about the advantages of longitudinal data through a brief consideration of a substantive research issue where data drawn from panel surveys can assist our understanding of micro-social change.

Transitions into and out of poverty is perhaps the area in which the potentials of panel data for social science and social policy have been most clearly established. First, only longitudinal designs can distinguish between the 'stock' and 'flow' of a social condition such as poverty. By tracing variations in income over time for the same set of individuals, panel studies can identify transitions into and out of poverty and attempts can then be made to test various hypotheses regarding causal factors in this process. For example, the American Panel Study of Income Dynamics (PSID) has documented both a striking rapidity of movements into and out of poverty and a close association between such transitions and changes in household composition. PSID data have shown that, in the USA, the great proportion of the poor at any one time are suffering temporary rather than long-term poverty, i.e. are moving into poverty through a crisis such as divorce, redundancy or illness in the household and out again on remarriage, re-employment or the recovery of good health. But it is also possible to obtain in this way a deeper understanding of the circumstances of persistent poverty.

PSID data have also demonstrated that only a small proportion of poverty is intergenerational. For instance, 46 per cent of the married male family heads who were poor (in the sense of being in the bottom quintile of the income distribution) in 1967 had become non-poor by 1973, while an unmarried female head who was poor in 1967 more than doubled her chances of leaving poverty by marrying. Taken together these findings have undermined assumptions about a 'culture of poverty' and the intergenerational transmission of poverty; they also raise doubts about the existence of an underclass. They therefore have implications for the way in which poverty is perceived, both by analysts and policy-makers, and thus for the design of policies towards its alleviation. We conclude this discussion of the importance of longitudinal data with concrete examples taken from the BHPS.

Table 12.1 Unemployed as a percentage of economically active men

September 1990	7.7
September 1992	11.5

Consider Table 12.1, which shows unemployment among adult men in our panel during the Septembers of 1990 and 1992. (This uses the retrospective question '*What was your employment status on September 1 last year?*' from Wave 1 of the panel together with '*What was your employment status on September 1 this year?*' from Wave 2 to get the 24-month spread.) We see a substantial increase in unemployment over the period, from 225 (7.7 per cent of those in the labour market) to 334 (11.5 per cent.) How does this relate to their level of education or other qualifications?

Table 12.2 suggests that there was in 1990 a relatively small but nevertheless quite clear difference in proneness to unemployment between those men with high qualifications (5.1 per cent of whom were unemployed) and those with low qualifications or none at all (of whom 8.8 per cent were unemployed). The 1990 cross-section on its own does not suggest a very great effect of level of qualification (though it is not inconsiderable); but, in the subsequent years, as the UK recession deepened, so the effect of possession of qualifications became larger. In 1992 the

Table 12.2 Unemployed as a percentage of economically active men by qualifications

	High level qualifications ('A'-levels or better)	Low-level qualifications or none	All
September 1990	5.1	8.8	7.7
September 1992	5.8	14.2	11.5

rates were respectively 5.8 per cent and 14.2 per cent. This indicates that the relationship between educational qualifications and unemployment became markedly stronger over the period. Apparently education became more important as a means of avoiding unemployment through this particular period of economic decline. But can we be sure that it really is education itself that is having this effect?

In fact we get a rather different view if, rather than considering the cross-sections, we *track individuals' positions through historical time*. It is not, of course, the case that all that has happened within our sample is a simple increase in unemployment from September 1990 to September 1992. The growth in unemployment indicated in Table 12.2 represents just the net change: the eventual balance that emerges from a much more complicated set of movements of people into and out of various economic statuses. The *net change* in unemployment numbers in Table 12.2 is much smaller than the *gross movements of individuals into and out of unemployment*.

The real strength of this sort of longitudinal evidence (and the particular reason for looking across this 24-month gap) is that we can use it to construct an altogether more powerful explanation of the incidence of unemployment. Table 12.2 was constructed just from the cross-sectional information contained in the two waves of data. It does not use any of the information about the previous circumstances of our respondents in Wave 2 that we can get from Wave 1 data.

Table 12.3, by contrast, does use the longitudinal information about our respondents. It classifies the men in the sample in 1992, by their employment status in 1990. Although the general unemployment rate for men in our sample in 1992 was 11.5 per cent, if we look just at that group of our sample who were in employment in September 1990, the 1992 unemployment rate for this particular group was only 6.3 per cent. More remarkably, if we look just at the group who were unemployed in September 1990, their 1992 unemployment rate was 61.2 per cent. Once we know about a man's (in this instance) unemployment history, we therefore know a great deal about his current risk of unemployment.

It appeared in Table 12.2 that those with low levels of qualification in 1992 were considerably more prone to unemployment than those with

Table 12.3 Percentage male unemployment in September 1992 by educational level and employment status in September 1990

Employment status	High-level qualifications	Other/none	All
All	5.8	14.2	11.5
Employed in September 1990	4.3	7.3	6.3
Unemployed in September 1990	25.0*	71.7	61.2

* Cell with fewer than 20 cases.

high levels of qualification; but when we look at unemployment in 1992 in the light of the previous unemployment history of our respondents we get a rather different picture. Education certainly makes a difference between the unemployment proneness of those with no unemployment record (4.3 per cent unemployed in 1992 for those with high-level qualifications as against 7.3 per cent for those without). But Table 12.3 also makes it clear that it is not education *alone* that produces proneness to unemployment.

Those with high-level qualifications who were *unemployed* in 1990, had an unemployment rate of 25 per cent in 1992 (although there are only seven cases here). But, of those with low-level qualifications who were unemployed in 1990, a remarkable 71 per cent were unemployed in 1992. Low-level qualifications on their own make for a marginal increase in proneness to unemployment. Low-level qualifications together with previous history of unemployment make for a dramatically high susceptibility to it. For those with low-level qualifications, unemployment in 1990 increases proneness to unemployment tenfold. The point is not that qualifications are unimportant (for those with high-level qualifications, 1990 unemployment only increases proneness to unemployment sixfold, i.e. from 4.3 to 25 per cent), but rather that its importance is only seen clearly in the context of (i.e. 'in interaction with') the historical information.

Unemployment two years previously is, of course, just one among many alternative ways of indicating a history of unemployment, but the same depressing result emerges whichever indicator we use: an unemployment history is the best predictor of present unemployment. In short, previous unemployment is a very good predictor of subsequent unemployment. Our view of the impact of education on unemployment – or perhaps of the mechanism through which it operates – is substantially changed once we introduce information about personal employment histories.

Of course the finding begs more questions than it answers; it raises issues about deskilling, employers' selection procedures, regional differences and motivational effects, among other issues. However, this is precisely our point: it is only once we have extensive access to information about various aspects of people's histories – not only descriptions of previous employment but also of marital and family histories, previous living arrangements and locations, attitudes and activity patterns – that we can really begin to develop an adequate understanding of their present circumstances. This is why we collect longitudinal data.

An employment example

We can conclude this discussion of the importance of panel data with another concrete example from the BHPS. Table 12.4 shows data on employment status in the BHPS in the years 1991 and 1993.

Table 12.4 Changes in employment status

Employment status	1993		1991 Totals
	Employed	Unemployed	
Employed	86.7%	5%	91.7%
1991 Unemployed	5.1%	3.2%	8.3%
1993 Totals	91.8%	8.2%	100%

If we imagined that these data had been taken from two separate samples (i.e. with a repeated cross-sectional survey rather than by a panel survey), the picture of change they would offer is that illustrated in Figure 12.1.

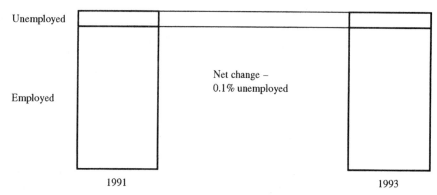

Figure 12.1 Changes in employment status: Cross-sectional

Figure 12.1 shows a net aggregate change of only 0.1 per cent. However, because the data are drawn from a panel study we can also observe the pattern of individual or micro change. This is shown in Figure 12.2 and reveals an overall change much greater than the one we see in Figure 12.1. Whereas the first figure showed only the changes in the proportions of those employed and unemployed in 1991 and 1993, Figure 12.2, because it contains individual level data, gives much more detail. We can see, for example, that 5 per cent of the sample changed their employment status from employed to unemployed and only 3.2 per cent constituted a hard core of unemployed.

Where Figure 12.1 shows only the pattern of net change, Figure 12.2 shows gross individual change. Not only do we see the stocks of the employed and unemployed but the flows between them too. This is vital to any analyses which attempt to explain why these changes take place. When linked with other information about the sample, we could begin to explore, say, who constitutes the hard core unemployed; or, as in our earlier example, the types of people who become unemployed, and why

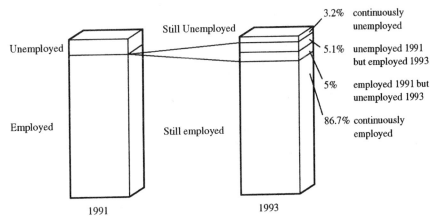

Figure 12.2 Changes in employment status: Panel information

this happens to them. In this way we can study not only the changes but the *changers*.

To summarize this short discussion of the benefits of longitudinal data, we can note that they derive essentially from the fact that data are collected from the same respondent at two or more points in time. This allows for more reliable measures of change than we can get from retrospective questions. In addition, there is a statistical advantage in estimating changes using panel data rather than regular or repeated cross-sections, since an element of sampling error is eliminated when we use the same sample at each time point rather than a new one. When it comes to substantive issues, we have seen that longitudinal data have the distinct advantage of allowing us to examine individual level change and to explain that change using dynamic models. However, these types of analysis are inevitably more complex than those which use only cross-sectional aggregate data. We turn now to discuss one of the main analytical procedures for the analysis of longitudinal data.

Event-history analysis

Event-history analysis is a comparatively recent methodology, particularly in the area of social research, where the collection of appropriate longitudinal data is also a relatively recent development. Put very simply, since longitudinal data are involved, the 'dependent variable' in event-history analysis can be thought of as the probability of an individual experiencing a particular event (marriage, redundancy, housing move, etc.) within a certain period of time. The forms of event-history models popular now are based on extensions of *life-table analysis*, which is a methodology widely used by demographers to calculate life expectancies from the so-called 'survival rates' of individuals in a population over time.

For instance, of so many people alive at time t, how many survive to time $t + 1$? From this the survival rate from $t - t_{+1}$ can be calculated. However, life tables like this are relatively simple. They deal with non-repeatable events (i.e. death), and the calculation of life expectancies does not depend on distinguishing between different causes of death. Once these parameters change, the mathematics of computation becomes very much more difficult, and more complex event-history models dealing with repeated and/or multiple types of event have to be used. As we have already said, we are *not* going to go into the intricacies of these models here. What we will try to do instead is to convey the basic similarity of their underlying form to multivariate models which you have already encountered in previous chapters. This is because, like the others, they fall into the general linear model (GLM) category (see pp. 200–2). By the use of a simple example, we hope to get across an intuitive rather than a formal understanding of the basic steps which are necessary in order to undertake event-history analysis.

Up to this point, we have only mentioned the nature of the dependent variable in such analysis: the probability of an event occurring within a particular time, more generally referred to as the **hazard rate**. As we have said, though, event-history models fall into the overall category of GLMs. We ought then to be able to somehow relate these individual probabilities to other, independent, variables which might affect them. For instance, the probability of the first housing move since leaving home occurring within a particular period of time will depend on a whole range of factors, among which might be age, income, education level, housing tenure, size of family, etc. All these factors might influence whether a housing move occurs, and, as with all GLMs, we should be able to estimate coefficients which indicate the relative contribution of each factor. Most models use procedures of 'maximum likelihood' to do this. In other words, coefficients for the factors are estimated which maximize the probability of replicating what was in fact observed in the data. This procedure can be likened to the attempt in log-linear analysis (see Chapter 11) to reproduce as closely as possible a set of observed cell frequencies from a cross-tabulation, using the most parsimonious combination of coefficients. For any particular model, those coefficients which contribute most to reproducing the observed frequencies represent those variables which are most important as 'explanatory' factors. In event-history analysis, however, the dependent variable is not a set of frequencies in a cross-tabulation, but the probability of an event occurring within a specific time.

Let us now consider the different types of variables, and how they are measured, before noting this down algebraically in a GLM-type equation. To return to our housing-move example; we saw that the dependent variable was simply the probability of an event occurring to an individual within a specific period of time (the hazard rate). In this example, it is the probability of the occurrence of the first housing move after leaving home. Hence for every year, say, that an individual contributes to the observations they are coded 1 if such an event occurs and 0 if it does not. (Of course, once it has occurred they do not contribute any more to the observations, since the *first* housing move is a non-repeatable event.) The independent variables are a mixture of factors representing both constant states and time-varying variables. The variables which to all intents and purposes we can take to represent constant states are level of education and housing tenure. We would not expect level of education to change much over the period of study, if we have defined leaving home as occurring *after* the completion of full-time education, and housing tenure is unlikely to change without a housing move. However, age, income and size of family are clearly things which could or do change over the period of study. They are known as time-varying variables and must be measured at each time point (e.g. every month or year, depending on the study).

So we might arrive at a linear model for an event-history analysis similar in form to many we have already seen:

$$P(t) = a + b_1 x_1^{ED} + b_2 x_2^{TEN} + b_3 x_3^{AGE}(t) + b_4 x_4^{INC}(t) + b_5 x_5^{FAM}(t)$$

where *P(t)* indicates the hazard rate (the probability that the event occurs during time *t*) and the $b_i x_i$ values represent the estimates for the effects of the various factors on this probability (education, tenure, age); *(t)* indicates a time-varying variable.

Having discussed the underlying formula we can now introduce an actual example of a simple type of event-history analysis, which has the advantage of looking quite familiar. This is the **logistic regression model**, in which the dependent variable is just the natural logarithm of the ratio of the probability (*P*) of experiencing an event during a particular period to the probability of not experiencing it $(1 - P)$. $\ln(P/1 - P)$ is known as the 'logit' of a probability, in this case the probability (*P*) of experiencing the event during a particular time (*t*). (In effect, this trick can be thought of as the same sort of thing as the log transformation used in log-linear analysis and referred to in Chapter 11. Basically all it does is to make the equation look more similar to other GLMs you have encountered.) So the equation now reads:

$$\text{Logit } P(t) = a + b_1 x_1^{ED} + b_2 x_2^{TEN} \ldots \text{etc.}$$

This is one of the simplest forms of event-history analysis, and should be relatively easy to understand now that we have looked at several different GLMs already. The underlying similarity of these models should by now be fairly evident to you. The logistic regression model is an example of a 'discrete-time' model, since time is measured in discrete units, e.g. years, and the dependent variable is the logit of the probability of an individual experiencing an event during that time. Any formulation in which the logit is used in this way must of necessity fall into the 'discrete-time' category. In fact, much event-history analysis is now done using 'continuous-time' models.

The continuous-time hazard rate is the *instantaneous* probability of the event occurring, i.e. not measured over a discrete period of time but at any single moment in time. To calculate the continuous time hazard rate, it is necessary to have data which give a more exact measure of the time of occurrence of the event concerned (for instance, day and month rather than just year), so this immediately imposes a practical constraint on their use. If in a panel study, for example, data are collected once a year from the participants (in other words, a series of 'cross-sectional' observations on the same individuals), then discrete-time models are appropriate, since all that will be known about any particular event is that it did or did not occur during that year. For instance, a change in an individual's marital state from single to married indicates that a marriage occurred at some point between time t (the date of the most recent survey) and time $t - 1$ (the date of the previous survey). If, however, retrospective event histories are collected for the year, then the exact occurrence of the event will be known (for instance, a retrospective marital history will reveal the actual date of marriage). In the latter case continuous-time models may be used, but the pay-off is always that the process of data collection itself will be more lengthy and consequently more expensive.

The continuous time hazard rate is the dependent variable in a model which has rapidly become one of the most popular and widely used techniques of event-history analysis in social research: the **proportional hazards model**. The model is called 'proportional' because for any point in time the ratio of the effect of being in one category of an independent variable (say, being married) relative to another (say, being single) is constant. Therefore the effect of a change in state on the hazard rate is always the same. It has become so widely used because it is particularly useful for assessing the impact of a range of independent variables on the hazard rate, an issue that social researchers are often interested in. For this purpose, the proportional hazards model has two major advantages: (1) it can deal with both constant and time-varying independent variables; and (2) it does not depend on the researcher specifying the relationship of the hazard rate with time. Many earlier types of event history models (referred to as *parametric models*) required the researcher to specify this underlying parameter, i.e. does the hazard rate increase linearly with time, decrease exponentially or what? In some circumstances, depending on the purpose of the analysis being undertaken, it may of course be useful to do just this. For instance, if the probability of finding a job for an unemployed individual was hypothesized either to increase with time (because the longer the period spent unemployed the more likely it becomes that *any* job will be acceptable) or to decrease with time (because the longer the period spent unemployed the less likely employers are to be interested) it is useful to be able to specify these relationships in order to test them. However, the proportional hazards model does not require the relationship with time to be specified, which simplifies life for the researcher interested primarily in the effects of independent variables! It is therefore often referred to as a *semi-parametric* or *partially parametric method*.

The basic equation for a proportional hazards model may thus be written as:

$$\log h(t) = a(t) + b_1 x_1^{ED} + b_2 x_2^{TEN} + b_3 x_3^{AGE}(t) + b_4 x_4^{INC}(t) + b_5 x_5^{FAM}(t)$$

where $\log h(t)$ = the log of the continuous-time hazard rate, $a(t)$ = the intercept, $b_i x_i$ = the effects of non-time-varying independent variables and $b_i x_i(t)$ = the effects of time-varying independent variables.

The coefficients are estimated in the proportional hazards model according to a *partial* (rather than maximum) likelihood procedure, and the relative magnitude of the *b* coefficients allows the relative contribution of each independent variable to the hazard rate to be assessed – the hazard rate being in the above example the chance at time *t* of experiencing the first housing move after leaving home.

There is an intuitively simple way of understanding the resulting coefficients. For example, if the *b* coefficient for size of family were 0.091, then the exponential of this value ($\exp^{0.091}$) gives the percentage increase in the hazard rate associated with each additional family member when controlling for all other variables in the model. $\text{Exp.}^{0.091} = 1.09$, which indicates a 9 per cent increase in the hazard rate for each additional member of the family. It is thus possible to directly compare the relative magnitude of the effects of the independent variables in the same way that in multiple regression analysis it was possible to compare directly the standardized partial regression coefficients (see Chapter 11). As with multiple regression, the coefficients can also be assessed in relation to their standard errors and their statistical significance determined. As always, these statistics are interpretative guides rather than ends in themselves, and will be meaningless if substantial errors have been made in the formulation of the model or the measurement of the variables. Particular consideration should be given to the potential effects of variables which may be thought to be important in the determination of the event concerned but have not been included in the model – perhaps because the necessary information was not collected in the survey. This consideration should, of course, be of primary importance in the assessment of any multivariate model.

Points to note

1 There are various ways of testing the violation of the assumption of proportionality of hazards for individuals in the study. In general, though, the model

is not very sensitive to such violations – and errors arising from other sources, e.g. omitted independent variables, are likely to have a far greater impact on the analysis anyway.

2 SPSS includes a procedure called COXREG in its Advanced Statistics facility which provides proportional hazards analyses. There are, in addition, a number of more specialized packages such as GLIM or LIMDEP.

3 The choice between the many types of model available depends upon a number of factors. In addition, as we noted at the end of Chapter 10 with respect to inferential statistics, the basic estimation procedures described here often require modification for complex sample designs. For those wishing to pursue these topics further a useful starting point is Allison (1984), which is relatively easy to follow and goes on to deal with more complex analyses than that described above. For a simple introduction to the idea of longitudinal studies see Hakim (1987): Chapter 8.

Acknowledgement

The support of both the Economic and Social Research Council and the University of Essex is gratefully acknowledged. The work reported in this chapter is part of the scientific programme of the ESRC Research Centre on Micro-social Change in Britain (the British Household Panel Study). We are grateful to Jonathan Gershuny for permission to reproduce analyses which he undertook on unemployment. A book discussing the initial findings from the BHPS – *Changing Households* – can be purchased from the Centre by writing to Hilary Doughty, BHPS, University of Essex, Colchester, CO4 3SQ (Tel. 01206-872938).

Key concepts

Make sure you have understood the following key concepts:

- micro-level change
- longitudinal studies
- unobserved determinants of behaviour
- event-history analysis
- hazard rate
- logistic regression model
- proportional hazards models

Multiple choice questions

1 What is the purpose of longitudinal analysis:

   (i)   to measure aggregate change at the population level?

   (ii) to measure gross change at the individual level?

   (iii) to produce retrospective data?

2 Which of the following *do not* produce prospective longitudinal data:

   (i)   panel studies?

   (ii) cohort studies?

   (iii) cross-sectional studies?

3 What is a 'hazard rate':

   (i)   the probability of surviving to age X?

   (ii) the probability of an event occurring within (or at) a particular time?

   (iii) the probability that the model fits the observed data well?

Exercise 5

Included on the data-disk in the file called EXAMPLE.SPS is an annotated set of SPSS commands which demonstrate how the data used in Table 12.4 were produced. These show the gross (micro-level) and net (aggregate) changes in employment status between waves 1 (1991) and 3 (1993) of the BHPS. You can run this file directly by bringing it into the scratch.pad in SPSS/PC+ or by opening it as a syntax file in SPSS FOR WINDOWS.

Table 12.5 lists all the variables that are available to you in the BHPS123 data files.

To complete Exercise 5 select any *other* variable from the BHPS123 data file (see below) and:

- construct a similar table to Table 12.4, showing the gross and net change in status between two waves of BHPS data
- comment in writing on the findings in respect of the gross and net changes shown; what does the longitudinal element of the analysis tell you that you would not have known from the net change?

Table 12.5 Variable descriptions; BHPS123.SYS/BHPS123.SAV

Wave variable	Variable name	Description
WAVE 1		
VARIABLES (1991)	ASEX	Sex of respondent
	AAGE	Age (continuous variable)
	AQFEDHI	Highest educational qualification
	AJSAT	Job satisfaction
	AJBSEG	Socio-economic group
	AJBGOLD	John Goldthorpe's social class categories
	AJBRGSC	Registrar General's social class categories
	AOPPOL4	From: 'If the government had to choose between maintaining living standards or protecting the environment, to which do you think it should give the highest priority?'
	ATENURE	Housing tenure
	AFIYR	Annual income (continuous variable)
	AMASTAT	Marital status
	AVOTE	Political party supported
	AOPFAME	From: 'Having a full time job is the best way for a woman to be an independent person' (scaled response)
	AOPFAMF	From: 'A husband's job is to earn money; a wife's job is to look after the home and family' (scaled response)
	AOPPOL1	From: 'If you had to choose among these political goals, which would be your first choice?'
	AJBSTAT	Employment status
	AHID	Weighting variable
	APNO	Weighting variable
WAVE 2		
VARIABLES (1992)	BQFEDHI	Highest educational qualification
	BJSAT	Job satisfaction
	BJBSEG	Socio-economic group
	BJBGOLD	John Goldthorpe's social class categories
	BJBRGSC	Registrar General's social class categories
	BTENURE	Housing tenure

Table 12.5 Continued

Wave variable	Variable name	Description
	BFIYR	Annual income (continuous variable)
	BMASTAT	Marital status
	BVOTE	Political party supported
	BOPPOL1	From: 'If you had to choose among these political goals, which would be your first choice?'
	BJBSTAT	Employment status
WAVE 3 VARIABLES (1993)	CQFEDHI	Highest educational qualification
	CJSAT	Job satisfaction
	CBJSEG	Socio-economic group
	CJBGOLD	John Goldthorpe's social class categories
	CJBRGSC	Registrar General's social class categories
	COPPOL4	From: 'If the government had to choose between maintaining living standards or protecting the environment, to which do you think it should give the highest priority?'
	CTENURE	Housing tenure
	CFIYR	Annual income (continuous variable)
	CMASTAT	Marital status
	CVOTE	Political party supported
	COPFAME	From: 'Having a full time job is the best way for a woman to be an independent person' (scaled response)
	COPFAMF	From: 'A husband's job is to earn money; a wife's job is to look after the home and family' (scaled response)
	COPPOL1	From: 'If you had to choose among these political goals, which would be your first choice?'
	CJBSTAT	Employment status
	CLRWGHT	Weighting variable

Concluding remarks

In this book we have tried to adopt an approach which is not too statistically complex for the beginner to follow, but which at the same time avoids the pitfalls of providing a 'cookbook' which shows how to perform relatively sophisticated analyses without putting sufficient stress on the assumptions that underlie them, and on their limitations. We believe that the key to this 'middle path' lies in demonstrating the basic principles of analysing data at the simplest level – and then going on to explain in a non-formal way how these principles apply at more sophisticated levels. It is assumed (i) that readers will have worked through the text in a logical way (i.e. from beginning to end!), since later chapters contain material which assumes that the content of previous chapters has been absorbed, and (ii) that we have made it clear that those who now wish either to pursue these topics to a higher level, or who wish to embark on applied multivariate analysis themselves will need to consult other more detailed texts before they are in a position to do so. Hopefully, though, those who were previously beginners in quantitative analysis will now be able to grasp the gist of such texts, which in turn will help them to develop a more formal appreciation.

We hope we have not left anyone floundering. The last two chapters in particular are relatively demanding, since we have tried to introduce the underlying principles of a vast range of complex analytic techniques in a concise and comprehensible way. We have attempted this within an introductory text because social science is developing extremely rapidly in terms of the quantitative skills expected of its students and practitioners. It is increasingly necessary to be able to understand and interpret multivariate analyses for all types of data. On the other hand, we would argue that it is dangerous to attempt to introduce detailed instructions on how to *perform* such analyses, without first ensuring that the underlying principles are firmly understood. An understanding of the basics is more important than an immediate ticket to doing multivariate analysis.

Remember that it pays to read and re-read pieces that seem difficult.

In some respects, learning about data analysis is a bit like learning a foreign language; it will inevitably appear obscure at first, but there is nothing so effective in becoming familiar with it as practice and constant repetition!

Appendix: use of the data disk

The disk enclosed with this book is a 3.5″ (1.44MB) cassette-type floppy disk. On it you will find nine files:

READ.ME
DEMO.DAT
CLASS.SYS
CLASS.SAV
BHPS1.SYS
BHPS1.SAV
BHPS123.SYS
BHPS123.SAV
EXAMPLE.SPS

containing information and data for you to use. A full description of what is contained in the last eight of these files is found in the file: READ.ME.

In order to start using the disk, then, you need to insert it into your floppy drive a: and at the DOS prompt (C:\>), type:

type a: read.me ¦more (The ¦more switch enables you to read through screen by screen.)

Alternatively, you can read the READ.ME file in the DOS editor, which allows you to scroll through it by typing:

edit a:read.me

at the DOS prompt.

The text contained in the READ.ME file will tell you what the files are, and how you can use them. If you want a hard copy of the READ.ME file you can print it using the DOS print command (remember that in a lab environment this command may vary locally, according to the location of specific printers), or directly from the File menu of the editor.

Glossary of methodological and statistical terms

aggregate change *See* micro-level change.

aggregate data Data produced for broad groups or categories (e.g. types of persons or households) and in which the characteristics of individual respondents are no longer identifiable. *See also* microdata; micro-level change.

algorithm Initially a word with equivalent meaning to formula, but under the influence of computing now regarded as the step-by-step procedure to solve a problem, usually supported by a mathematical proof. In sociology, the term is generally used more loosely than this, to describe the steps which must be followed to construct a new variable from a set of other variables. A good example would be the algorithm used by Erik Olin Wright to arrive at his social class variable, by combining particular combinations of ownership and decision-making responsibilities, said to characterize the various class locations (see Wright, *Classes*, 1985).

association coefficients Association coefficients consist of a number used to indicate the degree to which two variables or attributes are related. Two basic types are covariation measures and dis/similarity measures. Covariation measures (such as the Pearsonian product-moment correlation, r) are based upon the product (multiplication) of the data values, and indicate the extent to which the variables are associated ($0 =$ none and $1 =$ perfect), and the direction in which the variables vary with each other (positive, where one variable increases with another, or negative where one variable decreases as the other increases). Association measures should be chosen by reference to the level of measurement of the variables involved. Statistical associations and measures of correlation are not in themselves evidence of causal relationships, which must be identified by theoretical reasoning and models. In practice, statistical associations are often treated as equivalent to establishing causal links, with textbooks thus warning against spurious correlations. *See also* proportionate reduction of error (PRE); standardized measures of association.

bar chart A diagram for displaying frequency distributions of nominal level data. Bars are drawn proportional to the frequency in each category of a variable. Bars are of the same width and are separate from each other. *See also* distribution (statistical or frequency); histogram.

binomial distribution A probability distribution for the occurrence of a specific event which either occurs or not – such as winning a race. The binomial distribution is symmetrical (like the normal distribution), in certain cases, but is otherwise skewed. For the calculation of differences between sample proportions it can be approximated by the normal distribution. *See also* normal distribution; distribution (statistical or frequency).

bivariate analysis *See* multivariate analysis.

category A key aspect of the measurement process involves placing observations or measurements into groups or categories on the basis of unequivocally shared features. Hence a category is a homogeneous grouping of data. For example, the variable 'sex' would have two categories, male and female; the variable 'social class' might have three categories, upper, middle, and working. In the former case the rule for assigning cases or observations to the appropriate category is relatively simple. In the latter, the rules would be more complex and dependent upon the class theory being used. *See also* coding; operational definition; variable.

central tendency (measures of) A statistical term applied to the central value in a frequency distribution – commonly referred to as the average. Depending on the level of measurement of the variable (nominal, ordinal, interval or ratio), and the shape of the distribution (normal or otherwise), various measures of central tendency may be calculated. The mean is the most well known, and is obtained by adding together all the individual values in a set of measurements, then dividing the sum by the total number of cases in the set – to give the average age, height, income, or whatever. However, if a particular distribution is highly skewed (that is, if there are several numbers of extreme value at one or other end of the series), then it may make more sense to calculate the median. The median is literally the middle value in a series of numbers, and may be used in place of the mean when, for example, average income is calculated, since the distribution of income is generally highly skewed. The third measure of central tendency, the mode, is used to describe the most frequently occurring category of a non-numeric variable (for example, voting intention). It is less frequently employed than the mean or median.

chi-square tests *See* significance tests; statistical independence.

closed response Fixed choice answers to an interview question, which may be read out, or shown to respondents on a card, for them to choose the reply closest to their views or situation. *See also* open response, open-ended question.

codebook A complete listing of all categories, codes and descriptions for each variable in a dataset. Frequencies are often included, too. *See also* coding.

coding The assignment of responses to survey questions (or other data) into predetermined categories of a variable. For example, when a person answers a question on how they will vote in a general election by saying 'Conservative', we assign a numeral to this type of answer which distinguishes it from other types of answer – such as Labour or Liberal Democrat which could be identified by other numerals. Hence each type of answer is given a separate numeric code, usually for entry into a computer data file for subsequent analysis. *See also* category; codebook; closed response; open response; raw data file.

cohort, cohort analysis The term cohort originally referred to a Roman military unit, but it is now used to identify any group of people with a time-specific common experience, such as graduating from university in the same year, or cohorts defined by time of birth, marriage or widowhood. Hence cohort study is a variant of the panel study. Cohort analysis refers to any study in which there are measures of some characteristics of one or more cohorts at regular intervals after the defining event. Perhaps the best-known cohort study in Britain is the *National Child Development Study*, a cohort of people born in a particular week in March 1958. Data have been collected on this cohort at five different times, most recently in 1991. The critical problem of cohort analysis is to differentiate age, cohort and period effects. Age effects are associated with growing older; cohort effects are common to people born at the same time; period effects are due to the shared experience of particular historical events – for example the Second World War. Unfortunately there is no simple way of disentangling these. This is important substantively: because the effects are confounded, different interpretations of change are usually possible (for example, observed cultural, political or social changes may be due to cohort effects or ageing), and conclusions have to be correspondingly tentative. When informed by sound theory, however, cohort analysis is a powerful analytic technique. *See also* microdata; panel study.

component variables An aspect of an independent variable which produces differences on a dependent variable. For example, if we discover that a new method of teaching social science data analysis, in which computer-aided teaching forms a key component, obtains better results than a previous chalk and talk teaching method, computer-aided teaching would be a component variable: an aspect of the independent variable – the new teaching method – responsible for differences on the dependent variable (the results students obtain). *See also* dependent variable; independent variable.

computer packages Quantitative sociologists now have access to a huge variety of statistical packages for managing and analysing large-scale data-sets. The most widely used of these is probably SPSS (the Statistical Package for the Social Sciences), hence its use in this book. *See also* SPSS.

concepts The terminological means by which social scientists seek to analyse social phenomena, to classify the objects of the observed world, impart meaning through explanation to these phenomena, and formulate higher-level propositions on the basis of these observations. Concepts have themselves been categorized in many ways, for example one distinction is between those which describe directly observable phenomena, and those which signify inferred phenomena. The malleability of concepts is attested to by the fact that there is controversy over their definition and indeed there exists a class of such concepts termed 'essentially contested concepts'. Many concepts in the social sciences are both descriptive and evaluative and many carry emotional or theoretically loaded overtones. Such terms as exploitation, alienation, discrimination and even social class bring with them a heavy baggage of values.

confidence intervals The spread of values around the mean for a sample survey variable which, using the conventional 95 per cent confidence level, equate to the mean plus or minus two standard deviations, or standard errors of the mean. *See also* central tendency (measures of); variation (statistical).

contingency table Contingency tables, often referred to as cross-classifications or cross-tabulations, are tables of counts which describe and analyse the relationship between two or more variables in a data-set. They contain row variables across the horizontal axis and column variables down the vertical. Cell entries give the number of cases (persons, households, or other units of analysis) that occur in each cell. The cells themselves are formed by combining one category from each of the row and column variables. Marginal totals (or marginal frequencies) give the total number of cases found in each category of the variables – in other words they are the row and column totals. Normally, cell entries are expressed as either row or column percentages (depending on the point the analyst wishes to make), with the total numbers of cases shown in the marginals. These elements are shown in tabular form below.

COLUMN VARIABLE

		variable A	variable B	
R O W	V A R I A B L E	variable X	cell entry	cell entry	row marginal
		variable Y	cell entry	cell entry	row marginal
			column marginal	column marginal	Total number

The above is a template for a typical 2 × 2 cross-tabulation. However, contingency tables can take more complex forms, with three or more variables and several categories of each. In such complex presentations, it is often difficult both to determine the natures of the causal relationships to be found among the variables, and then to demonstrate these to the reader. For example, it may be hard to eliminate spurious correlations, or to establish three-way interaction effects, that is, those cases where two variables are associated, but the strength or direction of the association varies across different categories of the variables. For these reasons the analysis of complex contingency tables is nowadays normally undertaken using the mathematical techniques of log-linear analysis. *See also* log-linear analysis; multivariate analysis; tabular presentation.

control   Experimental research designs require that all cases are randomly allocated to either the experimental group which receives the treatment being tested, or to a control group which receives no treatment or an ineffective (placebo) treatment, and hence provides baseline information on spontaneous developments against which the effects of the experimental treatment can be measured.

control group   A group used for comparison with another, either because it represents the most common or typical case, or because it illustrates the absence of some phenomenon being studied. Human beings are not inert, lifeless matter, and hence cannot be studied simply by carrying out before-and-after studies around some experimental stimulus applied to them. Many other developments and changes will be occurring spontaneously at the same time, as people go about their lives, and it is difficult to disentangle the effects of one particular stimulus from all the others simultaneously affecting people, as individuals or as groups. The solution is to identify a group, or social aggregate, that serves as a control group in providing information on characteristics or changes in a baseline situation that is as close to 'ordinary' as possible, or illustrates social behaviour in the absence of the key factor of interest. Control groups can be created at the sampling stage, through statistical manipulation of the data-set, or during analysis. The most rigorous type is experimental controls, obtained by random allocation of cases. *See also* control.

control variables *See* elaboration.

correlation If a change in the amount of one variable is accompanied by a comparable change in the amount of another variable, and the latter change does not occur in the absence of the former change, then the variables are said to be correlated. Correlations may be linear (where there is a constant ratio between the rates of change in each of the variables) or curvilinear (where the rate of change of one variable is at an increasing or decreasing ratio to the rate of change in the other variable). They may be positive (increase in one variable is associated with increase in the other) or negative (increase in one variable associated with decrease in the other). Negative correlations are sometimes termed inverse correlations; positive correlations are occasionally referred to as direct correlations. When two (or more) variables are correlated, but there is no causal link between them, then the correlation is said to be spurious: both may be affected by a third (antecedent) variable. *See also* association coefficients; multivariate analysis.

covariation *See* association coefficients.

cross-sectional analysis, cross-sectional data Statistical analysis which provides information on the characteristics of, and statistical relationships between, individual units of study at a specified moment in time (the moment of data collection). Sometimes referred to as a 'snapshot' approach, cross-sectional analysis cannot therefore provide information on change or processes over time, for which purpose a longitudinal study design is required. However, for logistical reasons, the bulk of social survey data to date has been collected in a form suitable only for cross-sectional analysis. *See also* micro-level change; panel study; survey, social survey.

cross-tabulation, cross-classification *See* contingency table.

data Plural of datum, a fact or statistic. Hence data are records of observations. These might take a number of forms for example, scores in IQ tests, interview records, fieldwork diaries or taped interviews. All of these provide data, that is, observations from which inferences may be drawn, via analysis.

data analysis Whereas statistics refer to formal mathematical procedures as they are applied to data, data analysis refers to the practical application of such procedures to the analysis of social science data. That is, data analysis is concerned with sensitizing social researchers to the use, interpretation and evaluation of relevant data rather than with the more formal understanding of statistics. It involves the understanding of certain statistical techniques in terms of knowing which ones apply to which sort of data or which can best deal with certain kinds of problems in analysis; but this understanding takes the form of appreciation and awareness rather than any particular mathematical facility. The more familiar we become with techniques of data analysis, the better we can think about data in general. This is because a proper understanding of data analysis improves the way in which we think about, interpret, evaluate and plan empirical research. Data analysis is thus concerned with explaining variance, with explaining why there is variability in some particular characteristic in a population or sample which is of theoretical importance to social researchers.

data archive, data-bank   A storage and retrieval facility or service for social scientific data. Data archiving has grown in parallel with the development of secondary analysis as a recognized field of social research. The International Federation of Data Organizations for the Social Sciences (IFDO) was founded as recently as 1977 by four North American and seven European data archives. These archives act as lending libraries for machine-readable information collected by academics and government agencies. In the vast majority of cases, the information in question is derived from social surveys (most data archives are in fact survey archives), although there are now archives which store the taped interviews obtained by oral historians and others. Survey archives are often depositories for official statistics, including censuses, as well as non-official data-sets such as opinion polls and academic surveys. In the UK, for example, the Economic and Social Research Council established such a data archive at the University of Essex in the late 1960s. Similar archives exist at many universities in America and Europe.

data coding   *See* coding.

deduction, deductive   The use of logical rules to arrive at a set of premises from which certain conclusions must follow. Deduction begins with theory, moves to hypothesis derived from the theory, and then tests hypotheses via prediction and observations. This approach to testing and theory is often referred to as the hypothetico-deductive method, and since it emphasizes hypotheses, prediction, and testing, is sometimes held to be the method *par excellence* of science. *See also* induction, inductive.

dependent variable   Within a particular study, analysis or model, a dependent variable is the social element whose characteristics or variations are to be explained by reference to the influence of other, prior, so-called independent variables. For example, a person's income (dependent variable) may vary according to age and social class (independent variables). The value of dependent variables can often be predicted using some form of causal modelling. Whether a variable is treated as dependent or independent is determined by the theoretical framework and focus of a study. *See also* independent variable; variable.

descriptive statistics   *See* inferential statistics.

dichotomous variable, dichotomy   Any variable which has only two categories. In theory these categories are meant to be mutually exclusive. The variable 'sex', with its two categories of 'male' and 'female', is a good example. There are numerous well-known examples of dichotomies in sociology: Tönnies's *Gemeinschaft* and *Gesellschaft*, Durkheim's mechanical and organic solidarity, and so on. A variable with more than two categories is called a polytomy. Sometimes, in order to simplify analysis, polytomous variables are collapsed – the number of categories is reduced by merging adjacent codes – to a dichotomy.

distribution of repeated sample means   A normally shaped distribution defined by its mean and standard deviation, the distribution of repeated sample means is a hypothetical distribution used in statistical significance testing. The central value of the distribution is simply the population mean (μ), while the standard deviation (called the 'standard error') is given by: $\frac{\sigma}{\sqrt{n}}$ σ is just the familiar population standard deviation for the variable concerned (i.e. a measure of population variability), while n is the number of cases in the (repeated) sample. The shape of the distribution therefore depends on: (i) the size of the sample; and (ii) the variability of the variable in the population, indicated by the population standard deviation σ. *See also* normal distribution; statistical inference; significance tests.

distribution (statistical or frequency)   A series of figures presenting all observed values (as raw numbers or proportion of cases) for a variable in a quantitative data-set – enabling a quick visual appreciation of the distribution of the data. The frequency distribution may be further illustrated by use of graphics such as a bar chart or histogram. Frequency distributions from a survey data-set are usually the first output from the clean and edited data-set, showing the response totals for each possible reply to each question in the questionnaire.

dummy variables   In quantitative data analysis, researchers are sometimes interested in the implications of non-interval level variables for a dependent variable, as for example in the case of the relationship between sex and income. Although regression analyses normally require data scaled at the interval level, it is possible to include non-interval variables in a multiple regression by creating appropriate so-called dummy variables. In the example just cited, this would involve coding men as 1 and women as 0: or, where the independent variable comprises more than two (let us say n) categories, creating a dummy variable comprising $n - 1$ dummy variables. Thus, if the independent variable 'social class' contains the four categories 'upper', 'middle', 'working' and 'none', then in order to include these in a multiple regression analysis three dummy variables would have to be created: $v1$ 'upper' (coded 1) or 'not upper' (coded 0); $v2$ 'middle' (coded 1) or 'not middle' (coded 0); $v3$ 'working' (coded 1) or 'not working' (coded 0). The fourth category is represented by these three dummy variables since it can be described by the combination 000. Each category in the social class variable now has a unique combination of zeros or ones by means of which its presence or absence can be indicated. In a regression analysis involving dummy variables the resulting regression coefficients are then treated as if they were based on variables measured at the interval level. *See also* measurement, levels of.

elaboration   The method of studying correlations between variables by introducing control variables to see how the original observed relations are affected. This assists both in understanding the conditions under which a relationship operates and is necessary to detect spurious correlations. *See also* correlation; spurious correlation; partitioning variance, partial relationships; variable.

empirical   As applied to statements, particular research projects, or even to general approaches to research, the term 'empirical' implies a close relationship to sensory experience, observation or experiment. Sometimes the term is contrasted with abstract or theoretical, sometimes with dogmatic, or sometimes with scholarly. In its derogatory uses, lack of attention to matters of principle or theory is implied. As a term of approval, for example from the standpoint of empiricism, the term implies practical relevance, or testability, as against bookish scholasticism or groundless speculation.

error (sampling and non-sampling)   There are many sources of inaccuracy, or error, in a survey. Sampling error consists of bias in sample selection procedures, plus random sampling error. Non-response bias can be measured and analysed after interviewing is completed. There is scope for less visible and less measurable error in the interviewing process itself, and in the subsequent coding and classification of replies. Interviewer bias affects some interviews, and interviewers do occasionally make mistakes, such as overlooking a whole section of a questionnaire. Coding errors arise when data are prepared for analysis. They consist of simple mispunches, from striking the wrong key to code a reply, and misclassification, as when a job description is not read or understood correctly, and is allocated to the wrong occupation code. Edit and consistency checks after data preparation will identify some but not all coding errors. Surveys require rigorous attention to detail at every stage in the process to reduce error to the minimum. Even small inaccuracies at each stage can mount up to an appreciable amount of total error in the end.

event-history analysis   A form of longitudinal analysis in which the unit of enquiry is not the individual or social group but the socially significant event, for example, change of occupation, spell of unemployment, change of marital status, or other significant life-event. *See also* hazard model, proportional-hazard model.

fieldwork   Data collection for any study that involves talking to people or asking them questions about their activities and views, sometimes including attempts at systematic observation of their behaviour. Fieldwork ranges from large-scale survey interviewing by hundreds of professional interviewers, to the lone researcher recording information collected through participant observation in a small-scale case study. The term is sometimes extended to any research activity that takes one out of the office and into the 'field' that is the subject of the study.

frequency distribution   *See* distribution (statistical or frequency).

general linear models (GLM)   This refers to a group of statistical techniques or procedures, related by a similar underlying equation or 'model'. These techniques constitute the most well-known procedures of multivariate statistical analysis. The simple linear regression equation $Y = a + bX + e$ is the simplest example of a generalized formula which relates the value of a dependent variable (Y) to a systematic component made up of the linear effects of various independent variables (variance *explained*) and a random or error component expressing the variation not accounted for by the relationship between the dependent and independent variables (*residual* variance). The multiple regression equation for the simultaneous effect of two independent variables on a single dependent variable is, for example, $Y = a + b_1x_1 + b_2x_2 + e$. Here another 'slope' parameter, b_2, has been introduced into the equation, which expresses the effect of the second independent variable, x_2, on the dependent variable. With the growth of statistical knowledge, and in particular the development of more sophisticated computing software, the principles of analysis initially developed for analysing linear relationships between interval-level variables have been extended and developed so that it is now possible to utilize similarly structured models for the analysis of a wide range of different types of data and kinds of relationship. Well-known examples of procedures which fall into the category of GLMs are log-linear analysis (for the analysis of categoric cross-tabulated data), proportional hazards models (for the analysis of longitudinal event-history data) as well as analysis of variance, logit models, discriminant analysis, factor analysis, etc. SPSS includes capabilities to deal with most of these, but there are in addition computer packages available which are dedicated to GLMs, such as GLIM and LISREL.

goodness of fit   A statistical term used to indicate the correspondence between an observed distribution and a model or hypothetical mathematical distribution. In many statistical tests of significance, the hypothetical or expected distribution is a model based upon there being no relationship between the dependent and independent variables. The tests then measure whether any observed deviation from the expected model may reasonably be accounted for by chance sampling variation, or whether it is sufficiently large to indicate a real difference, generalizable to the population from which the sample was taken. *See also* significance tests.

gross change   *See* micro-level change.

hazard model, proportional-hazard model   A statistical technique for determining the 'hazard function' or hazard rate, i.e. the probability that an individual will experience an event (for example first employment) within a particular time period, given that the individual was subject to the risk that the event might occur (in this case, given continuing initial unemployment). *See also* event-history analysis.

hazard rate   *See* hazard model, proportional-hazard model.

histogram   A diagram which represents a frequency distribution of data, where the data are measured at least at interval level. Blocks proportional in width to the size of the interval or categories are raised along the horizontal axis. The height of each block is then adjusted so that its area is proportional to the relative frequency of its category. The diagram thus appears as a series of bars of varying height. *See also* bar chart.

hypothesis, hypothesis testing   A hypothesis is an untested statement about the relationship (usually of association or causation) between concepts within a given theory. Hypothesis testing involves the testing of a hypothesis in a scientific manner, and hence requires a precise statement of the supposed relationship between the concepts under investigation, and the data which would need to be collected for the testing to take place. It is normal in social science to assume the null hypothesis and to use statistical methods in the testing process. However, hypothesis testing is perhaps best seen as involving also an element of falsificationism. *See also* deduction, deductive.

independent variable   Within a particular study, analysis, or model, the independent (or explanatory) variable is the social element whose characteristics or variations shape and determine the dependent variable: for example, the age of marriage can help explain the likelihood of divorce. In an experimental situation, independent variables can be systematically manipulated, so that the effect on the dependent variable can be observed. Whether a variable is treated as dependent or independent is determined by the theoretical framework and focus of a study, but independent variables must precede the dependent variable, and should have causal powers. *See also* dependent variable; variable.

induction, inductive   The inverse of deduction. Induction begins from particular observations from which empirical generalizations are made. These generalizations then form the basis for theory-building. So-called analytic induction is common in qualitative studies within sociology. This method requires that every case examined in a piece of research substantiates a hypothesis. The researcher formulates a general hypothesis from observation of initial cases, investigates subsequent cases in the search for a negative instance and reformulates the hypothesis to cope with those confounding cases that are encountered. The process is deemed to be exhausted when no new discrepant cases can be found – a necessarily rather subjective judgement – and the (now revised) generalization is allowed to stand. *See also* deduction, deductive.

inferential statistics   Statistics which permit the researcher to demonstrate the probability that the results deriving from a sample are likely to be found in the population from which the sample has been drawn. They therefore allow sociologists to generalize from representative samples, by applying 'tests of significance' to patterns found in these samples, in order to determine whether these hold for populations as a whole. The other type of statistics in which sociologists are interested are descriptive statistics, which summarize the patterns in the responses within a data-set, and provide information about averages, correlations, and so forth. *See also* significance tests; statistical inference.

intervening variable   A variable, used in the process of explaining an observed relationship between an independent and dependent variable(s), such that $X \rightarrow TY$, where T is the intervening variable which is used to explain the $X \rightarrow Y$ relationship. For example, if X is age and Y is reading ability, the causal relationship between X and Y might be explained by the intervening variable T, say education, which explains the $X \rightarrow Y$ link. Hence X is an indirect cause of Y through the intervening variable T: T predicts Y but is simultaneously predicted by X.

logistical regression model   *See* regression, regression analysis.

log-linear analysis   A statistical technique for analysing relationships within contingency tables. Cross-classified tables of data are very common in sociology, for example cross-tabulations of political preference by sex, educational attainment by social class, and so forth. Conventionally, these tables are analysed by looking at departures from statistical independence by using the χ^2 test. This principle of independence can be written as:

$$\log n_{ij} = \log n_i + \log n_j - \log n$$

(hence involving the *logarithms* of the data combined in an additive or *linear* composition). This makes the analysis simpler, more akin to analysis of variance (*see* variation, statistical), and more easily generalizable to three or more variables. It also allows interaction effects to be studied; that is, the effect which both i and j together have, over and above the effect of i and the effect of j. Log-linear analysis begins with a (definitionally true but trivial) 'saturated' model, where all possible direct and interaction effects are specified. Simpler models are then examined which leave out some of these effects (on the basis of theory or hunch) to see whether good fits to the data can be obtained with fewer effects (that is, with a more parsimonious model), and in that way the researcher may infer what variables are most important and what the pattern of effect actually is in the data. It is a very flexible multivariate procedure, best adapted to analysing attributes (variables at the nominal level of measurement), and is only feasible using computer programs. *See also* contingency table; multivariate analysis; parsimony.

longitudinal studies   *See* cohort; micro-level change; panel study.

marginal frequencies   *See* contingency table.

mean   *See* central tendency (measures of).

measurement, levels of   Term used to describe different measurement scales in relation to the amount of information they convey and the methods which can be used to analyse them. Conventionally four levels are identified: nominal, ordinal, interval and ratio (N-O-I-R). Nominal measures simply express difference (e.g. sex – male and female); ordinal measures express degree but not precise amount of difference (e.g. social position – upper class, working class); interval and ratio levels express precise degrees of difference in numeric terms (e.g. age – 10 years old, 20 years old). Interval level data can be reduced to ordinal level data (e.g. age in single years can be expressed as age in banded groups) but data at nominal or ordinal level cannot be expressed at interval level.

measures of association   *See* association coefficients; proportionate reduction in error; standardized measures of association.

measures of dispersion   *See* variation.

median   *See* central tendency (measures of).

microdata   Data-sets containing information on individual respondents to an enquiry, be they persons, households, or organizations such as schools or companies. Microdata are virtually always anonymized, with not only names and addresses omitted to preserve confidentiality, but also detailed geographical or industry codes sometimes deleted or broadbanded to obscure identities. *See also* aggregate data; micro-level change.

micro-level change   We can make a basic distinction between the measurement of net or aggregate change, that is change at the macro-level, and the measurement of gross or individual change, or change at the micro-level. We can illustrate this distinction by reference to survey data. Most surveys are conducted at single points in time. As such they are cross-sections and so cannot tell us much about social change. However, regular or repeated cross-sectional social surveys, like the General Household Survey, in which the same questions are asked every year of a different sample of the population, are somewhat better tools for the study of change. They provide a time-series and thus permit analysis of net change at the aggregate or macro-level (for example, proportion of the population below the poverty line at time t could be compared with the proportion at time $t - 1$). However, in order to study change at the individual or micro-level, it is necessary to employ a longitudinal design and, therefore, a prospective method such as a panel survey in which the same individuals are interviewed repeatedly across time. The longitudinal data provided by a panel survey will then allow researchers not only to examine the proportion of the population at different times in states such as poverty but, because of their panel nature, these micro-data can also be used to examine flows into and out of these states, thus opening up a wider range of possibilities in terms of causal analyses and inferences. In other words longitudinal data tell us about change at the individual or micro level; cross-sections tell us only about populations at one time point. *See also* aggregate data; cohort, cohort analysis; cross-sectional analysis, cross-sectional data; microdata; panel study; time-series data.

mode   *See* central tendency (measures of).

model   This is a term which has been given a wide variety of different meanings by sociologists. In some cases it has been used as a synonym for theory, but in others as a reference to a system of abstract concepts at a more general level than a theory. Equally, it is used to refer to a statistical model, as in causal modelling. Whichever definition is used the essence of a model is that it requires the researcher to engage with theory and thus avoid empiricism. Whatever form it takes, a model is an aid to complex theoretical activity, and directs our attention to concepts or variables and their interrelationships. *See also* multivariate analysis.

model of no association　*See* statistical independence.

multiple correlation coefficient　*See* regression, regression analysis.

multiple regression　*See* regression, regression analysis.

multivariate analysis　Univariate analysis consists in describing and explaining the variation in a single variable. Bivariate analysis does the same for two variables taken together (covariation). Multivariate analysis (MVA) considers the simultaneous effects of many variables taken together. A crucial role is played by the multivariate normal distribution, which allows simplifying assumptions to be made (such as the fact that the interrelations of many variables can be reduced to information on the correlations between each pair), which make it feasible to develop appropriate models. MVA models are often expressed in algebraic form (as a set of linear equations specifying the way in which the variables combine with each other to affect the dependent variable) and can also be thought of geometrically. Thus, the familiar bivariate scatterplot of individuals in the two dimensions representing two variables can be extended to higher-dimensional (variable) spaces, and MVA can be thought of as discovering how the points cluster together. The most familiar and often-used variants of MVA include extensions of regression analysis and analysis of variance, to multiple regression and multivariate analysis of variance respectively, both of which examine the linear effect of a number of independent variables on a single dependent variable. Recently, much effort has gone into the development of MVA for discrete (nominal and ordinal) data, of particular relevance to social scientists interested in analysing complex cross-tabulations and category counts (the most common forms of numerical analysis in sociology). Of especial interest is log-linear analysis (akin both to analysis of variance and chi-squared analysis) which allows the interrelationships in a multi-way contingency table to be presented more simply and parsimoniously. *See also* log-linear analysis; parsimony, parsimonous; regression, regression analysis; variation (statistical).

net change　*See* micro-level change.

non-parametric statistics　A branch of statistical inference which makes no assumptions about the underlying distributional form of variables. While parametric statistics are based upon an ideal hypothetical mathematical form for the data (usually the normal distribution) some statisticians claim that for social science data the assumptions required to do this are hardly ever justified, and consequently that it is always preferable to use non-parametric statistics. A well-known example equivalent to the parametric *t*-test, is the Mann–Whitney U-test. *See also* parametric statistics.

normal approximation to the binomial distribution　*See* binomial distribution.

normal distribution　In common usage, normality is treated as synonymous with natural, conventional, acceptable or ordinary. In statistics, normality is defined as the most commonly occurring, the numerically most frequent type, which is then used as the baseline for identifying the unusual and the statistically rare.

A hypothetical mathematical distribution, the normal distribution provides an idealized model for comparison with observed variable distributions, and is the most commonly used mathematical model in statistical inference. In form it is a symmetrical, bell-shaped curve. The normal distribution for any particular variable is defined by its mean and standard deviation. The mathematical properties of the normal distribution can be used to estimate the proportion in a sample falling above or below any particular reading or measurement for any variable to which the model is being applied. It is said to be relatively 'robust' to non-normality in observed variable distributions: in other words, in many circumstances it will serve as a reasonable model, even in cases where observed variable distributions appear to be rather inadequate approximations to normality. Even when a population does not itself have a normal distribution, the distribution of sample means will tend to approximate to a normal distribution. *See also* central tendency (measures of); distribution of repeated sample means; variation (statistical).

null hypothesis   The principle underlying significance tests, which proposes that any differences observed between two samples, or sub-sections of one sample, are in fact due to a random sampling error rather than to real differences. *See also* sampling error; significance tests.

odds ratio   The odds ratio is the ratio of two odds. If, for example, there is an experimental process (p_e) and a standard process (p_s) then the odds ratio is defined as $p_e (1 - p_s)/p_s (1 - p_e)$. Unlike most measures of association, 1.0 represents a complete absence of relationship, with deviations in either direction representing an increasing relation. In sociology odds ratios have been most widely used in the study of social mobility, where their insensitivity to changes in the marginals of a mobility table is said by class analysts to have enabled the distinction to be made between relative and absolute rates of mobility. The mathematics and characteristics of the odds ratio are perhaps easiest understood in this substantive context.

open response, open-ended question   An interview question that has no predetermined reply categories. The respondent's reply must be written down by the interviewer verbatim, and coded after all interviews are completed, or grouped into broad categories of reply for verbatim quotes in a report. *See also* closed response; coding.

operational definition, operationalization   The transformation of an abstract, theoretical concept into something concrete, observable and measurable in an empirical research project. Operational definitions are pragmatic and realistic indicators of more diffuse notions. For example, one way of operationalizing the concept of social class might be to ask people for details about their occupation and employment status (as indicators of class) and then relate these answers to a matrix of all possible combinations of the two to code their class. This is the operational method used by both the Office of Population Censuses and Surveys for its classification known as Social Class based on Occupations and by John Goldthorpe for his class scheme. An alternative operationalization of the same concept would be to ask respondents to which class (if any) they felt they belonged. This would be a measure of self-assigned or subjective class position. As will be seen from these examples, operational definitions are crucial to the process of measurement, and are often the most controversial aspect of any research design.

panel study   A study that provides longitudinal data on a group of people, households, employers, or other social unit, termed 'the panel', about whom information is collected over a period of months, years or decades. Two of the most common types of panel are age cohorts, people within a common age band, and groups with some other date-specific common experience, such as people graduating from university, having a first child, or migrating to another country in a given year or band of years. Another type is the nationally representative cross-sectional sample of households or employers that is interviewed at regular intervals over a period of years. Because data relate to the same social units, change is measured more reliably than in regular cross-sectional studies, and sample sizes can be correspondingly smaller, while remaining nationally representative, as long as non-response and sample attrition are kept within bounds. These are the key problems for panel studies, as initial samples are eroded by deaths, migration, fatigue with the study, and other causes. Another problem is that people become experienced interviewees, leading to response bias. For example, they may report 'no change' since the previous interview, so as to avoid detailed questioning on changes that have in fact occurred. Because they yield longitudinal data, panel studies offer possibilities for examining the relationships between individual life histories, cohort effects, and period effects due to social change. A number of specialized techniques have therefore been developed for analysing these data. *See also* cohort, cohort analysis; cross-sectional analysis; event-history analysis; hazard models, proportional-hazard models; microdata; micro-level change; time-series data; unobserved determinants of behaviour.

parametric statistics   A branch of statistical inference which makes assumptions about the underlying mathematical distributional form of observed variables. The most familiar of these hypothetical mathematical distributions is the normal distribution. Binomial and Poisson distributions are also widely used. Some statisticians believe that these models are inappropriate to the social sciences, since they rest on assumptions that are violated by much social science data and prefer instead to rely on non-parametric statistics. *See also* binomial distribution; non-parametric statistics; normal distribution.

parsimony, parsimonious   The principle that the best statistical model among all satisfactory models is that with the fewest parameters. Hence, more generally, the principle which asserts that if it is possible to explain a phenomenon equally adequately in a number of different ways, then the simplest of explanations (in terms of the number of variables or propositions) should be selected.

partial regression coefficients   *See* regression, regression analysis.

partitioning variance, partial relationships   Once we have constructed variables (by defining them and assigning numeric values according to the observations we have made), we use data analysis to try and explain the variability we have observed. We call this partitioning variance, i.e. finding a way of categorizing a variable into two or more constants and thus explaining the observed variability. *See also* elaboration; statistical control; variable; variation (statistical).

polytomous variable, polytomy   *See* dichotomous variable, dichotomy.

pre-coding   *See* coding.

proportional-hazard models   *See* hazard model, proportional-hazard model.

proportionate reduction of error (PRE)   PRE measures are standardized measures of association used for assessing relationships between variables, and are based upon simple ratios of the amount of error made in guessing the value of one variable for an individual under two situations: (1) where the only information available is the distribution of the dependent variable; and (2) where we have additional knowledge about how the dependent variable is distributed among the categories of an independent variable. What a PRE measure does is to state the proportion by which one can reduce guessing errors made in (1) by using information from (2). An example of a PRE measure is *lambda*. *See also* association coefficients; standardized measures of association.

questionnaire A document containing all the questions, closed and open-ended, for a survey. Normally, a separate questionnaire is used for each respondent to a survey, providing enough space for answers to be recorded, and subsequently coded for computer-based analysis of all replies to each question. Questionnaires range from the postcard with a few questions to be filled in by respondents, to long documents to be filled in by trained interviewers. Good questionnaires require a great deal of care and effort, to ensure that the questions are clear and easy to answer, to exclude leading questions unless by conscious design, to prompt and probe respondents' recollections of events that may not always be very recent, and to shape the interview overall so that it is a pleasant and interesting experience for respondents. Special techniques have been developed for questions on sensitive topics, interviewing on life-cycle events and work histories, questions on attitudes, values and preferences. Questionnaires must also be structured to ensure that people are correctly filtered into or past particular sections – for example, someone who has not been in employment for many years should not be asked questions about their work, and so on. Questionnaires help to standardize interviews, increasing the consistency of enquiry and response, but they cannot completely eliminate interviewer bias. *See also* coding; closed response; open-response, open-ended question; survey, social survey.

raw data file The non-program-specific form in which data may be transferred between different computers and programs, a raw data file normally consists of rows and columns of numerals representing category codes (for categoric variables) and real numbers (for continuous variables). In such a file, the columns contain the individual variables, and rows comprise the cases, so that the information for each variable is found in the same columns for each case. Conventionally the format is 80 columns in width. These raw data can then be used to create a data file for analysis within a specific computer package. *See also* coding.

regression, regression analysis In statistical usage, regression refers in the simplest case (bivariate linear regression) to fitting a line to the plot of data from two variables, in order to represent the trend between them. Regression is asymmetric, that is, it assumes that one variable (Y, the dependent variable) is determined by the other (independent) variable X; that the relationship is linear (and hence that the variables are at the interval level of measurement); and that the fit is not perfect

$$Y_i = \alpha + \beta X_i + e_i$$

(that is, the value of the dependent variable Y for individual i varies in a straight line with the value of X, together with an individual error term, e). The slope of this line is represented by a constant multiplier weight or 'regression co-efficient', β, and a constant α, which represents the intercept or point at which the regression line crosses the Y-axis. Statistically, it is assumed that the error terms (e_i) are random with a mean of 0, and are independent of the independent variable values. The main purpose of regression analysis is to calculate the value of the slope (β), often interpreted as the overall effect of X. This is normally done by using the least squares principle to find a best-fitting line (in the sense that the sum of the squared error terms – discrepancies between actual Y_i values and those predicted by the regression line – is an small as possible). The correlation coefficient (r) gives a measure of how well the data fit this regression line (perfectly if $r = \pm 1$ and as poorly as possible if $r = 0$. Simple regression can be extended in various ways: to more than one independent variable (multiple linear regression) and to other functions or relationships (for example, monotonic or non-metric regression for ordinal variables, used in multidimensional scaling, and logistic and power regression). In the multiple linear regression, the model is written as:

$$Y_i = \alpha + \beta_1 X_1 + \beta_2 X_1 + \beta_3 X_1 + \ldots \beta_k X_1 + e_i$$

where the regression weights β_k now represent the effect of the independent variable X_i on Y_i, controlling for (or 'partialling out', that is removing the linear effect of) the other independent variables. These 'partial regression co-efficients' or 'beta weights' are of especial interest in causal models and structural equation systems. The Correlation Coefficient is replaced by the multiple correlation coefficient which gives the strength of the linear relationship between all the independent variables in the equation and the dependent variables. *See also* multivariate analysis.

regression coefficients   *See* regression, regression analysis.

regression line   *See* regression, regression analysis.

reliability   When sociologists enquire as to the reliability of data, or of a measurement procedure, they are questioning whether the same results would be produced if the research procedure were to be repeated. Reliability embraces two principal forms of repetition: temporal reliability (the same result is obtained when the measurement is repeated at a later time); and comparative reliability (the same result is obtained when two different forms of a test are used, the same test is applied by different researchers, or the same test is applied to two different samples taken from the same population). Reliability raises many technical problems for the sociologist. For example, having once interviewed someone, a repeat interview may be contaminated by the earlier experience. Reliability is usually contrasted with validity – whether or not a measurement procedure actually measures what the researcher supposes it does. However, the two are not perfectly independent. One may have a highly reliable measure which is not valid: for example, we might measure IQ by standing subjects on a weighing machine and reading off the numbers, an extremely reliable procedure in both senses; but bodyweight is hardly a valid indicator of IQ. A highly unreliable measure, on the other hand, cannot be valid. *See also* validity.

representativeness   The ability to give a reasonably accurate portrayal of the research subject's characteristics and known diversity. As applied to survey samples, or case-study samples, this is judged by the extent to which key characteristics of the sample are the same as the characteristics of the population from which the sample was selected. In relation to single cases, the criterion would be the typicality of the case selected. The term is also applied to research reports, for example to assess whether verbatim quotations, incidents described in detail, or other selectively reported results reflect the full variety and weight of the results obtained. *See also* sampling; sampling error.

research design   The strategic plan for a research project or research programme, setting out the broad outline and key features of the work to be undertaken, including the methods of data collection and analysis to be employed, and showing how the research strategy addresses the specific aims and objectives of the study, and whether the research issues are theoretical or policy-oriented. Hence also, the process of developing such a document, choosing between alternative types of study, their relative size, whether triangulation will be employed, and adjusting plans to the available resources and timetable.

research ethics   The application of moral rules and professional codes of conduct to the collection, analysis, reporting, and publication of information about research subjects, in particular active acceptance of subjects' right to privacy, confidentiality and informed consent. Until recently, sociologists (and social scientists generally) often displayed arrogance in their treatment of research subjects, justifying their actions by the search for truth. This trend is now being redressed, especially in industrial societies, with the adoption of formal codes of conduct, and greater emphasis on ethical research procedures. Ethical issues are most salient in relation to case studies and other research designs which focus on very few cases (with the risk that they remain identifiable in reports). Public opinion now resists invasions of privacy for genuine research purposes just as much as for publicity-seeking mass-media stories, as evidenced by periodic increases in survey non-response, despite the fact that anonymity is effectively guaranteed in large-scale data collections.

residual variance   *See* general linear models (GLM).

response rate   The percentage of an eligible random sample that agrees to participate in an interview survey. There is no response rate for a quota sample.

sampling   A method for collecting information and drawing inferences about a larger population or universe, from the analysis of only part thereof, the sample. There are a variety of sample designs. A random sample, or simple random sample, is one in which each case has an equal chance (or equal probability) of selection so that the techniques of probability statistics can then be applied to the resulting information. A common variation on this is the stratified random sample: the population being studied is first divided into subgroups or strata, and random sampling is applied within the strata. Another common variation is two-stage or multi-stage sampling. For example, random sampling is first used to select a limited number of local areas for a survey, and then a second stage of random sampling is applied to selecting persons or households or companies within the random sample of areas. All these sampling designs use random sampling in the final selection process, producing a list of persons from the electoral register, household addresses, company names, or other cases which constitute the final issued sample. All of them must be included in the study, with no substitutions allowed, in sharp contrast with the procedures for obtaining quota samples. Once the sampling fraction and sample size are known, probability theory provides the basis for a whole range of statistical inferences to be made about the characteristics of the universe, from the observed characteristics of the sample drawn from it. Most of the relevant calculations and significance tests are supplied in the SPSS software package. Statistics textbooks supply details of the underlying calculations.

sampling error   The principal aim of any sampling procedure is to obtain a sample which, subject to limitations of size, will reproduce the characteristics of the population being studied, especially those of immediate interest, as closely as possible. In practice, two types of error will arise from any sampling procedure: first, sampling bias may arise in the way the selection is carried out; and second, random sampling error may arise in the sample obtained, due to chance differences between the members of the population included, or excluded, from the sample. Total sampling error in the sample issued for interviewing consists of these two taken together. The key difference between the two is that random sampling error decreases as the sample size is increased, whereas sampling bias is not eliminated or reduced in that way: it is a constant characteristic unless steps are taken to improve the quality of sample selection. An important source of sampling bias is a sampling frame (a list of the members of the total population of interest from which a sample for study is to be drawn) which does not in fact cover all of the intended population. For example, there may be systematic differences between people who do or do not enter themselves on the electoral register or own a telephone, so that lists of such persons are not completely representative of the adult population. Another source of bias is random sampling that is not in practice completely random, because the lists and records used as the sampling frame are not put together randomly, but presented in some systematic manner not known to the researcher using them. After interviewing is completed, non-response bias may be discovered in survey results. The combination of sampling error and survey non-response bias together determine the representativeness of the survey data produced by the study. *See also* representativeness.

scatterplot   Sometimes referred to as scatter diagrams or 'scattergrams', these are two-dimensional representations of the relationship between pairs of variables, achieved by plotting each individual case on a graph. The diagram thus represents the points at which the two variables intersect for each case in the sample. These diagrams can be routinely produced by most statistical computer packages. They allow easy and visual representation of three aspects of a pairwise relationship: whether or not it is linear; whether it is positive or negative; and the strength of the association. They can be useful aids to the understanding of the idea of correlation but are rarely reproduced in the published results of sociological analyses. *See also* regression, regression analysis.

scientific/non-scientific samples   *See* statistical inference.

secondary analysis   Any further analysis of an existing data-set which presents interpretations, conclusions, or knowledge additional to, or different from, those presented in the first report on the data collection and its results. Some disciplines, such as economics and demography, rely almost entirely on data collected by others, especially official statistics. With improved access to micro-data from major government surveys, sociologists are also using secondary analysis of such data to complement, or replace, analysis of new data-sets.

significance tests   A variety of statistical techniques are used in empirical social research in order to establish whether a relationship between sample variables may be inferred to apply to the population from which the sample was drawn. Significance tests form the central core of statistical inference: they are the technique of analysis by which statistical inferences concerning the relationship between two or more variables in a sample can be generalized to a population. They are therefore subject to the same conditions concerning sampling procedures as apply to all statistical inference. The starting point is the null hypothesis, which states that interesting differences in the research results are due to sampling error, rather than to genuine differences: in other words there is no relationship in the population between the variables under test. Significance tests offer various levels of significance or confidence: they state that a particular statistical result would only occur by chance less than one in a hundred times (the 0.1 level), or less than one in twenty times (the 0.5 level). The latter is referred to as the 95 per cent level of significance and the former as the 99 per cent level of significance. Depending on the degree of certainty required by the researcher, results at any of these levels might be accepted as significant, but the 'less than one chance in a thousand' level is regarded as the safest assurance that research results would so rarely arise by chance that they must be true reflections of the real world. There are two major types of significance tests belonging to two major branches of statistics – parametric and non-parametric statistics. In parametric statistics, assumptions are made about the underlying distributional form of the variables in the population. Examples of parametric tests of significance are the z-score tests and the t-test. The best-known example of a non-parametric test of significance is the Mann–Whitney U-test. A textbook should be consulted to ensure a test appropriate to the data-set is chosen. The two best-known tests are probably the chi-square, which makes only some very simple assumptions about underlying distributional form, and is suitable for simple nominal variables, and Spearman's rank correlation coefficient, one of the earliest to be developed, and the most widely used for variables consisting of ordinal or interval scales. *See also* distribution of repeated sample means.

simple linear regression   *See* regression, regression analysis.

skewness   A measure of asymmetry in frequency distributions. The skew in a distribution is the degree to which frequencies trail towards extreme scores in one direction away from the majority of cases. Negative skew means cases trail to the left and positive skew involves trailing to the right. It is important in order to know what measures (for example of central tendency) can best describe it. *See also* central tendency (measures of).

social statistics   Quantitative information about social groups, including census and demographic data, used for descriptive policy and inferential analysis. As an application of statistical theory, increasing attention has been given to models of influence and measurement, and to multivariate models of analysis.

socio-logic   In the social sciences there are many competing theories and a wide range of methods or techniques, but nevertheless it can be argued that there is a similar underlying logic to the process of social research regardless of the particular theory and method being used. In other words, there are general points we can make about theories, concepts and forms of explanation in social research. Thus, while there is not one methodology, it can be argued that there is one 'socio-logic'. Socio-logic is the knitting together of theory, concept formation, the derivation of hypotheses, operationalization, observation, data analysis, causal inference and back to theory again.

SPSS   The Statistical Package for the Social Sciences, commonly know as SPSS, is the most widely used software package among academic sociologists. Developed in the United States by social scientists, it provides a range of facilities, including tabulation, multivariate analysis, and virtually all the tests of statistical significance appropriate for sample survey data. SPSS was originally developed for mainframe computers, and at the time of writing, the latest version (SPSS-X) is still only usable on such machines. However, versions for IBM-PC compatible machines are now also available (SPSS-PC+ and SPSS FOR WINDOWS), and these have gradually gained in popularity. Market researchers who require report quality output, and researchers working with large government-produced statistical surveys and censuses, usually use other, more efficient and more powerful software and programme languages. *See also* computer packages.

spurious correlation   A correlation between two variables when there is no causal link between them. A famous spurious correlation often quoted in the literature is that between the number of fire-engines at a fire (X) and the amount of damage done (Y). Once the size of the conflagration (T) is controlled for – that is, large fires cause more damage, and therefore require more fire-engines to extinguish them – the original relationship disappears. Hence the $X \rightarrow Y$ relationship becomes $T \rightarrow X, T \rightarrow Y$, but X and Y are not causally related, where T (the size of the fire) is an antecedent variable. Note also that it is not really the correlation which is spurious, but rather the implicit causal model: there are indeed more fire-engines at fires where the greatest damage is done, but it is not the fire-engines which cause the damage.

standard deviation   *See* variation, (statistical).

standard error of the mean   *See* statistical inference.

standardized measures of association   Normed or standardized measures of association are association coefficients which allow us to make valid comparisons between different variable associations in the same way that standardizing by percentaging allows us to compare different frequency distributions. Characteristically such measures vary from –1.00 (for negative associations), through zero (for no association), to +1.00 (for positive associations); the larger the value of the measure in either direction from zero, the greater is the degree of association between the relevant variables. Different standardized measures of association exist for different levels of measurement of variables, and for both symmetric and asymmetric relationships between variables. Well known examples of such measures are phi, lambda and gamma. *See also* association coefficients; proportionate reduction in error.

statistical control   Statistical techniques for excluding the influence of specified variables in an analysis. For example, if the data from a sample survey showed a strong association between unemployment and clinical depression, one might want to control for the effect of social class. Partitioning the data by class (middle versus working) would establish whether or not the relationship between unemployment and depression is constant across all classes. Similarly, an observed association between class and clinical depression might well disappear, once a control is introduced for unemployment. (Working-class people are no more likely to suffer from depression than middle-class people, but they are more likely to be unemployed, and the unemployed are more likely to be depressed than are those in work.)

statistical independence   Two variables (i and j) are statistically independent if the proportion who are both i and j (p_{ij}) is equal to the proportion who are i multiplied by the proportion who are j ($p_{ij} = p_i \times p_j$ or $p_{ij} - p_i \times p_j = 0$). This principle forms the basis of the popular χ^2 (chi-square) test.

statistical inference   The process by which results from a sample may be applied more generally to a population. More precisely, how inferences may be drawn about a population, based on results from a sample of that population. Inferential statistics are generally distinguished as a branch of statistics analysis from descriptive statistics, which describe variables and the strength and nature of relationships between them, but do not allow generalization. The ability to draw inferences about a population from a sample of observations from that population depends upon the sampling technique employed. The importance of a scientific sample is that it permits statistical generalization or inference. For example, if we survey a simple random sample of university students in the UK and establish their average (mean) height, we will be able to infer the likely range within which the mean height of all university students in the UK is likely to fall. Other types of sample, such as quota samples, do not allow such inferences to be drawn. The accuracy with which we are able to estimate the population mean from the sample will depend on two things (assuming that the sample has been drawn correctly): the size of the sample and the variability of heights within the population. Both these factors are reflected in the calculation of the standard error of the mean. The bigger the standard error of the mean, the less accurate the sample mean will be as an estimate of the population mean. Strictly speaking, therefore, inferential statistics is a form of inductive inference in which the characteristics of a population are estimated from data obtained by sampling that population. In practice, however, the methods are called upon for the more ambitious purpose of prediction, explanation and hypothesis testing. *See also* distribution of repeated sample means; inferential statistics; significance tests.

statistical interaction   A statistically established relationship between two (or more) variables such that the values of one vary in some systematic way with the values of another. Statistical interactions between two or more independent variables can significantly complicate certain types of multivariate analyses where independent variables are assumed to be independent of (orthogonal to) each other.

statistical significance   *See* significance tests.

survey, social survey   A research design in which a sample of subjects is selected on a systematic basis from a population and interviewed in order to draw inferences about the whole population. Interviews may be conducted face to face or by telephone using either a paper-and-pencil method in which respondents' answers are entered on to a printed questionnaire or (as is increasingly the case) using a computerized method in which the questionnaire is contained within a computer program and answers are keyed directly into the computer by the interviewer.

***t*-test**   *See* significance tests.

tabular presentation   Quantitative social science results are most commonly presented in the form of an analytical table. Tables should fulfil two main criteria: they should be easy to read; and they should support the inference drawn by the analyst. All tables should have a clear self-explanatory title; give the number of cases on which the statistics are based; and should include only the critical information relevant to the point that the table illustrates. The most basic type of analytical table is the percentage table. The simplest percentage table is the univariate type which presents the distribution of answers to a single question. A two-way (or two-variable) table shows the relationship between a dependent and independent variable. *See also* contingency table.

theory, social theory   A theory is an account of the world which goes beyond what we can see and measure. It embraces a set of interrelated definitions and relationships that organizes our concepts of, and understanding of, the empirical world in a systematic way. Thus, we may establish a statistical relationship between poverty and crime, but to explain that relationship we might have to employ a number of theories: about people's motivations, and social meanings attached to poverty and crime, and the structural constraints which keep sections of the population in poverty. Generally speaking there are three different conceptions of theory in sociology. Some think of theory as generalizations about, and classifications of, the social world. The scope of generalization varies from theorizing about a particular range of phenomena to more abstract and general theories about society and history as a whole. Others believe that theoretical statements should be translated into empirical, measurable, observable propositions and systematically tested. Thus, in the example above, we should test assumption and motivation, social meanings, and so forth. This approach is usually characterized (rather unhelpfully) as positivism. Finally, yet others argue that theory should explain phenomena, identifying causal mechanisms and processes which, although they cannot be observed directly, can be seen in their effects. For example, Marxists might use the alleged contradiction between the forces and relations of production (unobservable) to explain fluctuations in the levels and development of class struggle (observable). The label 'realism' is sometimes attached to this view.

time-series data   Data about a social phenomenon or phenomena which are ordered in time. In sociology, the most common forms of time-series data are those derived either from population censuses or panel studies, although repeated government cross-sectional surveys, certain opinion-poll surveys and some administrative records also offer opportunities for time-series study. Occasionally, two or more unrelated *ad hoc* surveys have asked similar sorts of questions of similar populations, and allow an approximation to time-series analysis. In the UK, the Office for National Statistics (formerly the Central Statistical Office and Office of Population Censuses and Surveys) hosts both a time-series data-bank which contains information on some 2000 variables, and a longitudinal study of the Census with records of 1% of the population taken from each Census since 1971. *See also* micro-level change; panel study.

Type I/Type II error   A Type I error occurs in tests of statistical significance where the null hypothesis of no association is rejected and it is concluded too readily that a statistically significant difference does in fact exist. This problem tends to arise where sample sizes are large, which has the effect of increasing the probability of a statistically significant result. In this case, it is thought to be good practice to rely only on the 'one-in-a-thousand' level of statistical significance ($P < 0.001$) in order to conclude that a sample estimate may reasonably be generalized to the population. The Type II error occurs where too stringent criteria of statistical significance are applied, with the outcome that a difference which really does exist in the population is not discerned using tests of statistical significance on the sample. In this instance, no evidence is found to reject the null hypothesis, when in fact there is a real difference.

unit of analysis   *See* unit of enquiry.

unit of enquiry   This is the unit – for example individual, household, corporation or whatever – about which information is required in a research project. Students often confuse the unit of enquiry (sometimes called the 'unit of analysis') with the sampling unit. The two need not be the same for any particular study. Thus, one may sample households and then collect information (from one or more of its members) about all individual residents. Here, the sampling unit is the household and the unit of enquiry is the household member.

univariate analysis   *See* multivariate analysis.

unobserved determinants of behaviour   Longitudinal data allow analysts to control for certain unobserved determinants of behaviour on which no data have been collected, in particular those unobserved factors which vary across individuals but remain the same across time for any given individual. These factors are referred to as individual-specific effects and their presence as population heterogeneity. For example, we know that individuals unemployed at time t have a higher probability of being unemployed at time $t + 1$. Is this because there is something about unemployment that increases the likelihood that the unemployed will remain in that state (for example, demoralization)? Or is there something about the unemployed themselves which puts them and keeps them in that state? We need longitudinal data to begin to tackle such questions. *See also* panel study; micro-level change.

validity   The property of being genuine, a true reflection of attitudes, behaviour or characteristics. A measure (such as a question, series of questions or test) is considered valid if it is thought to measure the concept or property which it claims to measure. For example, it might be contested whether the answers to a question about job satisfaction are a valid indicator of alienation from modern society; holding paid employment on the part of a woman is a valid indicator of a feminist consciousness; or that the divorce rate in the United States is a valid indicator of the extent of social stress in that society. The validity of an attitude scale, or of the answers obtained by a question in an interview, is ultimately a matter for judgement, but techniques have been developed to supplement a researcher's own views, which may not be representative. *See also* reliability.

variable   In the physical sciences, variables are the characteristics of entities which are physically manipulated, such as the heat or volume of a substance. In the social sciences, the term refers to attributes which are fixed for each person or other social entity, but which are observed to be at different levels, amounts, or strengths across samples and other aggregate groups. Variables measure a social construct (such as social class, age or housing type) in a way which renders it amenable to numerical analysis. Thus, the key feature of a variable is that it is capable of reflecting variation within a population and is not a constant. There are various difficulties involved in the process of creating variables from constructs (operationalization). The central considerations here are validity (that the variable is a true measurement of the construct it is aimed at) and reliability (that measurement is reliable). Variables may be measured at different levels of measurement, but the basic distinction is between continuous variables such as income and categoric or discrete variables such as class. Relatively few social variables are continuous – forming interval scales such as income or age. Most are discrete, forming ordinal and nominal scales such as highest educational qualification obtained, or sex, respectively. The different levels of measurement have implications for the types of analysis that can be undertaken. *See also* component variable; dependent variable; independent variable; intervening variable; measurement, levels of; operational definition, operationalization; reliability; validity.

variance *See* variation (statistical); data analysis.

variation (statistical) The greater part of empirical research is concerned with the characteristics of groups, or aggregate social entities, rather than individual cases; that is, with men or women in general, rather than any particular man or woman. A range of statistical measures of association are employed to describe the features of groups, or types of case in the aggregate. Most of them are based on the normal distribution, the binomial distribution, or the Poisson distribution, from which a number of statistical summary measures are derived. The mean, mode and median provide measures of central tendency, the most common or typical value in the distribution, which coincide when the distribution is normal. Measures of dispersion attempt to concentrate information about the general pattern in single summary statistics. These include the range, mean deviation, quartile deviation, decile range and the standard deviation, which is by far the most important. One of the properties of the normal distribution is that about 68 per cent of all cases are contained within one standard deviation on either side of the mean, about 95 per cent lie within two standard deviations and some 99.73 per cent lie within three standard deviations on either side of the mean. The standard deviation of a distribution thus summarizes a great deal of information about the overall dispersion, the degree of clustering or concentration around the mean. The variance is the square of the standard deviation and has the property of being additive. Analysis of variance measures variance within sub-groups in the data-set, and between the averages of these sub-groups. *See also* binomial distribution; central tendency (measures of); measurement, levels of; normal distribution; sampling.

Acknowledgement

We are grateful to Oxford University Press for granting permission to use extracts from *The Concise Oxford Dictionary of Sociology* (Marshall, 1994).

Answers to multiple choice questions

Chapter 5
1 (ii)
2 (i)   interval and ordinal
   (ii) nominal and ordinal
   (iii) interval
3 (iii)
4 (i)   68.26 per cent
   (ii) 97.73 per cent up the distribution
   (iv) the individual score, the mean score and the standard deviation

Chapter 7
1 (iii)
2 (iii)
3 (i)

Chapter 8
1 (iii)
2 (ii)
3 (i) and (iv)

Chapter 9
1 (iv)
2 (v)
3 (ii) and (iii)
4 (iii)

Chapter 10
1 (ii)
2 (ii), (iii) and (iv)
3 (iv)

Chapter 11
1 (ii)
2 (i)
3 (iii)
4 (i) and (iv)

Chapter 12
1 (ii)
2 (iii)
3 (ii)

References and select bibliography

Allison, P. (1984) Event history analysis: regression for longitudinal event data, *Sage University Papers: Quantitative Applications in the Social Sciences*, 46. Beverly Hills and London: Sage.

Bottomore, T. and Rubel, M. (eds) (1963) *Karl Marx: Selected Writings in Sociology and Social Philosophy*. Harmondsworth: Penguin.

Bowen, B. D. and Weisberg, H. F. (1977) *An Introduction to Data Analysis*. San Francisco: W. H. Freeman & Co.

Bryman, A. and Cramer, D. (1990) *Quantitative Data Analysis for Social Scientists*. London: Routledge.

Buck, N., Gershuny, J., Rose, D. and Scott, J. (eds) (1994) *Changing Households: The British Household Panel Survey 1990–1992*. Colchester: ESRC Research Centre on Micro-Social Change.

Cochrane, W. G. (1977) *Sampling Techniques*. New York: John Wiley (3rd edn).

Conover, W. D. (1980) *Practical Nonparametric Statistics*. New York: John Wiley (2nd edn).

Dale, A., Arber, S. and Proctor, M. (1988) *Doing secondary analysis, Contemporary Social Research: 17*. London: Unwin Hyman.

Davis, J. A. (1971) *Elementary Survey Analysis*. Englewood Cliffs: Prentice Hall.

de Vaus, D. A. (1991) *Surveys in Social Research*. London: Unwin Hyman (3rd edn).

Dobson, A. J. (1990) *An Introduction to Generalized Linear Models*. London: Chapman & Hall.

Durkheim, E. (1951) *Suicide: A Study in Sociology*. London: Routledge.

ESRC Research Centre on Micro-social Change (1991) *Technical Paper 1: ESRC Research Centre on Micro-social Change*. Colchester: University of Essex.

ESRC (1991) *British Household Panel Survey: Interviewer Instructions*, Main Stage Panel 1. Colchester: University of Essex.

ESRC (1992) *British Household Panel Survey: Technical Report*, Main Stage Panel 1. Colchester: University of Essex.

Evans, J. (1979) Causation and control, in *Research Methods in Education and the Social Sciences*. Block 3A. Milton Keynes: Open University Educational Enterprises.

Fox, J. (1984) *Linear Statistical Models and Related Methods with Reference to Social Research*. New York: John Wiley.

Gilbert, G. N. (1981) *Modelling Society: An Introduction to Loglinear Analysis for Social Researchers, Contemporary Social Research: 2*. London: Allen & Unwin.

Goldthorpe, J. H. (1980) *Social Mobility and Class Structure in Modern Britain.* Oxford: Clarendon Press.

Hakim, C. (1982) *Secondary Analysis in Social Research, Contemporary Social Research: 5.* London: Allen & Unwin.

Hakim, C. (1987) *Research Design, Contemporary Social Research: 13.* London: Allen & Unwin.

Hirschi, T. and Selvin, H. (1967) *Principles of Survey Analysis.* New York: Free Press.

Hughes, J. A. (1980) *The Philosophy of Social Research.* London: Longman.

Loether, H. J. and McTavish, D. G. (1974) *Descriptive Statistics for Sociologists.* Boston: Allyn & Bacon.

Mann, M. (1981) Socio-logic, *Sociology*, 15(4), 544–50.

Marsh, C. (1982) *The Survey Method, Contemporary Social Research: 5.* London: Allen & Unwin.

Marsh, C. (1986) Social class and occupation, in R. G. Burgess (ed.) *Key Variables in Social Investigation*, pp.123–52. London: RKP.

Marsh, C. (1988) *Exploring Data.* Cambridge: Polity Press.

Marshall, G. (ed.) (1994) *The Concise Oxford Dictionary of Sociology.* Oxford: Oxford University Press.

Marshall, G., Rose, D., Newby, H. and Vogler, C. (1988) *Social Class in Modern Britain.* London: Unwin Hyman.

Moser, C. and Kalton, G. (1971) *Survey Methods in Social Investigation.* London: Heinemann.

Norusis, M. (1988) *The SPSS Guide to Data Analysis for SPSS/PC+.* Chicago: SPSS Inc.

Norusis, M. J./SPSS Inc. (1993) *SPSS/PC+ Release 5.0 Users Guide.* Chicago: SPSS Inc.

Norusis M. J./SPSS Inc. (1994) *SPSS for Windows Release 6.1 Users Guide.* Chicago: SPSS Inc.

Norusis M. J./SPSS Inc. (1995) *Guide to Data Analysis in SPSS for Windows Release 6.1.* Chicago: SPSS Inc.

Payne, C. D. (ed.) (1987) *GLIM System Release 3.77 Manual.* Oxford: Royal Statistical Society (2nd edn).

Plewis, I. (1985) *Analysing Change: Measurement and Explanation Using Longitudinal Data.* Chichester: John Wiley.

Rose, D. (1993) European Household Panels, *Working Papers on Panels*, No. 1. Siena: Nuova Imagine.

Rose, D. (ed.) (1995) *Innovation: the European Journal of Social Sciences*, 8(1) (special issue on Household Panel Studies).

Rosenberg, M. (1968) *The Logic of Survey Analysis.* New York: Basic Books.

Saris, W. (1991) Computer-assisted interviewing, *Sage University Papers: Quantitative Applications in the Social Sciences*, 80. Newbury Park and London: Sage.

Siegel, S. and Castellan, N. J. (Jr) (1988) *Non-parametric Statistics for the Behavioural Sciences.* McGraw-Hill International Editions Statistics Series, Singapore: McGraw-Hill.

SPSS Inc. (1994) *Base System Syntax Reference Guide Release 6.1.* Chicago: SPSS Inc.

Tabachnick, B. G. and Fidell, L. S. (1983) *Using Multivariate Statistics.* New York: Harper & Row.

Upton, G. J. G. (1978) *The Analysis of Cross-tabulated Data*. Chichester: John Wiley.

von Eye, A. (1990) *Statistical Methods in Longitudinal Research*. New York: Academic Press Inc.

Wallace, W. (1971) *The Logic of Science in Sociology*. Chicago: Aldine.

Wright, E. O. (1979) *Class, Crisis and The State*. London: Verso.

Wright, E. O. (1985) *Classes*. London: Verso.

Index

TRENDS IN BRITISH PUBLIC POLICY
DO GOVERNMENTS MAKE ANY DIFFERENCE?

Brian W. Hogwood

Do Conservative governments tax more and spend less than Labour? Which governments have had the most effect on the sizes of the armed and police forces in the post-war years? Which governments have carried through the most legislation? These questions, and many more, are answered in this book which examines how British public policy and its effects have changed in the post-war years, and over the last two decades in particular.

The book shows in graphical and tabular form the trends in a variety of indicators including public expenditure, taxation, public sector employment and legislation. The author discusses the causes and implications of these trends in the light of influences such as social and demographic developments and, most importantly, changing governments. Comparisons are made with trends in other countries. Throughout the book the author encourages the reader to develop a healthy scepticism about how politicians and others portray trends in public policy as well as some constructive skills in interpreting information and government activity.

This will be a unique text and valuable source of reference for all students of politics, public administration, economics, sociology and social policy.

Contents
The sea and the lifeboat, the key and the lamppost – Public expenditure – Tax expenditures – Taxes – Funding the gap – Public employment – Legislation and regulation – Organizational change – Alternative policy instruments – Influences on policy trends – Future prospects and issues – Appendix – References – Index.

272pp   0 335 15629 0 (Paperback)   0 335 15630 4 (Hardback)

DOING YOUR RESEARCH PROJECT (2nd edition)
A GUIDE FOR FIRST-TIME RESEARCHERS IN
EDUCATION AND SOCIAL SCIENCE

Judith Bell

If you are a beginner researcher, the problems facing you are much the same whether you are producing a small project, an MEd dissertation or a PhD thesis. You will need to select a topic; identify the objectives of your study; plan and design a suitable methodology; devise research instruments; negotiate access to institutions, material and people; collect, analyse and present information; and finally, produce a well-written report or dissertation. Whatever the scale of the undertaking, you will have to master techniques and devise a plan of action which does not attempt more than the limitations of expertise, time and access permit.

We all learn to do research by actually doing it, but a great deal of time can be wasted and goodwill dissipated by inadequate preparation. This book aims to provide you with the tools to do the job, to help you avoid some of the pitfalls and time-wasting false trails that can eat into your time, to establish good research habits, and to take you from the stage of choosing a topic through to the production of a well-planned, methodologically sound and well-written final report or dissertation on time.

Doing Your Research Project serves as a source of reference and guide to good practice for all beginner researchers, whether undergraduate and postgraduate students or professionals such as teachers or social workers undertaking investigations in Education and the Social Sciences. This second edition retains the basic structure of the very successful first edition whilst incorporating some important new material.

Contents
Introduction – Approaches to educational research – Planning the project – Keeping records and making notes – Reviewing the literature – Negotiating access and the problems of inside research – The analysis of documentary evidence – Designing and administering questionnaires – Planning and conducting interviews – Diaries – Observation studies – Interpretation and presentation of the evidence – Postscript – References – Index.

208pp   0 335 19094 4 (Paperback)

THE EVERYDAY WORLD AS PROBLEMATIC
A FEMINIST SOCIOLOGY

Dorothy E. Smith

A new sociology from the standpoint of women is the exciting possibility explored in *The Everyday World as Problematic*. Using feminist theory, Marxism, and phenomenology to examine the structure of our everyday world, the author develops an alternative to traditional modes of thinking about and understanding social relations in a patriarchal society. Her analysis derives from the premise that women continue to be excluded from the ruling apparatus of culture – a culture manufactured by those in power who shape the ways we view ourselves and our society. In essays encompassing both theory and practice, she concentrates on shifting the focus of traditional sociological inquiry to a standpoint that makes women the subject and not merely the object of analysis. The result is a radical incorporation of women's interests and perspectives into contemporary sociological discourse.

Contents

256pp   0 335 15881 1 (Paperback)

This edition for sale only in the UK, Ireland, Europe and Commonwealth (excluding Canada).